THE COMMON FLAW

THE COMMON FLAW

NEEDLESS COMPLEXITY IN THE COURTS
AND 50 WAYS TO REDUCE IT

THOMAS G. MOUKAWSHER

BRANDEIS UNIVERSITY PRESS

Waltham, Massachusetts

Brandeis University Press
© 2023 Thomas G. Moukawsher
All rights reserved
Manufactured in the United States of America
Designed by Richard Hendel
Typeset in Miller and New Yorker by Passumpsic Publishing

For permission to reproduce any of the material in this book,
contact Brandeis University Press, 415 South Street, Waltham MA 02453,
or visit brandeisuniversitypress.com

Library of Congress Cataloging-in-publishing Data
available upon request
cloth ISBN 978-1-68458-164-1
ebook ISBN 978-1-68458-165-8
5 4 3 2 1

Dedicated to the memory of my father,

Joseph E. Moukawsher, Harvard Law '49,

because you were right all along, and in

memory of my brother,

CDR E. James Moukawsher, USCG (1955–95),

because you were the best and

brightest of us all

CONTENTS

PREFACE

There are perfectly good reasons not to read this book. For instance, you may think the courts are no more complex than required. That might be a good reason not to trouble yourself with it—unless you want to test the strength of that belief.

Another more common reason might be that you recognize that going to court is needlessly complex, but you believe there is nothing to be done about it. That's just the way courts are. We aren't likely to change them, so why bother talking about it?

But what if this book was mostly about changes any lawyer or judge could make without anyone's help or permission? If that interests you, keep reading.

And, of course, we can all question the author's credentials. A book by a US Supreme Court justice might be interesting. But a book by a trial judge in a state court—especially one who isn't in my state? Will it be relevant?

Fortunately, this book has mostly modest and certainly universal goals. To place things in context, it tries to understand some of the higher thinking that led courts to where they are today, but its real focus is on fifty practical steps derived from around forty years of researching, drafting, and litigating all kinds of cases all across the country capped by about a decade of judging them. If you work in a courtroom or if you don't and simply want to understand what goes on in them, this book might interest you. Whatever it does, it speaks for nobody except its author. It's pure opinion, so you can take it or leave it.

This book isn't political. If you see disagreement with judges you admire, try to withhold judgment. If you see what you view as a partisan red flag concerning the consequences of a court's ruling, you will also find a flag you might view as representing the opposite camp in the book's preference for the plain language of a statute over its legislative history.

The only thing this book cares about is getting people who work in courts to question whether courts are needlessly complex and encouraging them to consider what they might do to make them more comprehensible—more worthy of respect and more able to solve problems than create them, to do the job in ways we can understand, and to show concern for the humans and humanity that ought to be our focus in court.

While many of this book's lessons apply to criminal court, it's basically about civil litigation of all types in state and federal courts. And it's mostly about the everyday cases. With a few exceptions, it's not about the cases that get attention from the media.

This book gets pretty far down in the weeds. It goes there because it's the weeds that are choking the litigant-centered humanity out of courts—with snarled complaints, tangled motion practice, choking discovery, smothering trials, and stultifying legal rulings. These weeds have always been there. The problem is they're getting thicker and more prolific.

The weeds keep the courts from seeing their duty to the people in front of them and the people at large. Courts should worry that too often they simply get rid of a case or that, when forced to address it, the court and the lawyers talk around the issues the parties want addressed rather than thoughtfully resolving them. We should worry that needless complexity strangles the village elders who sit on the bench and replaces them with medieval monks—lost in their manuscripts, exalting their procedures, incanting their prior sayings, and laying everywhere traps of tortured logic for the unwary.

This book identifies the problem, including through an analysis of Justice Alito's 2022 majority opinion on abortion that focuses on his process-centered thinking, not his result. It notes that one cause of needless complexity is that, unlike Justice Alito, many lawyers and judges have no unifying and organizing vision of how to decide cases. Most visions, including his, have failed us, so instead we cling to busy work as a way to appear thoughtful, organized, and dispassionate.

Next, the book suggests a new way for lawyers and judges to reimagine their work by focusing on the people in front of them and the humanity of which they are a part. It asks them to consider that the rules take us only so far and to consider the credibility we might gain by admitting that, for the rest, we apply fallible human judgment to address problems. This book then walks through the lawsuit stage by stage, naming specific ways the courts seem to disconnect from humanity and practicality. Most importantly, this book proposes fifty specific solutions intended to be simple and fast and to make the law more relevant to life and more credible to the public.

The author has only one aim: to recognize lessons from many years in court and pass them on. Make of them what you will.

ACKNOWLEDGMENTS

When my parents, Joseph and Patricia Moukawsher, came home to raise six children after serving in World War II, they never stopped serving. They worked for decades to better their state, their region, and their town on boards, commissions, and in office. All six of their children went on to serve their country, their state, their town, or their community. We had learned from our parents that being part of a community means trying to right wrongs, ease pain, lift spirits, and serve others. The belief that this is a duty has driven my life and this book.

My life has been about grappling with those values within the grubby and grand experiences of life. I spent seventeen sessions observing the Connecticut General Assembly, mostly while representing clients but also as a member of the Connecticut House of Representatives and as counselor to the president of the Senate. When that president went to Congress, I got glimpses of how Congress runs too, especially when my friend and former client Congressman John Larson was chairman of the House Democratic Caucus.

Despite glimpses of the legislative branch and a brief stint in the Connecticut governor's office, most of my experience has been in court. I owe many of those experiences to my father and to my former law partner and long-time friend Mike Walsh, a well-loved Hartford litigator. For twenty years, as litigation found me in courtrooms across the country, we were perhaps the only law partnership in America never to have a disagreement.

I owe my experience as a judge to a gracious nod from Governor Dannel Malloy but wouldn't have it without the guidance and support of Tim Shearin, the best of friends and the best of litigators; Andrew McDonald, previously the governor's legal counsel and now the honorable associate justice of the Connecticut Supreme Court; Rep. John Larson; and one more, whom I will mention last. If you don't like the book, don't blame them. I didn't consult them, and they couldn't have known what I would get up to.

You can credit this book to Sue Ramin, my acquisitions editor at Brandeis University Press, who saw merit in my work and has given me a chance to give it voice. I am eternally grateful to her and to Roz Kabrhel and Dan Breen at Brandeis for their suggestions and support, and I thank Anthony Lipscomb, Hannah Krasikov, Ben Woollard, and the others who helped push the project along. I am grateful for encouragement as I entered the publishing world from my friends at the Library of Congress, including Sue Siegel and Becky Clark, and I thank Carla Hayden, librarian of Congress, for being so welcoming to authors and so determined to share the library with the broadest possible audience.

My immediate family, an eclectic group of children, swans, snapping turtles, dogs, and cats who grew up on the river in Mystic, Connecticut, deserve special mention. But most of all I give thanks, love, and the rest of my life to my wife, Betsy, who has given the world Jackie, Kate, Ted, and Alex; her support to my work; her political clout to my judgeship; her service to her town as its clerk; and her food and love to the world.

THE COMMON FLAW

1 : PREFER HUMANITY
TO COMPLEXITY

Needless complexity is the rule

This is the age of the meme. Memes are instant. They're pithy. They're often trenchant. Like tweets, they make life more direct, more focused, more immediately accountable. Sometimes too much so. But they're here to stay. They often convey wholly formed ideas in the blink of an eye—some valuable, some silly, some dangerous.

Courts can't keep up with them. And we don't exactly want them to. We can't resolve human problems with a meme, a tweet, a bumper sticker, or a slogan. The real trouble with the courts is that while the rest of the world is hurtling through virtual worlds—gathering new ideas and new values—courts are becoming more out of touch than ever. Many do nothing about a problem until it is too late to matter, and when they do, increasingly we can't understand what they say or why they say it.

This doesn't keep us from learning about the Supreme Court's rulings on abortion or gay marriage, but those rulings have taken decades to happen, and when they are announced, few of us rush for copies of the decision—someone has to translate even those decisions for us.

The bigger problem is that in the 99 percent of cases that aren't sweeping and socially relevant, it's hard to see the courts even addressing the problem that prompted the lawsuit in the first place. Instead, we sense that courts more often deflect the issues with procedural rulings, smother them in unsatisfying settlements, or address at great length everything about a case except its heart. This makes it harder to see the courts' contribution to democracy at a moment when faith in our institutions is at a dangerous low point.

1

Wouldn't we rather see courts at their best than their worst? We can see them at their best when they are timely problem solvers in everyday life and business—when they try to understand a dispute by finding facts about its core and when they resolve the dispute by transparently applying values enshrined in law to those facts.

But instead of vindicating established values plainly, firmly, and convincingly, courts can easily appear to be damaging their own relevance and credibility. We find them hiding more than ever behind long, slowly produced decisions full of unexpressed or arcane reasoning. Increasingly, it's possible to see the typical court decision as an indirect and sometimes inexplicable resolution of a direct dispute. For most of us observers, this has left contemporary legal maneuvering and legal decisions at all levels appearing deliberate, scholarly, and mechanical rather than responsive, principled, and transparent.

Courts aren't merely slow. The most worrying thing is that they give in more than ever to the vice for which they have always been mocked—exalting form over substance. This happens when courts strain and expand basic questions about who may sue (standing), when they may sue (statutes of limitation), which court can hear them (jurisdiction), whether their complaint sounds like a winner (plausibility), whether they sued too soon (ripeness), and whether they sued too late (staleness). When courts are preoccupied with increasingly complex mechanics, they resolve fewer cases on their merits. In other words, courts resolve too many cases without ever answering the actual questions the parties raised.

It's no secret that the courts try only a tiny number of cases. Over 99 percent of all federal civil lawsuits end without a trial.[1] Many are settled unsatisfactorily because the parties would rather be unhappy than broke. They would rather be dissatisfied with the courts than pay the crushing cost of maneuvering around the procedural obstacles between them and a trial. When cases don't settle, statistics show courts usually dispose of them, particularly in federal court, by granting a preliminary motion rather than by deciding the merits of the case.[2] And while courts try far fewer cases, trials are protracted and financially crushing. As we will see later, when judges decide cases, it now takes longer than ever to get a written decision, and the decisions themselves are much longer.

FIGURE 1.1. *"Damn it, Fenton! We can't refuse to hear every case."*
See Illustration Credits on page 241.

Of course, it would be one thing if these longer decisions were wiser for the wear. But the worst part of all this busyness in decision writing may be that it happens without us seeing evidence that judges have thought deeply about the issues and without them saying anything meaningful about the case.

And this leads to a dangerous possibility. It's hard to measure. It won't show up in statistics. But the preoccupation with avoiding trials and obscuring meaning through needless complexity suggests that courts — and lawyers too — may be subconsciously avoiding responsibility for making hard choices.

Rather than discussing the value judgments, the credibility determinations, or the human conflict that is supposed to decide a case, those who work in the legal profession may have found it easier — particularly in these tense times — to disguise the disposition of cases as technical matters having nothing to do with the merits of the case. This often happens in tandem with efforts to avoid the reality and accountability of a ruling by pushing the litigants into settling before any decision is made.

Those who do this suggest to the participants that what happens in court comes from something other than human judgment about facts and legal argument — that is to say, there is no one to blame, so there is no blame at all. Some think that this minimizes conflict. But we should question whether this merely deflects it, and deflecting conflict doesn't always resolve it. Sometimes it merely leaves it smoldering, waiting to flare up again.

In recent years, some lawyers have made the problem worse by serving up ever more creative excuses for judges to avoid the basic issues in a case. When judges accept these excuses, they deflect; they dodge—they don't decide. Claimants resent it when rulings are about who may make a claim and how to make a claim rather than anything about the claim. Many times, this resentment leads to more litigation and dissatisfaction, not less.

The formalism that gave us needless complexity and how to replace it

Now let's look deeper at the problem by looking not at just what's going wrong, but at the clash of ideas that may have led us into needless complexity in the first place. Of course, we know that lawyers and judges don't spend much time thinking about the higher causes of why we file what we file and why we rule what we rule. Instead, what we do may best be seen as reflecting habit and subconscious assumptions.

We turn a screw to the right because we want to tighten it. We give it no thought. Somewhere in our heads, we think, "righty tighty, lefty loosey." Somebody told us this long ago—or more likely, someone showed us this. Yet whoever showed us this didn't invent it and likely hadn't given it any thought either. The origin of the behavior is somewhere in the dark recesses of time where someone invented the screw and decreed, "it shall turn to the right." We don't know anything about that moment in time, and we don't care.

What judges and lawyers do is likely similar. Someone in law school and later at work showed us what a brief looks like, what a complaint looks like, and what kind of motions lawyers file, and we followed their example. We didn't ask why. We had long since stopped being two-year-olds with their incessant questioning why. After all, we have work to do and bills to pay.

After we mastered imitation, some of us sought to take the forms we had been following and "improve" them. We filed more motions, and the motions were more complicated. We aimed for the perfect brief. But still, what we asked the courts for and how we asked for it remained in the same form, backed by the same thinking—whatever that is—that has long animated the choice of what motion to file and what to say in a brief or pleading. What happened was merely a more "beautiful" version of the same basic form—maybe it had more background about the applicable law or cited more cases that sounded like the one at issue. Maybe it mentioned law review articles and statistics. We became pleased with our work. We created, in the abstract, the perfect filing. Maybe it had nothing to do with winning the case, but it was beautiful.

It's much the same with judges. Before they reach the bench, most of them have learned to read briefs and write briefs like those they have read. Before taking the bench, judges have also likely read hundreds of decisions by other judges. So when they assume the bench, they have many models in mind. They know how judges write. The first instinct of many new judges is quite logical—to be accepted as a judge. So they write like one. Again, they don't have time to question the model. They just get on with the job.

But if we think things aren't working so well in court, we may have to rethink some of those assumptions. Fundamental problems require fundamental change, and to embrace that change may mean we had better understand where our customs come from and the competing ideas that led to them.

So, what theory supports the way most of us do things today? Why so many preliminary motions? Why avoid deciding hard cases in ways the parties and the public can understand? Why are briefs and opinions such a thicket? Why do we miss our big chance so often—the chance to justify the choices we make rather than leaving them unexplained beneath a compost of superfluities? In short, why is our system *needlessly* complex?

The road to an answer leads us through a place we'd rather avoid: legal philosophy, or jurisprudence. Jurisprudence is sometimes needlessly, but very often needfully, complex. All we can be sure of is that whatever we say about jurisprudence, it will invite caveats and diversions we haven't time for here.

So, let's make no pretense of a deep dive. We can simply use some basic concepts about legal thinking to show how competing legal theories have left us with needless complexity and how rethinking our approach might get us out of this mess.

In this spirit, let's dare to put a label on the thinking behind needless complexity, not to expound on philosophy but only to have a name for the thing we oppose. Let's call what goes on in too many courts in too many cases "legal formalism"—where formalism suggests form over substance.

Needless complexity in the courts is likely a product of a kind of legal formalism. *Formalism* is a useful word to describe the root cause of needless complexity because legal formalism is known to be concerned with forms and formulas. Formalism is devoted to the kind of mechanical method of decision-making that identifies a rule, runs the facts through a controlled experiment, and then produces a judgment.[3] The process is clinical. It includes subjective calls and has implications for real people and social problems, but it smothers them in process. It suggests the existence of an inevitable, objectively correct answer that was not fashioned by living, breathing judges but discovered by them through the process of formal reasoning, science, or both.

Legal formalism likely explains today's disappointing legal writing and thinking. To decide if formalism is to blame for needless complexity, we will consider it after looking at specific complaints, motions, briefs, and decisions. We will find that legal writing seldom focuses on the pivotal human judgment that is the core of a case. Judges' decisions discuss tangential matters at great length, appearing to produce an inevitable result, but only conclude as they do because of a human judgment call they never discuss—often an unexplained assumption. The deliberative part of the decision is merely derivative of the unexplained, unjustified assumption.

Let's consider one example now. Justice Alito's 2022 opinion for the Supreme Court majority in *Dobbs v. Jackson Women's Health Organization* overturned the court's earlier decision in *Roe v. Wade*—the ruling limiting states' rights to regulate abortion.[4] Regardless of how you view abortion rights, there are things wrong with the decision that are typical of legal formalism.

We know the constitution doesn't mention the word *abortion*. Justice Alito recognized this. Starting with that observation is called "textualism."[5] *Dobbs* was not about a right explicitly named in the Constitution. Ultimately, it was about what interests the Constitution protects with the provision concerning "liberty" under the Fourteenth Amendment.

After not finding the word *abortion* in the Constitution, Justice Alito further framed the question. He said that whatever liberty a woman had in an abortion at the time of his opinion depended chiefly on her legal right to an abortion in the history and tradition that preceded *Roe*. This is called "originalism."[6]

It's this second assumption that's telling. Justice Alito framed the question this way even though the court in *Roe v. Wade* didn't base its decision on a historically recognized *right to an abortion*. It based its decision on the historically recognized right to *privacy*. In *Roe*, the court held that this already-recognized right was broad enough to embrace a woman's rights concerning abortion.[7]

By changing the right being examined under his originalist study of history from privacy to abortion, Justice Alito created an easier target to aim at. He knew that, before *Roe*, privacy was recognized in history as a "right," but abortion was not. So, the case was over the moment he adopted his assumption. We might call this part of his jurisprudential approach "stacking the deck."

Justice Alito didn't ignore the long-recognized right to privacy. But when the opinion reached the privacy issue, another unexplained assumption emerged. Barely addressing the court's earlier liberty-based privacy rulings about marriage, contraception, family, and so forth, Justice Alito noted that the court has always talked not about mere liberty, but "*ordered* liberty." Then, without explaining the role of the word "ordered," Justice Alito concluded: "Our Nation's historical understanding of ordered liberty does not prevent the people's elected representatives from deciding how abortion should be regulated."[8] But why? What about "ordered" liberty in our historical understanding means the privacy-based right to contraception recognized in 1965 in *Griswold v. Connecticut* is part of "ordered" liberty, but abortion isn't?[9] More on this in a moment.

But first, what was most important constitutionally in *Dobbs* was whether we *should* measure a woman's right to liberty in the form of privacy today by measuring her right to liberty, and more specifically to abortion, in history and tradition. Justice Alito treated this as a settled question. He said all liberty rights that deserve constitutional protection must be proved to be deeply embedded in our history and tradition. For this proposition, he quoted the court's 1997 decision in *Washington v. Glucksberg* as holding that to find a right guaranteed but not named by the constitution, it must be "deeply rooted in this Nation's history and tradition."[10] He could have chosen other cases that called it "history and conscience."[11]

But the real trouble is that Justice Alito didn't say much about why he chose *Glucksberg* when he could have chosen other cases that don't look at history at all. Justice Alito could have confronted the reality recognized in a case he cited but, on this point, didn't quote—*Brown v. Board of Education*. In that case, Chief Justice Earl Warren wrote for a *unanimous* court that racially segregated public schools denied minority children the equal protection of the laws under the Fourteenth Amendment. In doing so, all nine members of the court underscored the importance of looking at rights as they should stand in light of today's realities, not yesterday's: "In approaching this problem, we cannot turn the clock back to 1868, when the Amendment was adopted, or even to 1896, when *Plessy v. Ferguson* was written [saying separate but equal schools were constitutional]. We must consider public education in the light of its full development and its present place in American life throughout the Nation. Only in this way can it be determined if segregation in public schools deprives these plaintiffs of the equal protection of the laws."[12]

Regardless what part of the Fourteenth Amendment was in play in the two cases (liberty versus equal protection), the *Dobbs* decision is less convincing because it ignored the easily made argument that history was a bad measure in *Dobbs* for the same reason it was in *Brown*.

Black Americans had no history of schooling in this country. During most of our history, they had no rights at all. And, as the *Dobbs* dissent pointed out, neither did women.[13] In fact, the Fifteenth Amendment to the Constitution gave Black Americans the right to vote around fifty years before the Constitution granted women that right. They may have been put in doubt by interference, but no one

doubted that a woman had no federal right to vote until the Nineteenth Amendment was ratified in 1920.

The Fourteenth Amendment's guarantee of equal protection of
the laws was also known to apply to Black Americans when it went
into effect in 1868. The Supreme Court didn't apply it to women until
more than one hundred years later, and at common law, a woman's
legal existence was mostly subsumed by her husband under the doctrine of coverture.[14]

Justice Alito warned against imposing through the constitution "our
own ardent ideas" about what liberty the Constitution protects.[15] He
suggested that the dissent would simply enforce its own view of right,

FIGURE 1.2. *"I interpret the death penalty according to the times."*

wrong, and liberty, while he was controlled not by his own views but "history and tradition." He ignored that he was enforcing his own view of right, wrong, and liberty when he chose to be guided by "history and tradition" and when he said the test applied to abortion, not privacy.

Justice Alito's opinion was an example of today's formalism. His opinion gave the appearance of deliberation without focusing convincingly on what actually decided the case—by focusing on history rather than justifying his focus on history as the measure of the rights of people with no historic rights. By claiming he was forced to choose "history and tradition" despite the illogic of doing so, Justice Alito gave his decision the appearance of being compelled and not the product of human judgment despite its depending entirely on his unexplained human judgment to apply that ill-fitting standard rather than another.

Now let's return to Justice Alito's discussion of privacy. In the original draft of the decision leaked to the press, Justice Alito didn't bother much with why "ordered liberty" recognized a fundamental right to use contraception and marry persons of the same sex or a different race but granted no fundamental rights related to abortion.[16]

In the final version, he reflected more on this question—or his writing reflected the concerns of the other justices who joined in his opinion. In any case, Justice Alito explained that privacy rights related to abortion were different because a potential life was involved in a way it was not when the issue was who may marry and whether people may use contraception.[17]

This yielded a kind of pushmi-pullyu opinion. It headed in two different directions at once—toward history and tradition while also giving weight to the court majority's view on the sanctity of life.

That the case involved a potential life may have been an important distinction, but not under the "history and tradition" approach that Justice Alito relied on. As the dissent points out, there was no "history and tradition" of allowing Black Americans to marry Whites, men to marry men, and contraception to be used by anyone, yet the Supreme Court has held that all of these are constitutional rights under the same clause at issue in *Dobbs*.[18]

Only Justice Thomas was forthright about the implications of the history-and-tradition approach. He said it required the court to discard the idea of substantive due process altogether and look potentially elsewhere in the Constitution when considering claimed rights regarding contraception, gay marriage, and interracial marriage.[19]

Justice Thomas may worry some of us about what he might do, but Justice Alito should worry us with what he meant.

In *Roe v. Wade*, Justice Blackmun didn't do much better at focusing on the real issues than Justice Alito did in *Dobbs*. That decision turned on its own unexplained assumptions. The decision discussed disputed historical sources to suggest that history has not always frowned on abortion. Justice Blackmun wrote, "we feel it desirable briefly to survey . . ."[20] But unlike Justice Alito, Justice Blackmun didn't say what significance history had for the decision, if any.

What is more concerning is that Justice Blackmun identified privacy as the constitutionally protected right in play but, having done so by citing examples, he spent little time justifying his pivotal conclusion that this privacy right is "broad enough to encompass a woman's decision whether or not to terminate her pregnancy."[21] The best we can say is that he went on briefly to discuss the psychological and physical burdens pregnancy imposes on a woman. The connection between recognized privacy rights and this claimed right should have been the main focus of the decision, but it got short shrift and inevitably fed criticisms of the court's reasoning.[22]

The puzzling thing about both decisions is why they didn't adequately justify their main assumptions. With both of them, with so much at stake, we should expect a thorough justification. The two decisions represent conflicting judicial views about what matters— the past or current reality. It makes it easier to discredit these important choices when their authors don't join the battle candidly or adequately.

Roe's implications for sociological and biological concerns might have been a good chance for Justice Blackmun to display legal realism. Realists frankly confess that judges exercise judgment and often use contemporary science to justify those judgments. Still, a judge might not want to confess to being a realist these days because, in caricature, realists suggest that courts' judgments are more subjective than scientific—a decision is more about what a judge ate for breakfast than it is a reasoned attempt to take established values and apply them to a set of facts. It nakedly admits what Justice Alito refused to acknowledge—the justices enforce their own views.

But what if Justice Alito at least admitted he was applying reason—the collective judgment of the court majority—to the recognized fundamental right of privacy while balancing that right against the right of the state to protect an actual or potential life? Justice O'Connor candidly admitted that was the job when *Roe* was modified in 1992 in *Planned Parenthood v. Casey*. She said the decision "may call upon the Court in interpreting the Constitution to exercise that same capacity which by tradition courts always have exercised: reasoned judgment."[23] But then again, *Dobbs* overruled that decision too.

Still, Justice Alito could have admitted that we can't measure the rights of the historically oppressed by their historic oppression. Instead, he could have simply argued that *Roe* struck the balance wrong between the state and a woman.

Nothing is more fundamental in law than life. Life is listed first in the Fourteenth Amendment sequence of protections of "life, liberty, or property." The law reserves the harshest punishments for the taking of life. Would he have gotten closer to the heart of the issue by concluding that the importance of life—actual or potential—outweighs the liberty/privacy right?

He might have argued that privacy may attach to matters like marriage and contraception but that the stakes are different with life or potential life. It could have led him to hold that the balance favoring life means that the fundamental right to privacy does not embrace abortion, and thus, it may be regulated by states.

Alternatively, with more pronounced legal realism, Justice Alito could have argued that science has taught us more about how quickly a fetus develops and how much sooner it can live outside of the womb. He might have observed that science has greatly expanded the means that women have to control their own bodies without abortion—particularly late-term abortion. These changes, he might have argued, mean that the states' interests in protecting the unborn has grown while a woman's need for constitutional protection has shrunk. Again, he could have claimed the balance needed to be restruck. Again, he mentioned these developments, but again, they didn't matter under his "history and tradition" approach to constitutional interpretation.[24]

Regardless of whether we agree that these explanations would be the "right" decision, they are a rationale on the pivotal question that would show us the court's sincerity and help us respect it. Wouldn't that be better than predetermining the outcome by picking without justifying a standard the court didn't have to apply to a situation where it was so obviously a bad fit?

As Justice O'Connor said, judges must use judgment. But this doesn't mean that rejecting formalism means that law is merely judges enforcing their own views of right and wrong. For now, the thing to understand is that the abortion debate shows how needless complexity often creates a smoke screen concealing the deep issue in a case.

Is that a good thing? Not if law gets its legitimacy from being principled, understood, and respected. This book argues that, in a democracy, law should be principled, understood, and respected. It tries to show why this is a good thing and how we might get closer to achieving it.

But first, there's more bad news. Most contemporary legal work is far less focused than Justice Alito's *Dobbs* opinion. The bulk of his opinion at least supported a proposition—mostly that women had no historic right to an abortion. What makes the formula behind too many motions, briefs, and rulings worse is that most of what they say is given over to process rather than argument in favor of any proposition.

As we will see, typical motions, briefs, and decisions are dominated by discussions of the court's jurisdiction, the standard under which the court examines the case, the case's history in court, the background of the claims, the contentions of the parties, the law that might apply, and the law's background.

When we read legal filings, we are too easily left thinking that they spend most of their energy giving the appearance of arguing or deliberating without arguing or deliberating at all. When we see the proposed answer or the answer to the case, it's as if it appears out of nowhere. It's discovered as if by magic. Much legal writing appears to assume that by enduring the typical formalistic gyrations, we are bound to discover the answer. After all that effort—at whatever it was we were doing—we don't have to explain. We can simply say: "There it is."

The suggestion that a case outcome is inevitable connects to an-other idea important in the minds of many legal thinkers and prac-titioners: that there is only one right answer to a case. Some believe it can be discovered through rational exercises about the subject at hand while others suggest we can discover an appropriate outcome merely by showing how much process we went through to achieve it—things like a review of the case's procedural history, the parties' contentions, or the background law.

We should ask: Is this a meaningful process?

Today, most of us still think of the concept of "discovery" in its non-legal sense as a scientific process, but the debate about discovering the "one right answer"—the one that exists independent of human judgment—is as old as time. Both Plato and Aristotle believed that truth, beauty, justice, greenness, and other concepts are not relative things—they have an independent existence we can discover through intellectual exercise. Plato believed we can find them intuitively. Ar-istotle and later thinkers, like Saint Thomas Aquinas, argued that we can find what is true, what is beautiful, and what is the "right" answer to a case through a formal reasoning process.

The idea that there is a single *right* answer to be discovered shows up in the way most lawyers and judges approach cases. They dig, dig, dig for it. We'll see this in action later when we consider the use of similar-sounding cases in particular. Done right, these cases are marshaled to prove a point. But too many times, cases are dug up, exposed, and then included in complaints, motions, briefs, and deci-sions as a kind of background ultimately used for little more than to show how much work the party did.

Anyway, many legal professionals think that the answer to any given case is out there and can be discovered from a process of rea-soning involving a search through the sacred texts—through case decisions or perhaps history or even legislative history. These prac-titioners imagine that the decision in the case doesn't come from the judge: it is found in the law.

Needless complexity lives and breathes concern about there being a difference between what judges do and what law is. Legal realism repudiates it utterly—and yes, perhaps too much so sometimes, as realism can suggest that judges' decisions in hard cases reflect only

FIGURE 1.3.
*"My English teacher
says there are many
ways to solve a
problem and my
math teacher says
there is only one way
to solve a problem."*

their personal opinions and not a sincere attempt to reflect the values
that lie behind the case law, the statutes, and the Constitution.

Formalism leads some lawyers and judges to discover answers
whenever possible solely by reading texts. Whenever the text is clear,
this makes sense. This is textualism. But for others, the plain language of the text is never enough. For them, the law and the right
answer to a case are never just what a statute or a precedent says. Instead, they seek the Platonic "just" or "right" answer in the sense of
its being the one and only correct answer. Indeed, in that connection,
they would say that in some cases, we must disregard the plain words
of a text in favor of a "good" answer—in favor of a moral answer. They
believe in "natural law." They believe that a thing is not law if it is immoral. It is far less mechanical than the kind of formalism we're concerned with here.

Natural law supports the eighteenth-century Enlightenment belief
that no allegiance is owed to an immoral king. It inspired, in our own

Declaration of Independence, the assertion of the *"self-evident"* truth that "all men are created equal" and that men are *"endowed by their creator* with certain *unalienable* rights."

Natural law theory suggests many different ways of discovering law, but in the formalist sense, we can still see the formulas as a hunt for the one true answer, not merely a precedent or an applicable statute.

In philosophy, natural law was the study of men like Immanuel Kant.[25] In law, a form of it was urged more recently by Ronald Dworkin.[26] The natural law belief that an immoral law is not law was challenged and, for a time, overtaken by a close relative of textualism—legal positivism.

Positivists posit that law isn't a matter of what ought to be—what is morally correct—it's a matter of what lawmakers say it is, especially in legal codes. Law isn't discovered. It's decreed. It can't be judged beautiful or correct. It doesn't draw any of its legitimacy by being understood and accepted by the public. Indeed, as a textualist and originalist, Justice Alito asserted in *Dobbs* that courts can't be concerned about public reaction.[27] The law is what it is. This means that judges can apply it without higher thinking about right and wrong and without worrying too much about the human beings it will affect.

The consequences of the positivist view were explored at the end of World War II. Its implication for judges was the subject of the classic film *Judgment at Nuremburg*, where Nazi judges mounted the positivist defense. They claimed that they only enforced the letter of the law and that Nazi law's lack of moral content was irrelevant to what they had to do. The victorious Allies imprisoned some Nazis and hanged others for holding and implementing this morally impartial view. This put a damper on legal positivism for a time despite the mighty efforts of its most ardent postwar advocate, Professor H. L. A. Hart.[28]

Perhaps as a consequence, legal realism continued to grow. Its high priests were Karl Llewellyn and Jerome Frank.[29] Legal realism peaked in the 1970s, and over the years, its adherents' willingness to admit that judges apply judgment led to the charge that some judges were ignoring what statutes said and simply deciding cases with sole regard to their own—decidedly liberal—views. This gave judges favoring a positivist, formalist, textualist, originalist view, like Justice Antonin Scalia, fuel as Justice Scalia and others argued that the courts were plagued by judges pushing partisan social agendas and rewriting statutes and the Constitution to serve their ends. Their favorite bugbear was *Roe v. Wade*, and, at last, they slew it in *Dobbs*.

Under assault, legal realism went into hiding beginning in the 1980s. Judges didn't want it to appear that the troubling questions at the heart of most cases were being manhandled by social do-gooders or influenced by their preference for oatmeal over eggs. But they couldn't exactly fall back openly into the moral vacuum of legal positivism either. Some invented a textualist and originalist substitute for legal positivism.

Many more judges simply floundered. The lack of a dominant way of thinking about law has contributed much to needless complexity in the courts today. With no guiding philosophy about how to fill gaps in the law, it seems as if many lawyers and judges have fallen back on process—on the appearance of deliberation and objectivity—and too many times, this has meant they have left out the most important assumptions and conclusions in their work because they don't have an accepted construct to justify how they reached them. This has led to a reign in too many courts of a content-neutral formalism. The real issue gets ignored altogether or disposed of with a footnote or an unexplained judgment.

So, let's say you're a postmodern judge. You don't want to be labelled a "realist," a "textualist," or an "originalist." You want to look objective and thoughtful. How can you explain your method for resolving ambiguities in the law? What model do you have left?

As we dissect legal decisions later in this book, we'll see that many judges appear to be unconsciously mimicking a kind of scientific method to fill these gaps. Even though faith in science isn't what it used to be, at least it hasn't sunk as low as faith in politics has, and the last things judges want to be seen as is political.

Remember what a typical legal case goes through. Long and technically detailed complaints. Multiple motions challenging the form of the pleading. Revisions. Challenges to standing, jurisdiction, venue. Vast reams of data called "discovery" get collected. And then there is the crucible of the trial, where, after elaborate setting-up exercises in pretrial motions and the like, the trial subjects the facts to heat—if not light—while every word is recorded and documents entered as

exhibits pile high. Finally, for a case without a jury, the judge recites
these procedural things again at length before reaching some brief
and often inadequately explained conclusion.

At least from what we learned in middle school, the record of a science experiment looks much like this. Scientists try to ensure objectivity through methodical attention to what unfolds in the lab.

Before they experiment, scientists record the tools they will use,
the participants, the location, and the conditions. Then they detail
each step they plan to take—exactly how much from what beaker
will be added when. At last, the experiment begins. Next, lab workers
dispassionately record what their senses detect from the steps they
take—every fizz, every pop, increases in temperature, decreases in
temperature, color changes, smells, sounds, whatever they can feel.
They record it all with exquisite particularity and complete dispassion.

Only after they have extensively documented their work, turned
the burners off, removed their goggles, and stroked their chins do
scientists reach their conclusions. They assume that their meticu-
lous records help them deliberate and permit others to replicate their
work. They also believe that what they do affirms their objectivity and
bolsters confidence in their conclusions.

Are judges trying to appear to be doing the same thing? As we will
see later, many of them start by recording the date the complaint was
filed, the dates and nature of motions, the evidence offered by one
party, the evidence offered by the other party, a history of the applicable law, and the arguments of counsel. Even if it's only subconscious,
perhaps they assume this scientific appearance bolsters confidence in
their work.

But we might question this assumption for two reasons. First,
many judges spend most of their time recording things that have no
bearing on their decisions. It's like scientists recording the color of the
lab walls, the dimensions of the room, the times they checked in and
out of the building, the background of the company they work for,
and the history of boric acid.

Second, and most important, we must ask ourselves, is a judge's decision really science—or is it art? Isn't the final decision more human
judgment than an ineluctable, objective conclusion drawn from rote
process?

After all, it doesn't pay to confuse the mere collection of data with wisdom. When a judge applies the law to a set of facts, isn't it more likely that judgment about the facts decides the case, not the collection of the facts themselves? If it is, then the missing element in most legal opinions is an adequate explanation of how that judgment was applied to produce a result.

The truth is that with science—as opposed to the imitation of science—judges decide cases using their experiences and insights and those of the entire legal system. Experience and insight applied to determine what evidence is relevant. Experience and insight applied to determine what witnesses may be believed. Experience and insight applied to determine the consequences caused by certain rules—with whether these rules are effective because enforcing them creates a better, or at least a more orderly, society.

Deciding a case, like deciding so many things, usually ends with an incorporeal synthesis of experience and judgment that can't be measured with scientific instruments. This being so, judges should explain their rulings—how everything in front of them combined to create an impression that hardened into a decision. Why do we think a punishment is cruel and unusual? Why do we think a trade practice was unfair? The standard is plain enough, but what's most important in the case is how we apply it and how we justify the way we apply it.

We might do this at the outset of a decision by saying: "the defendant Millicent Murgatroyd was 'negligent' because she was driving sixty miles an hour in a small parking lot while wearing a blindfold and playing the slide trombone." We can then go on to explain how we know Murgatroyd was doing this and why it's dangerous.

This is how a decision could be structured if we focus on judgment rather than process—when we emphasize reflection on and justification of the result. We might hope that this would represent applying wisdom to circumstances. But merely reciting the testimony, naming the exhibits, belaboring the applicable law, and declaring a winner leaves the decision focused almost entirely on circumstances. Because these activities are entirely needless, they are doing something even harder to support than what Justice Alito did when he didn't explain his assumptions but explained their inevitable consequences for the case at length.

So where can we turn for a way of thinking about cases? Legal positivism can justify evil. The law shouldn't be evil. Natural law theory pretends we can know more than we can—that we can discover the one true moral answer to a question and ignore public officials and public opinion that don't follow it. Legal realism is subject to the follies of the bogus science experiment on the one hand and politics on the other—science and wisdom aren't the same.

What about common sense? It's been used before. Nobody has better described what a complaint should say, what a motion should be about, how a brief should be written, and how a judge should rule better than Thomas Jefferson did when he explained why he wrote the Declaration of Independence. He said its goal was to place "before mankind the common sense of the subject, in terms so plain and firm as to command their assent."

Jefferson's focus on common sense suggests another school of legal thought: pragmatism. Pragmatism is associated with one of America's most celebrated judges, Justice Oliver Wendell Holmes. Like common sense, pragmatism is an especially American idea. Its roots may be with the Englishman Francis Bacon, but its best branches grew from the minds of the Americans Charles Peirce, John Dewey, and William James.[30] It focuses on whether things work in a practical setting. It is the view that Justice Stephen Breyer offers in his book *Making Our Democracy Work*—as an alternative to the originalism and textualism espoused by Justice Alito in *Dobbs* and by the late Justice Antonin Scalia everywhere.[31]

Pragmatism is pretty close to the mark. It is reflected in Justice Holmes's famous repudiation of the "discovery" of law—the idea that it exists and must be found rather than fashioned and interpreted by humans. The law, Holmes said, "isn't a brooding omnipresence in the sky."[32] To fill gaps when the law isn't clear, pragmatism examines the purposes of a law and then applies it with a view to its contemporary consequences.

Pragmatism may, as its name suggests, be useful. Yet it's still hard to swallow pragmatism whole. First, it shares roots with positivism that can be bitter because they are entangled not just with Nazis but with the roots of utilitarianism. Utilitarianism, most famously espoused by the English philosophers Jeremy Bentham and John Stewart Mill, can also be seen as pragmatic. Its driving force is utility, a desire to bring the most happiness to the largest number of people.[33]

These utilitarian roots can be bitter because they can justify the sacrifice of the one for the many. This is what the Nazis thought they were doing. But is sacrificing the one for the many consistent with the individuality Americans prize? Utilitarianism can be used to undercut the notion that there are some things the many may not take away from the few—no matter how many of the many are benefited. Indeed, this flawed concept of pragmatism may explain Justice Holmes's now discredited support in *Buck v. Bell* for sterilizing the intellectually disabled with the conclusion that "three generations of imbeciles are enough."[34]

We can further question pragmatism and utilitarianism when we see them in league with those who favor the law and economics movement. The epicenter of this movement has been the University of Chicago, and its high priest on the bench was Judge Richard Posner when he served on the Seventh Circuit Court of Appeals. For this group, "it's the economics, stupid." Law should be structured so that goods get to those who value them most. Liability should be placed on those—in accident cases, for instance—who can most efficiently handle it economically.

We can best explore possible flaws in this movement and thus the imperfection of pragmatism by examining two contrasting things Judge Posner wrote. The first is from his book *How Judges Think*.[35] There, we can see Judge Richard Posner in gleeful and unrestrained eggheadedness.

In *How Judges Think*, Judge Posner invokes Bayesian decision theory—naturally, you've heard of it—to suggest how we might predict whether a witness will be believed. The theory, developed by the eighteenth-century English statistician Thomas Bayes, describes the probability of an event with reference to prior knowledge that might affect it.

Judge Posner's use of the theory admitted that a judge starts with a preconception that might have various origins but is called "prior probability" and that this affects his "posterior probability"—the probability of truth telling perceived by the judge after hearing the actual testimony. Judge Posner then revealed a formula that illustrates how each piece of evidence might affect prior probability. Unfortunately, it looks like this:

$$\Omega(H \backslash x) = p(x \backslash H)/p(x \sim H) \times \Omega(H)$$

Do you want to know how it works? If you do, read his book. His explanation begins at page 65 of the 2008 Harvard University Press edition. It takes a lot of explaining.

But what it turns on shows us why it doesn't turn most of us on at all. It turns on the idea that we can attach a precise numerical probability of truthfulness to every additional piece of information a witness might give after taking the oath—not to mention a precise percentage to be assigned to the aspect that is prejudging. For example, we might unconsciously decide that before testifying, the witness had a 0.25 percent chance of telling the truth. Judge Posner later explained the point of the exercise: "Bayesian theory is a way of systematizing the elementary point that preconception plays a role in rational thought."[36]

But this rather gives the game away. For those of us who tried to understand him, we may have experienced much head-banging cogitation over what each symbol means and how it relates to the others, only to illustrate a point he admitted is "elementary." "But why?"—the nearest two-year-old might ask. Did "systematizing" this *elementary* point—one we already knew—really help us understand it? Equally important, when we realize that the numbers in the formula are wholly subjective and can thus be manipulated to ensure any outcome, the exercise proves useless. It might even invite a bit of teasing.

So, here's a bit of teasing—to make a point, of course. Many of us haven't heard much about Thomas Bayes, but many of us have seen the movie *Dead Poets Society*, where Robin Williams's character tackles useless science physically when considering the introduction to a poetry book written by the fictitious Evans Pritchard, PhD. Dr. Pritchard told us how to understand poetry in ways we might see as similar to the way Judge Posner told us how to understand witness credibility:

> To fully understand poetry, we must first be fluent with its meter, rhyme, and figures of speech, then ask two questions:

FIGURE 1.4. *"The beauty of this is that it is only of theoretical importance, and there is no way it can be of any practical use whatsoever."*

1. How artfully has the objective of the poem been rendered and
2. How important is that objective?

Question 1 rates the poem's perfection; question 2 rates its importance. And once these questions have been answered, determining the poem's greatness becomes a relatively simple matter.

If the poem's score for perfection is plotted on the horizontal of a graph and its importance is plotted on the vertical, then calculating the total area of the poem yields the measure of its greatness.

A sonnet by Byron might score high on the vertical but only average on the horizontal. A Shakespearean sonnet, on the other hand, would score high both horizontally and vertically, yielding a massive total area, thereby revealing the poem to be truly great. As you proceed through the poetry in this book, practice this rating method. As your ability to evaluate poems in this matter grows, so will your enjoyment and understanding of poetry.

Robin Williams's character, the prep school teacher John Keating, then speaks up for humanity in the study of the humanities: "Excrement. That's what I think of Mr. J. Evans Pritchard. We're not laying pipe. We're talking about poetry. How can you describe poetry like American Bandstand? 'Oh, I like Byron. I give him a forty-two, but I can't dance to it.' Now, I want you to rip out that page. Go on. Rip out the entire page. You heard me. Rip it out. Rip it out! Go on. Rip it out!"[37]

Those were the days before digital books. We've missed some ripping good times by giving up our hard copies.

Whatever we've missed, we shouldn't miss this questionable aspect in some realist, utilitarian, and pragmatist thinking. It makes science king and pretends that law is entirely objective. To too many people, science being king merely suggests that process is king. When process is king, we get needless complexity.

Wouldn't we be more believable if we admitted that judging whether a witness is telling the truth isn't a science—it's an art? If we did, then there is a point to be made: we can't pretend science can explain what is actually poetry.

Judge Posner proved he knew about poetry when he wrote his decision on same-sex marriage in *Baskin v. Bogan*. You don't have to agree with the result to admire his writing, his reasoning, and his beating heart:

> At oral argument the state's lawyer was asked whether "Indiana's law is about successfully raising children," and since "you agree same-sex couples can successfully raise children, why shouldn't the ban be lifted as to them?" The lawyer answered that "the assumption is that with opposite-sex couples there is very little thought given during the sexual act, sometimes, to whether babies

may be a consequence." In other words, Indiana's government thinks that straight couples tend to be sexually irresponsible, producing unwanted children by the carload, and so must be pressured (in the form of governmental encouragement of marriage through a combination of sticks and carrots) to marry, but that gay couples, unable as they are to produce children wanted or unwanted, are model parents—model citizens really—so have no need for marriage. Heterosexuals get drunk and pregnant, producing unwanted children; their reward is to be allowed to marry. Homosexual couples do not produce unwanted children; their reward is to be denied the right to marry. Go figure.[38]

It's because of the many passages he has written with humanity and wit that Judge Posner should be remembered as a great American judge—not because he understood Thomas Bayes.

So, it appears that much needless complexity comes from lawyers' and judges' unconvincing efforts to appear clinical, methodical, and neutral even when they take sides. This view reflects nineteenth- and twentieth-century worldviews about pragmatism that evoke the American tinkerer Thomas Edison, for instance—the world of experiment and discovery. But tinkering also gave us the atomic bomb, agent orange, and body counts in Vietnam. It gave us Judge Posner's Bayesian adventure. It's dominated by calculation and process rather than imagination and human sympathy. As with the other ways of thinking, pragmatism, however useful, is too closely linked to needless complexity to be an entirely adequate model.

With postmoderns having no belief in governance by God and knowing the limits of science, where can they turn? How can we describe for them a view that might refocus the lawsuit?

One possibility is what we've been talking about all along. Humans could be our focus when we are talking about how to organize a lawsuit. Not the beautiful disembodied ideal of the perfect brief. Not the search for the one truth. Not the process that produces a heartless, mechanical result.

Humans. Humanity. Humanitarians. Humanism. These words sound sweet to us. Of course, we could sharply distinguish each of these words from each of the others, but together they evoke things most of us identify as worthy concepts for a justice system.

There are real people in front of us in court. They have real problems. Delay hurts them. Expense hurts them. Humanity suffers when we forget those people and say to them: "Sorry, that's just the system." And, in America, corporations are people too, so they are also part of the humanity we must consider when reasoning about law.

The word *humanism* evokes a previous rejection of empty form and ceremony. The Renaissance, which began in Europe in the 1300s, was the great age of humanism. Humanist thinking threw off scholasticism, with its formulaic struggle to discover, as Aristotle and Aquinas would have it, the one true answer to any question.

Scholastics were at home in dimly lit monasteries populated by men who saw as few other humans as they possibly could. But don't human dilemmas require mindfulness of human consequences more than bloodless exercises?

In law, concepts like "reasonable" behavior, "due" process, and "malice" aren't self-defining any more than are religious edicts like "honor thy father and thy mother." They can't suggest a single course of action for all times, for every person, under every circumstance. Context and consequences matter. Human judgment matters.

Renaissance humanism rejected the scholastics' other-worldly thinking, reviving again the Greek and Roman belief that humanity is our focus—humanity became again, as the Greek philosopher Protagoras said, "the measure of all things."

Legal humanism existed during the Renaissance. Its chief focus was inadequate. It was concerned with reviving the study of the original Roman texts for the code known as the *corpus juris civilis*.[39] The movement never matured. We might have profited from it had it focused on a human-centered rather than a text-centered revival of classical rules.

Today, a human-centered legal system might suggest reasons to reduce needless complexity in court. It could start with us recognizing that unless the humans who are subjected to the legal system—inside and outside of business organizations—understand and have faith in it as a system, it will fail.

Besides belief in the basic fairness of a system, what can sustain it? Force? Every tyrant has found out that force doesn't last forever. Pragmatists are right to focus instead on the consequences of what happens in court for humans, but it's not enough. If they are to survive, courts should also consider the human spirit.

His failure to consider that spirit is why Justice Alito's *Dobbs* decision may be unpersuasive to those who have read his words rather than his media.

We all know that *Dobbs* replaced one view of a highly sensitive human question with another. Yet Justice Alito presented his analysis as though the court was merely realigning the law with a dispassionate, unavoidable, precedent-dictated result. He even went so far as to say that the court mustn't care what the public thinks. Its hands were tied. It merely examined the sacred and ancient texts and announced the answer.

The trouble is that this claim leaves many of us feeling he wasn't being straight with us. Justice Alito might have better justified himself by focusing on how best to sort out the balance between the rights of the living and the unborn or even saying he thinks abortion is murder — anything but a decision dominated by a tour of ancient abortion rights. When people admit their subjectivity, we might forgive them more readily when we don't agree with them. But when they insist they are dispassionate machines of justice, they fail to persuade. We know they are only human.

In most cases, the job is easier than the one Justice Alito faced. Most court cases are about who is on the right side of an unquestioned community value. These values are in statutes. They are in the common law.

We forget sometimes, but Americans still share a bedrock of these unquestioned values. We believe in the individual rights we enjoy regardless of whether they benefit the community as a whole. This means things like free speech, freedom of religion, freedom of association, the right to bear arms, and personal physical liberty. We believe people should keep their word. We have contract law to carry out that value. We believe people should tell the truth. We expect courts to punish liars. We are against theft and random violence, and we still favor enterprise more than entitlement.

When we go to court, we most often go there over these values.

Lawyers and judges might strengthen the legitimacy of our legal system by openly using and explaining human judgment to sort out relationships to values like these. Justice Alito was unwilling to recognize that this usually means focusing more on the future than the past. Many litigants, lawyers, and judges don't recognize this either.

Of course, a kind of justice can be fashioned from rearward-looking retribution. We can punish people for what they have done. And punishment has its place. But if the law is to focus on humans and humanity, it has to look ahead more than it looks behind. After all, humans must carry on, and mere punishment may close a chapter, but it won't certainly open a new one. If justice looks ahead, we can too.

Let's consider some quick examples to see how a human focus might drive a case better than a process focus. Take a hypothetical case where a former employee stole secret candy formulas and started making his own product and pedaling it around the country. Trade secret law can be interpreted as backward looking and purely punitive. But it's better seen as chiefly forward looking regardless whose side we take. The owner of a trade secret wants to start again from the position the owner enjoyed before the theft. The owner wants to be made whole, to deter others from stealing, and to avoid facing unfair competition in the marketplace. Workers want to work. They want to know that when they work harder or smarter, they will be rewarded for it.

The judge's job is to sort out these clashing interests in light of the community value placed on trade secrets and individual freedom. The judge must balance the liberty and enterprise of the worker against the property rights of the company. If workers can walk off with secrets they got paid to create for a company, the company isn't likely to pay for the secret to be created. This is bad for the worker and bad for the company. If the court interprets the law in a way that makes "the secret" so broad that it means the workers can leave but will never work in their field again, they aren't likely to lend their talent in creating the secret in the first place. The price is too high. The price is servitude. The court must consider the values vindicated along with the human cost of its rulings.

Now consider a hypothetical divorce. The husband is the breadwinner. The wife works at home raising two children. He has made millions in a high-tech start-up but squandered them on a one-hundred-foot yacht he couldn't afford and many other luxuries. He has been unfaithful to his wife and exposed his entire family, including two children, to financial ruin. His wife wants the remaining couple of million in the bank, along with a large sum of alimony and child support. His boss wants the two million because he borrowed the money from her. He owes the IRS a fortune as well.

The wife has plainly been wronged, and if retribution were most important, she would get the remaining millions.

But there are four people here. The husband still has his job and a good salary. His boss will fire him if he doesn't make hefty payments to her on the loan. Being fired will make it hard for him to find work. So will bankruptcy. So will pursuit by the IRS. The only thing to do is to keep the engine running. Sell the yacht. Use the remaining couple of million to hold the boss off with installments. Work out a payment plan with the IRS, and pay enough alimony and child support to get the wife a new home for her and their children. Make him wholly responsible for cleaning up the mess, but don't make more of a mess. Look forward.

Why this is the right answer can't be found in the words in a statute, nor can it be discovered by a rigid formula. It certainly has little to do with looking back over the filings in the case. Instead, reaching this judgment requires a judge to use judgment. We might profit from admitting it. We might openly accept that judgment of this kind is incorporeal. It's fallible. It reflects that in every human endeavor, there is something beyond calculation.

This includes even calculation itself. Ask anyone enamored with advanced mathematics, and they'll tell you that at its most sublime, math becomes an art, not a science. Ask a civil engineer why tolerances are built into every design—it's to account for the unknowable elements that only judgment on the spot can ultimately fix but that may be incapable of advance measurement. A good surgeon knows all the steps standard to an operation. A great surgeon knows what to do when something goes wrong and no rules apply. The mechanics of any discipline, whether math, medicine, engineering, lawyering, or judging, can take us far, but most disciplines recognize that mechanics can't always take us all the way home.

Let's consider one last example of how decisive a role individual, indefinable humanity plays in life and should be admitted to play in law. Erich Maria Remarque gave it to us from experience on a World War I battlefield in *All Quiet on the Western Front*:

> By the animal instinct that is awakened in us we are led and protected. It is not conscious; it is far quicker, much more sure, less fallible than consciousness. One cannot explain it. A man is walking along without thought or heed; — suddenly he throws himself down on the ground and a storm of fragments flies harmlessly over him; — yet he cannot remember either to have heard the shell coming or to have thought of flinging himself down. But had he not abandoned himself to the impulse he would now be a heap of mangled flesh. It is this other, this second sight in us, that has thrown us to the ground and saved us, without our knowing how. If it were not so, there would not be one man alive from Flanders to the Vosges.[40]

It is most likely the refusal to openly recognize the role played by our human instinct for justice—our judgment—that has left needless complexity in control of so much of legal proceeding. It's why pragmatism, with its utility and tinkering, isn't enough. It's why realism, with its science and cynicism, isn't enough.

Human judgment in court doesn't have to mean judges are either political or self-absorbed. It can mean instead that judges try to connect a case to the common values we've been talking about as contained in statutes, case law, and constitutions, with due recognition of our humanity and the humanity of those in front of us. It's what causes a judge to respect the law of contract while refusing to enforce a contract for a killing.

If lawyers and judges look at a lawsuit with this human spirit, they will likely find it harder to justify bloated, indecipherable complaints, endless motion practice, process obsession, and disingenuous decisions.

But what can we do to bring this about? Is it likely legislatures or the courts are going to adopt rules addressing needless complexity in the courts? Who knows?

But what if we don't need them? What if all we have to do is change our own habits—what we file, what we write, what we decide, and how we explain what we decided?

Habits might change; rules might be harder

Getting those at the top of the judicial establishment to address these frustrations may prove as difficult as passing controversial laws through Congress. Courts are often run by people at later, less flexible stages of their careers. They are set in their ways. They may be reluctant to change what they know and slow to see that formalism threatens our institutions. And some of them might, with perfectly predictable reasoning, see continuity as an important end and not merely a means.

Bar associations face obstacles to change too. They agglomerate competing groups of lawyers whose principal job is to gain favor or fees from courts, not to lecture them on how to do their jobs. To many lawyers, the system is beyond their control, like the weather. They may have trouble imagining or arguing for changes because they see how courts work as something to endure, not to reform.

Many of those who actually consider changes will understandably imagine obstacles to making them. They will worry about the rules of practice, and they will point to precedents that might be offended. Many legal professionals are also acutely aware that the way things are done is the result of committees and courts of appeal enshrining in the rules important compromises among competing interests.

And these competing interests are a major obstacle. Some stakeholders in the courts want longer lawsuits that yield larger fees. Some want shorter lawsuits with lots of settlements. Others want to discourage lawsuits altogether. Still others don't care about any of these things. They use the system asymmetrically not to resolve disputes, but to punish or delay their foes by exploiting the flaws in the system—delay, expense, and so on. In short, they enjoy needless complexity as an end in itself.

With all these competing interests, many rule makers find themselves discouraged from picking a side. As a result, in formally adopted rules, in instructive rulings, and in habit, judicial authorities have adopted compromises that have left us with a process few of us may like—they have left us with needless complexity.

Interestingly, they have also left us rules with a lot of wiggle room. We can interpret many rules to accomplish a wide variety of approaches because they have been written broadly. They frequently include significant exceptions or are offset by some equally potent but opposite rule. Procedural rules often say things like "unless the court orders otherwise."

Asking rule makers and broad groups of appeals courts to change these rules in some organized way may be fruitless. There will be problems adopting principles against needless complexity and imposing them from the top down.

But given the breadth of the rules, do we really need a top-down solution? What if we seek instead to change the habits that govern the behavior of judges and lawyers in individual cases under those rules? After all, with many of the rules being so loose, individual judges and lawyers control the average lawsuit, not courts of appeals and not committees.

Of course, the lower courts aren't free agents. They must apply the basic legal principles enshrined in law from above by courts, committees, and legislators. But those doing the day-to-day business of arguing and judging decide how to deploy and apply these often broad and flexible principles. Nothing stops lawyers and judges from trying to apply the established rules constructively. Nothing prevents them from using these principles as a tool to resolve rather than avoid disputes. No one is forcing them to becloud and belabor their work until the litigants stomp out of the courthouse in frustration.

What if judges and lawyers simply changed habits—case by case? They might embrace change if we could convince them that the system will serve them better when they act as problem solvers.

Wouldn't it be good for them if we got closer to producing for the people and businesses who come to court what *they* want: swift, fair decisions they can understand and live by? Meaningful decisions— more on merits than motions, and more on the evidence than on the plausibility of complaints. Reducing needless complexity could help make the legal profession what it says it is: judges and juries, helped by lawyers, sorting out people's everyday troubles. It could be fair and fast enough that people might be more willing to pay to come to court.

We can have our doubts about what to do or whether to do anything, but let's hold out hope for a bit and see what we can come up with. Let's explore the common flaw of needless complexity as it winds its way through a lawsuit and creeps into legal reasoning and writing. We can start where a lawsuit starts and follow it step-by-step through to the courts of appeal.

We'll explore ways to disentangle things as we go: fifty specific points. All of them suggest how we might resolve disputes by openly applying human judgment to core values enshrined in law.

2 : RETHINK 90 PERCENT OF THE TYPICAL COMPLAINT; MAKE IT ABOUT KEY FACTS, NOT LAW

Let's start where the problem starts—unintelligible, unfocused complaints—the documents that start lawsuits by describing who is suing whom and why. Are we eager to read them?

Someone believes they have been wronged. Someone struck their car, dishonored their contracts, cheated them out of money, broke their marriage, drove them out of business, or stole their trade secrets. They hire a lawyer to take their case to court. The lawyer drafts the lawsuit—that is, the lawyer drafts the complaint and files it in court. Unfortunately, these complaints have become something to complain about.

Thanks to legal rulings from the first decade of the 2000s—rulings purportedly aimed at clarity and precision—complaints have become less clear, less precise, and, above all, more deflectively complex than ever.

Ever since the Supreme Court's rulings in *Bell Atlantic v. Twombly* and *Ashcroft v. Iqbal*,[1] the story of complaint writing has gone from comedy to tragedy. Defense lawyers and the lower federal courts have taken up with gusto the high court's approval of increased complaint scrutiny. And state courts have taken to mimicking them. The result has been more work, not less. More delays, not fewer. The complaint is more than ever about form and formula. It is needlessly complex.

Most complaints are about something a third grader could explain. Personal injury: "She wasn't looking where she was going and hit my car with her car. My leg was broken. It cost me money. I missed work and will miss more. It hurt. I was very upset." Construction: "I hired a company to build a building for $10 million. The job got done late. The pipes leaked, the plaster didn't hold, and I have to repair it." Intellectual property: "I have a secret recipe for chicken, and they stole it by hacking into my computers." Discrimination: "I was fired because I am from India. My boss said Indians are all dishonest and that he had to get rid of me before I robbed him."

Because courts have allowed scrutiny of the complaint to be an endgame in itself, lawyers have come to believe that the more they stuff in the complaint, the better. More facts—no matter how trivial. More causes of action—especially redundant ones. More damage claims—we don't want to leave anything out; we might get thrown out of court. And besides, the more complex the complaint is, the stronger it superficially appears, and the more we get paid for writing it. No one knows what we're saying, so no one can blame us for it. It just looks like good business.

This obsession with the complaint leads to endless skirmishing about process and pleading rather than a resolution of the problem complained about. Fights that might have been resolved on the facts within a year or so get resolved instead on the paperwork—the "pleadings"—after two or three years. It takes that long to fight over layers of motions in many courts, with parties desperately making serial refilings after courts dismiss lawsuits "without prejudice"—that is, while giving them a chance to refile them again.

Complaints could start instead with the third-grader explanation. It could be placed in a one or two-sentence summary at the head of the complaint.

A person reading a complaint should see the material facts that one person claims make another person responsible for some injury. This means the facts that make the difference between winning and losing. This means the claims—not the evidence that supports them. At its best, a complaint is a short story of a human problem. Someone reading it should conclude: "Well, if this is all true, something should be done about it."

Yes, most court rules say things like this. But *Iqbal* and the cases after it have left these rules being ignored—not necessarily as a consequence of these rulings but because of overactions to them.

Let's look at *Twombly* and *Iqbal* for a moment without concern for the reactions that followed them.

Federal Rule of Civil Procedure 8 (a)(2) requires only "a short and plain statement of the claim showing that the pleader is entitled to relief." *Twombly* holds that a complaint "does not need detailed factual allegations" to avoid dismissal but needs at least something more than "labels and conclusions." Not merely suspicion. Not merely speculation. It must plausibly suggest the basic deficiency claimed.[2]

Iqbal adds to this: "A claim has facial plausibility when the pleaded factual content allows the court to draw the reasonable inference that the defendant is liable for the misconduct alleged." *Iqbal* says that courts don't have to assume "threadbare recitals" are true.[3]

The message in these two cases has been interpreted in disturbing ways. Does "pleaded factual content" mean evidence? Is a claim "plausible" because judges feel it's a winner in their guts? Some think so.

And if it's about evidence, those who do think so don't adequately account for the reality that in many cases only a defendant has the key evidence, and a complaint can only go so far without a court-supervised chance to find it—the process known as "discovery." That seems true in cases where the motives of government officials are challenged and a conspiracy alleged without access to the information needed to allege it in detail.

We might solve this narrower problem best with an improved and efficient process for filing bills of discovery. That is, prior to filing suit, a party might request a court to order a limited number of documents and depositions in a case where a party has reason to believe something might be found. The requests would have to be closely monitored by the courts. They would require the court to write a carefully crafted order for discovery rather than grant a wide-open opportunity for it. Delays associated with appeals would have to be limited, or the process would become meaningless because a party could file a dilatory appeal.

But putting the narrower issue aside, *Iqbal* and *Twombly* were hailed as a way of addressing the crushing federal docket. And that was the first mistake.

In reality, in most years, the civil work in federal courts has been easing rather than crushing. Over 2018 and 2019, the last two years unaffected by the COVID-19 pandemic, federal judicial-caseload statistics show no avalanche of new cases. Instead, the courts' own statistics show a net 2 percent decrease in new cases filed in the district courts, with 2018 cases dropping 5 percent and 2019 cases increasing 3 percent. Indeed, the same pattern held for the three years prior, with a net decrease of 3.5 percent during that period and cases up 6 percent in 2017 but down 2.5 percent in 2016 and down 7 percent in 2015.[4]

Not only are fewer new cases being filed, but the caseload being managed has dropped too. The same federal court statistics show that the total number of long-pending civil cases dropped by 20 percent between September 30, 2018, and March 31, 2019.[5]

And they didn't drop because of *Iqbal* and *Twombly*. According to a law and economics study written by William Hubbard and published by the University of Chicago, courts are dismissing more cases now. But the important thing is that they are dismissing them without prejudice—for technical, not substantive reasons. They can and are being refiled. So, what we get are more motions and more refiled, amended complaints.[6] More is added to them.

The federal statistics bear this out. Even with fewer new cases coming in and fewer cases on the docket to handle, between September 30, 2018, and March 31, 2019, the number of motions filed—many of which led to new complaints—increased by over 3 percent.[7]

So, while it is clear that *Iqbal* and *Twombly* weren't needed to save the courts time and the parties money, the latest statistics show a rise in motions being filed. The courts' increased obsession with the adequacy of complaints has only slowed lawsuits down even more and focused the lawsuits on themselves—a formalist, formulaic approach to complaint writing—rather than having complaints focus on the human conflicts that sparked them. What we got was needless complexity.

Studies show complaints are now longer than ever. A study of two thousand civil complaints published in the *Journal of Empirical Legal Studies* in 2013 shows lawyers abandoning the simplicity inherent in the rules and reaching ever further to add length and superficial breadth to complaints—particularly with respect to the facts. The study can be laconically summarized with the article's quotation from

Judge Posner: "The idea of 'a plain and short statement of the claim' has not caught on."[8]

So, more complaints start out longer in the first place and only get longer when they are dismissed without prejudice. Lawyers move to dismiss more often, and we will see that a single motion can hold up a case for years. That motion may be followed by a second motion to dismiss the amended complaint—more years disappear. Another still longer complaint is filed. It's not unheard of for another motion to attack the second amended complaint. And even if a court finally dismisses a complaint with prejudice, the case has ended on a point of law—a tempting ground for appeal to a higher court.

So, federal complaints have become more obsessed with getting the formula right, and these destructive practices have rubbed off on state courts too.

Now let's see the problem with complaints in action. Let's choose a random complaint and see how its needless complexity buries the matter at issue while entangling the parties in fights over process. We'll change the names and circumstances of the complaint to be fair to its well-intentioned author.

Snack-food companies sometimes grant other companies the exclusive right to bake and sell their goods in designated territories. They also give them control over the price of the goods in these areas.

The rise of mammoth national retail chains put pressure on these snack prices. The big chains pushed snack companies to make price-cutting deals with these chains in exchange for their buying more snacks. The snack companies complied. According to the baker in this case, this particular snack-food maker was trying to coerce the baker into lowering its prices to conform to the national deal, sometimes so low that the baker lost money.

The baker sued in federal court. The baker's complaint reflects many of the problems with complaints all over the country. It isn't worse. It's typical.

The first thing the complaint does is plant a thicket to hack through before we can get a glimpse of what the lawsuit is about. This first part of the complaint reflects widespread and often undue focus on the rule that federal courts hear only cases about federal law or significant suits by citizens of different states—they are courts of "limited jurisdiction."

This means that rather than learn anything about the case, we must first hum to ourselves or drum our fingers through long paragraphs about jurisdiction.

It doesn't have to begin like this. Nothing prevents a party from preceding the jurisdictional opening with a brief summary that gets to the core of the case. It might go something like this: "Bob the Baker is suing Acme Cake for $2 million for breaching an exclusive sales contract to sell cakes in Camden County, South Carolina."

At least we know it isn't a dog-bite case. We're already thinking about the merits and how they might be resolved. Yes, a federal complaint must also say why it was filed in federal court. But the facts alleged in these usually overlength sections are often undisputed. When they likely won't be disputed, there is no reason to belabor them. They should say what they must. This particular complaint burned up over two pages introducing the parties—and for some reason several non-parties—giving their complete addresses and bestowing on them the usual confusing acronyms before invoking the court's jurisdiction.

The complaint filed had six paragraphs on jurisdiction and venue. It could have settled for this: "This court has diversity jurisdiction because Bob the Baker is claiming $2 million in damages for breach of contract against Acme Cake, and it has its principal office in South Carolina, while Acme Cake has its principal office in Florida. Venue is proper in this court because all of the acts alleged happened in this district." Nervous lawyers may cite the jurisdiction and venue statutes, but they might consider that federal courts already know what they are.

What do judges want to learn from a jurisdictional statement? Facts, not law. Facts showing it's a diversity case. The amount in demand must be enough; the different states must appear. Yes, with multiple parties, lawyers should be careful to show complete diversity.

When appropriate, a complaint should allege facts indicating the claim is under federal law—lawyers should name the law. But especially when a lawyer has every reason to believe jurisdiction and venue are agreed, they shouldn't spend too much time on it.

The "cake" complaint then goes on to have too much detail about peripheral matters and not enough about pivotal matters. The complaint sounds complicated—we can barely hear the beat of its distant heart.

The complaint explains to us the history of cakes in North America. It belabors the minutiae of the parties' business arrangements over the years with dates, documents, attachments, participants, clauses, and product details that turn out to have no particular use when we scrutinize whether the complaint states a permissible ground for a lawsuit—whether it states a "cause of action." The complaint goes on like this for twenty pages or so while we wonder which bit of detail will matter and which won't.

Lawyers should give details in the contested parts of the complaint. They should give short shrift to the uncontested parts. Yet today, uncontested points take up most of the typical complaint.

Rather than use up twenty pages, after the summary and the jurisdiction language, the claim could have been stated with not much more than the following:

> Acme is a global snack-cake company with its main offices in Florida. In 2016, in exchange for a slice of the sales revenue, Acme awarded South Carolina–based Bob the Baker the exclusive right to make its cakes in Camden County, South Carolina, along with the right to sell them to retailers at prices of its own choosing within that county.
>
> Instead of honoring its agreement, Acme made deals for lower prices with large retailers in Bob's territory. It then blamed Bob for not adhering to these prices and told the retailers that Bob's refusal to cut its prices meant they would get no cakes.
>
> The loss of sales to these major retailers has cost Bob $2 million so far with additional losses mounting every day.
>
> Acme has breached its contract by refusing to honor its commitment to let Bob set its prices.
>
> Acme has also breached the covenant of good faith and fair dealing that attaches to all contracts by using its discretion to make discount deals with large retailers in other territories to force Bob to make large discount deals in its territory.

FIGURE 2.1. *"You don't call this a legal document, do you?
I can understand every word of it!!"*

Bob asks the court to order Acme to stop these practices and to award Bob money damages of at least $2 million.

This would have gotten to the heart of the issue. What the complaint actually says is breathtaking, and yet it is routine. Instead of taking the case for what it is—a contract dispute—Bob's tries torturing it into something that might generate punitive damages and attorneys' fees.

This is tempting. Most cases don't allow the party suing to recover its attorneys' fees, nor do they allow punishment damages—dollar amounts beyond what a party lost that might be imposed to punish serious wrongdoing. Where the facts fit laws permitting this kind of recovery, it's fair to ask.

But too often parties drag a lawsuit away from its core issues for years over long shot claims for extra damages. The case becomes about a lawyer's hope to make a case into a different case. It eats up

time and money, and when the claims inevitably fail, the party who
paid to make them has one more thing to blame judges and lawyers
for. Yet it's almost always done anyway. It makes a complaint look
bold when it isn't. It makes fees look justified when they aren't.

It proved so here. In addition to its contract claims, Bob sued Acme
for several forms of antitrust violations, fiduciary breaches, defamation, and for trademark abuse under the Lanham Act. Hours of study
of these convoluted claims doesn't show how they ever had any chance
of success. When that's the case, lawyers shouldn't bother. The client
will benefit, and no malpractice carrier will object. Remember, this is
no minor problem. Today, most complaints are needlessly doing this.

In this case, the result for the reader was another twenty pages of
head-banging attempts to see some possibility in these claims. The
result for the client was merely a waste of time and money. The court
struck all but the contract-related claims. A year was lost while this
went on—and that was a quick ruling. This is a consequence of lawyers fixating on legal claims rather than focusing on a persuasive core
of facts. It is about the appearance of substance—on form, on formula, on formalism—rather than about sound human judgment that
omits claims that are bound to fail.

Not all the needless complexity in the complaint is about higher
damages. Some of it is merely mindless repetition of claims in case a
party might win on multiple legal grounds rather than just one. The-
oretically, lawyers bring claims under multiple legal theories out of
concern that if one ground fails, another might succeed.

This again reflects that lawyers and judges spend more time on
legal theories than on the facts that relate to genuine human problems. A lawyer might bring a simple breach of contract claim while
also describing it as being brought separately for unjust enrichment,
quantum meruit, bad faith, fraud, negligent misrepresentation, and
unfair trade practices. The complaint is longer but too often it sheds
more heat than light.

There are cases where we can't quite tell what law covers them.
Sometimes a contract claim will fail, but a court will award damages because one party got a thing of value without paying anything
for it—a car, a renovated house, or what have you. The problem is
that this duplication happens today in almost every case—no matter

how straightforward. It keeps the court from seeing the core issue in the complaint. It discourages the court from reading the convoluted thing at all. It sucks the oxygen out of an ordinary human problem.

Judges should encourage lawyers to pick a claim. They shouldn't punish them for picking the wrong one by refusing to let them amend their complaints. It's the basic facts that shouldn't keep changing in a lawsuit, not so much the claims of law. Now let's see how a court might deal with the problem of a needlessly complex complaint by actively taking responsibility for it.

A self-represented plaintiff in a case decided to mimic a federal complaint in a filing in state court. The result was an indecipher-able 149-page amalgam of facts and law and arguments and witness lists. Around ninety-nine filings on the docket later, the parties were still battling over the complaint language—paragraph by paragraph, count by count. Five versions later, it was still being attacked as legally insufficient. The case languished.

Ultimately, a judge realized that the mimicry itself was the problem. Under the court's practice rules, the court on its own initiative ordered the plaintiff to scrap his entire complaint. The court ordered him to file a new one with one separate section—one "count"—against each person he had sued. It ordered him to say in each count, in his own words, the "who, what, when, where, why, and how" of what each person he was suing did to wrong him. The complaint was to focus on the facts of the wrong, not the pigeon holes a lawyer might place the claim in.

The complaint that resulted was just seven pages long. The plaintiff was complaining that the people he sued defamed him by saying he regularly filed frivolous lawsuits. No one attacked the complaint again. The case moved on and resulted in a summary judgment for the defendants.[9]

In short, by resorting to needless complexity, lawyers can get the case off on the wrong track from the very beginning. The problem begins as soon as the complaint is filed. Too many lawsuits immediately become about the lawsuit itself—about process. The words chosen. The applicable law invoked. What should stay. What should go. All with no attention paid to a real conflict hiding beneath the surface. When the courts avoid that conflict, they become strangers to the human beings and the human interests in front of them.

3 : ADDRESS BASIC PLEADING AND PROOF DEFICIENCIES WITH A SINGLE MOTION

People who get sued want to stop being sued as soon as possible—they hope to do so by getting the case thrown out of court. This is where preliminary motions come in. But are there too many of them? Are they leading to the wrong kinds of rulings?

Motions are requests to the court. They might ask for more time or orders regarding evidence gathering, or they might address more important matters—like preliminary motions to dismiss the case.

The trouble is that the more motions the parties file, the less momentum a case has. Of course, some hourly billing lawyers like more motions. But rather than enriching themselves thanks to more motions, those lawyers may be jeopardizing the prospects of the whole profession by taking too much time and money to get the job done.

Why do insurers hire outside audit firms to cut the fat out of their lawyers' bills? Why are they increasingly hiring in-house counsel to defend personal injury cases? Why have so many personal injury defense attorneys abandoned the practice and become plaintiffs' lawyers?[1]

What explains the rise in arbitration clauses? They have come to cover everything from phone service to employment contracts to buying a television. What has caused the Supreme Court, in the name of judicial economy and the economy in general, to enforce arbitration clauses with such relish?[2]

It's simple. Going to court takes too much time and money. Too many motions mean too much money without ever getting to trial. If going to court were cheaper and faster, more people would go to court. Court is a punishment. People avoid punishments.

44

FIGURE 3.1. *"By the way who's paying for all this?"*

Perhaps it's partly the number of motions holding up the march toward trial. Certainly, some are perfectly legitimate. The most important motions might decide a case. When there is no legal or factual basis for a claim to be in court, a party may move to have it thrown out—dismissed—or they might ask for a "summary judgment." Motions to dismiss are usually filed early in a case and relate to legal issues more than factual issues.

The federal system uses a single motion to dismiss to address preliminary legal issues. Connecticut, by contrast, has a motion to dismiss (challenging the court's right to hear the case—its jurisdiction), a request to revise (clarification requests—God knows why), and a motion to strike (failure to adequately allege violation of a recognized legal right). This creates a triple roadblock in front of the case core. Consider a fairly typical scenario:

- Lawsuit begins: January 1, 2023.
- Motion for sixty-day extension of time: March 1, 2023.
- Motion to dismiss for lack of standing. Response due: April 1, 2023.

- Motion for thirty-day extension to respond to motion:
  May 1, 2023. Response due: May 15, 2023.
- Motion for fourteen-day extension on reply brief: June 1, 2023.
- Court and parties maneuver about oral argument. Oral
  argument set for September 1, 2023.
- Court issues a decision on the motion: January 1, 2024.

Unhappily, this example is fairly fast. Many federal judges take four months to get a fully briefed motion to argument. Some federal judges may take a couple of years to decide a motion like this.

But let's assume this speedier scenario—it's bad enough. Now multiply it by three motions aimed at knocking the case out of court by attacking the sufficiency of the complaint. Assuming none of them are granted—they are almost always filed—there goes three years just on the complaint.

A single motion directed to the complaint and covering multiple grounds, like jurisdiction and legal sufficiency, solves the problem of multiple motions aimed at legal issues.

Better yet, a single motion for summary judgment may be all we need. Even in federal court, this is a separate motion, and it can raise both questions of fact and law.

Most courts have the discretion to allow a motion for summary judgment to be filed at any time. Courts could use their case-management powers to make these the sole means to defeat a case short of a trial.

The motion might address only the law. It might address only the facts. It might address both. It might be filed at the outset of the lawsuit or after discovery—or both.

When the motion is about the law, it might be indistinguishable from contemporary motions claiming the court lacks jurisdiction or asserting that the party suing has failed to make a legally recognized claim.

When it addresses only the facts, a party might complain that they haven't had enough time to gather evidence. This is easy to address. The party suing need only lay out the facts that warrant more time to discover evidence. Federal Rule 56(f) provides for this. But that shouldn't be necessary. The court can head off frivolous summary-judgment motions on the facts by ordering specific documents both sides must turn over at its initial conference about the case along with other vital discoveries. It might indicate at this preliminary conference that it will allow the motion to be heard after the discovery is completed.

But let's say it's the case, not the motion, that's frivolous. Summary judgment is as fast as moving to dismiss, but a dismissal is often without prejudice and another complaint follows hard upon the last. Summary judgment is final. It means the case is over because it has no merit rather than implying that it is just unartfully drafted.

Courts are most efficient when they resolve cases on the facts. Courts anxious to get rid of lawsuits too often focus on the pleadings as a way to get rid of cases they see as baseless. This often makes things worse. Courts would do better to move *most* cases along to some form of decision on their merits—for weak claims, summary judgment. This is better than dropping litigants through a trapdoor in some meritless ruling based on the "plausibility" of the complaint or some technical failure in the complaint.

Our focus on pleadings has two effects: (1) making lawsuits that should be decided on their facts longer and (2) undercutting the social function of courts by suggesting there are too many wrongs without remedies and too many rulings that deprive people of their day in court. Form first. Parties last.

Take the case of an unsuccessful lawsuit over pollution from a power plant. It was dismissed twice by other judges. The first time was for failing to adequately allege personal harm—"lack of standing." The second time was based on the claim no longer mattering because the challenged permit had already expired—a dismissal for "mootness." Twice the rulings were overturned. Over ten years later, a judge finally ordered a trial. After a few days, the trial was over. The claim failed. A fact-centered opinion followed within a few days. It was upheld on appeal.[3]

Or take the case of several courts that—purely on the pleadings— sided with insurance companies who insisted that COVID-19 contamination caused no "physical damage" to property and that, therefore, the insured's losses weren't covered by their policies. Without the benefit of a fact discussion, those courts assumed that if a thing wasn't burned or broken, it wasn't physically damaged, thereby creating a bad precedent for mold cases, graffiti damage, water surges, and the like, which leave all the molecules of a thing in place but certainly qualify as physical damage in most people's view—and indeed in most rulings that address those scenarios.[4] The various fact scenarios could have been considered on summary judgment with minimal effort. Deciding it on the pleadings, by contrast, created bad law on no facts.

Finally, let's consider the example of the developer's grudge. Some lawsuits reflect a single grievance a party won't let die. This often means the person bringing the lawsuit had a single claim. Instead of bringing it as a single claim, they brought multiple claims. They lost. They bring the same claims dressed up in new clothes. They lose and do it again.

In the case of the developer's grudge, government officials with power over land use, together with a rival company, frustrated a developer's plans, so he sued, and sued, and sued—through the normal routes of appealing the rulings, but he also sued for fraud, corruption, antitrust, defamation, breach of contract, a judgment declaring his property rights, and more. The developer tried lawsuits in his own name, but to avoid the obvious appearance of redundancy, he also brought lawsuits in the name of half a dozen business entities he owned and sued people as well as the entities they served. Thus, each lawsuit looked like it was someone new suing. But all of them were about the same thing—the developer was angry that he lost the right to the full use of his land.

A case like this fairly begs a judge to dismiss it without considering its merits. The defendants offered a full plate of reasons to dismiss, including the case's being filed too late (being barred by the statute of limitations), failing to allege harm (failing to allege contractual relations that were frustrated), and being barred by the "Noerr-Pennington" doctrine (a doctrine granting immunity in circumstances involving petitioning government action).

A judge faced with such a full plate might do well to consider the facts of the case. If, as in the case of the developer's grudge, technical defects are joined by a lack of merit, the court could bring the saga to a close by considering the facts on summary judgment rather than dismissing the case solely for being legally defective.

In the developer's grudge case, the first thing the court had to do was recognize what all these lawsuits were—a single grievance by a single man. Next, the court was best advised to rule on what was most powerful and what was most final. Many of the technical objections were good grounds—but why rule on the least rather than focus on the best?

Three things were obvious. The cases were really one case. The one case had been decided four times already. Most importantly, the developer couldn't prove the one case he kept bringing. He had suspicions about shady dealings; they infuriated him—but he lacked what should matter most: evidence. A summary judgment focusing on these three points was entered, appealed, and upheld, and review—that is, *certiorari*—was denied by the Supreme Court.

Again, the single motion focused the case on its key issues and resolved it once—and permanently.

4 : DECIDE CASES ONCE;
USE AGENCY REMANDS
SPARINGLY

In some cases, claimants can get what they want from government without going to court. Courts have rightly held that claimants should ask for the remedy from the agency before they sue for it. If you criticize how the Department of Motor Vehicles classified your driver's license, the department likely has a process to fix the problem. Rather than suing immediately, you must try to address the problem through the agency process first. We say you must "exhaust the administrative remedy" first.

But today, overuse of this doctrine has proved another unsatisfying way to get rid of a lawsuit without considering its merits. Courts too often accept the argument that sending a matter back to an administrative agency is an easy and official-sounding way to get something off the docket—even when there is no real remedy to give and even when the party making the administrative judgment has no business making it.

Most of the rulings involve government agencies. Let's take an environmental agency. It may be an expert on pollution. If a party wants the agency to do something or stop something, its thoughtful consideration on what pollutes and how much pollution to endure is something a court should pay attention to. But its view of the law— including the regulations that apply to it—is usually self-interested. Courts shouldn't defer to it.

The driver's license scenario isn't the problem. The problem is that when a party claims something against an agency, government lawyers typically say the matter should be remanded—sent down—for a decision by the agency itself. But when the constitutionality of a statute, a regulation, or an administrative action is being challenged, no court should give way to an administrative agency, nor should it fall victim to the claim that the agency can somehow create some useful fact-findings.

For instance, during the COVID-19 pandemic, governors across the United States assumed emergency powers granted them by legislatures in contemplation of a nuclear war or some natural catastrophe during which a legislature either couldn't assemble or couldn't assemble fast enough.

Governors used these statutes during the pandemic to close stores; limit public gatherings; and require the public, including school children, to wear masks. Naturally, lawsuits followed. They alleged many violations of state constitutions and the federal constitution. In many of them, those suing claimed that governors had usurped the legislature's exclusive power to pass laws—the governors had violated the doctrine of the separation of powers.

When parents sued governors over the school mask mandates, many government lawyers began their assault on the claims with typical procedural maneuvers that had nothing to do with whether the governor had overstepped the mark. One of them was the claim that the parties had failed to exhaust their administrative remedies. Lawyers claimed that the cases should be remanded to administrative agencies so that they might consider the claims and render a decision—after what might prove lengthy consideration of whether to declare that the government itself was wrong in any way, including constitutionally.[1]

But what the constitution requires is a matter exclusively for the courts. Chief Justice John Marshall established that in his foundational opinion in *Marbury v. Madison* in 1803.[2] Arguably, the courts in the mask cases could have remanded the claims in the hope that some related facts might be found or a compromise would be achieved or the thing would become moot because the mandate ended while the matter was still being pondered by the agency. But the idea of shunting the cases aside would likely have meant that, even in an emergency, the courts would have moved so slowly as to become irrelevant to the public need. So, some courts focused on the balance of powers between the executive and legislative branches. Some held that

the governor's power could not continue indefinitely and had to ultimately be submitted for approval or rejection by the legislature and
to be limited to matters vital to the emergency at hand.[3] At root, the
matter was what the law says, and that's a job for the courts.

A painful example will show that this problem isn't limited to constitutional issues and can lead to the worst sort of mischief.

To protect against a remand order in a pension case, lawyers for a
group of retirees sought to exhaust remedies with a state retirement
commission on a simple question of statutory interpretation involving a pension calculation. With the issue firmly in its self-interested
hands—despite it being a pure question of law—the agency ran riot
running the retirees round and round while some died and others
ceased to care.

The exhaustion took five years to make its way through the agency's
purpose-built labyrinth. The process included the pensioners filing a
claim, the agency filing a preliminary rejection, the pensioners petitioning for a declaratory ruling, the agency ruling, the pensioners appealing the agency ruling at another level of the agency, the agency's
adoption of a committee recommendation, the pensioners' request
for reconsideration, the agency's evidentiary hearing, the pensioners'
petition for reconsideration, the agency's decision to deny reconsideration, the pensioners' second petition, and the agency's declaratory
ruling.[4]

When the pensioners finally got to court, the whole thing smelled
terribly stale, especially since the matter languished in court for another five years. In the end, the agency successfully argued the case
was barred by the statute of limitations—it was brought too late.[5] Despite the pensioners' complaints, no court even commented on the
agency's hedgehog administrative process. This is an egregious example, but lesser versions of this happen all the time. They waste time.
They decrease faith in the judiciary because they place formalism
over humanism.

Deference to agency opinions on the law is embodied in what federal courts call "*Chevron* deference" by virtue of a Supreme Court case
involving that company.[6] The idea is that—beyond constitutional issues and administrative remands—the agency's view of the statutes
they apply matters, indeed, that courts should defer to it. In *Mak-*

ing Our Democracy Work, Justice Breyer goes so far as to say that when Congress is unclear when it writes an agency-administered law, courts should infer that Congress delegated the power to fill in the gaps in the law to the agency.[7]

But they shouldn't. Courts say what the law is, including when the law isn't clear, not administrative agencies. It is their expertise in their field we value, not their forays into ours. If it is a question of agency expertise, it isn't a question of law. If it's a question of what the law says, it's a question for the courts.

Still, because exhaustion is such a temptingly easy way to dispose of a case, clever lawyers have served this up regularly even in other contexts, and judges have too often swallowed the arguments—one more case off the docket—for a while. One of the most frustrating uses of remands is in employee-benefits law when an employee seeks some coverage or benefit under the terms of a benefit plan—typically medical or disability benefits.

The process imposed in this context involves stake-holding corporate agents designating themselves as trustees—benefit-plan fiduciaries—who then grant themselves in the benefit-plan documents discretion over who deserves benefits under the plan's terms.

Unfortunately, for decades, federal courts have bought the argument that these "experts" should not only be deferred to but that the administrative procedures they set up—rulings, appeals, or what have you—must be "exhausted" before the poor plan participant can go to court. Sometimes the decision is made by the very insurance companies that have to pay money if they rule in the employee's favor. An enormous mesh of case law has been woven around just how much deference the courts should then grant to this process and when.[8] Much billing, much needless complexity, goes on—at the expense of judicial credibility.

If employees don't deserve the benefits they are suing to collect, courts should say so. These employee-benefits cases are basically contract cases and should be treated like them. The decisions usually aren't hard. Courts shouldn't allow the claims to be needlessly delayed, nor should the courts defer to biased "experts."

5 : RECONSIDER STANDING CHALLENGES; THEY INVITE MORE LAWSUITS

Standing is the notion that people who sue other people should have a real stake in the matter being litigated. When someone hits a person with their car and breaks that person's leg, the person hit will have standing in court—if nowhere else. But if a neighbor sues an acquaintance because the acquaintance struck their own child, the neighbor has no standing to sue. The neighbor has no legal claim because the neighbor's concern is too much like the concern of the general public. It's a matter for the police or others.

Those distinctions aren't the problem. The problem is that standing has become another way of defeating a lawsuit without the courtesy of vindicating, for either party, human right over human wrong. Long ago, in law school, standing used to be explained in terms like the ones just used, but today it's remarkable how frequently defendants challenge plaintiffs' standing to sue. More remarkable is how increasingly courts buy ever-more-strained standing challenges.

There are many examples. An early one was an expansive view of the notion under federal retirement law. A pensioner claimed that his company benefits counselors lied to him about his retirement options and cheated him out of his rightful benefit. Since the applicable federal law allowed "plan participants" to sue, the case went to federal court.

The initial judge in the case and many other judges in similar cases held that, having left employment, the plaintiff was a *former* plan participant, not a plan participant, and therefore he had no standing to sue. It was an example of form over substance—of process defeating justice. For the judge, at least it got rid of the case.

The case ultimately took over ten years to resolve. After years in the appellate court, the original judge was overturned. The case went to trial. A different judge took over four years to decide the case after trial. The combined fees and expenses—all ultimately paid for by the defendant—approached one million dollars. The value of the dispute: $35,000.[1]

Some courts have begun using standing as a way to limit class actions—where a small number of people suing seek to represent a larger group. A good example comes from a case about monopoly behavior in the prepackaged ice business. Rather than wait to raise the issue in opposition to class certification, the defense moved to dismiss the case, saying the proposed representatives were inadequate to represent the class. They claimed the proposed representatives lacked claims typical of or in common with some potential members because the proposed representatives never bought ice in each state affected by the lawsuit.

While having a claim typical of the group and having common issues with the group are criteria for deciding whether a judge should certify a lawsuit as a class action, the court in the ice case seized on the issue and decided it before the lawsuit even got going by labelling it a question of standing bearing on the court's jurisdiction to hear the claim at all.

It's easy to recognize that a party must be injured to sue, but the ice-case plaintiffs claimed real personal harm—which should have been enough to get over the standing issue. The question for class certification was whether their harms were enough like the harms suffered by ice buyers in other states to let them represent those other people in a class claim about activities in their states.

But by treating the commonality and typicality claims as standing issues, the court cut out whole categories of potential victims without even permitting the parties to offer evidence at a class action hearing, where they might have proved that their claims were similar enough regardless of local legal variations.[2]

This case suggests that every class action can be attacked at the pleading stage because, it could be argued, with no common claim, no representative can have standing. Once again, a question of fact is turned into a question of law.

The lesson here is the same as elsewhere. Resolving cases on their facts is usually faster and almost always more credible than leaving lawyers telling their clients they lost for an obscure legal reason. It's also more permanent. Legal rulings are easier to overturn on appeal.

6 : REDUCE FIGHTING OVER SUBJECT MATTER JURISDICTION; THE UNHEARD WILL NOT REMAIN UNSEEN

Challenges to standing are just one example of the cottage industry that's cropped up around attacking the court's right to even hear a claim—attacking, in the technical jargon, its "subject matter jurisdiction."

Defendants love subject matter–jurisdiction challenges. They bring cases to a screeching halt. Courts hold that parties can't gather evidence or do any other thing until these motions are decided.[1] So, when they are filed, a court happy to get rid of a case is tempted to grant them.

Rulings about government officials' immunity from suit often come dressed as decisions about subject matter jurisdiction. In our system, citizens have no right to sue the federal and state governments without permission. This means courts assume government officials are immune from being sued, and anyone suing them must show they fit some of the exceptions to the rule carved out over the years or passed into law by legislative bodies. Such exceptions include cases where officials have violated a clearly established constitutional or statutory right.[2]

This general immunity has encouraged courts to shortcut cases against government officials by saying the courts have no jurisdiction over cases against immune government officials. The trouble is that this practice amounts to a preemptory judgment that the party suing doesn't have a case. Courts wind up holding that the official is immune because the official hasn't violated a clearly established right—a fact question—and therefore the court hasn't got jurisdiction.[3]

The reasoning is circular. A court must take up a subject matter–jurisdiction issue at once before reaching the merits, but it then reaches the merits by saying that what a person claims doesn't violate their rights. Therefore, the court has to dismiss the case on jurisdictional grounds.

In practice, this is often a convenient way for courts to get rid of frivolous lawsuits prisoners and others sometimes file against the government. But by dismissing the cases on jurisdictional grounds, the courts give the impression the claim was never heard at all.[4]

Take the case of the prisoner with the uncomfortable bed. He claims that by denying him his favorite mattress, the warden has inflicted on him cruel and unusual punishment in violation of the Eighth Amendment to the United States Constitution.

The warden responds by claiming the prisoner should have exhausted administrative remedies. The warden claims he is immune from suit. He doesn't say that the Constitution doesn't guarantee prisoners their choice of mattress and ask for a summary judgment.

But that's what the court should say in granting summary judgment: "Even if the prisoner had exhausted remedies—even if the warden weren't immune—the warden didn't cruelly and unusually punish the prisoner by refusing to give him his favorite mattress. This is a small inconvenience. Small inconveniences in prison aren't unconstitutional." The case is over. Exhaustion won't save it. Repleading around the immunity issue won't help. The prisoner likely won't win an appeal. The prisoner can't claim the court threw him out on a technicality. The message to the public and the prisoner alike is that courts hear and decide cases. They don't needlessly avoid them.

7 : ORDER DISCOVERY
WHEN A CASE BEGINS;
POLICE IT WITHOUT
WRITTEN MOTIONS

Courts often dismiss cases because they don't want to subject a party to punishing discovery—the formal process by which one party seeks evidence from another in documents, testimony, and so forth. But what if discovery wasn't punishing?

It wouldn't be as hard as you might think. The process need only be humanized rather than formalized. Lawyers billing by the hour should consider—and courts should remind them—that crushing

FIGURE 7.1. *"During discovery we found five more things to bill about."*

bills for discovery are actually crushing the long-term prospects of the lawyers who serve them. They make going to court—they make hiring a lawyer—something to avoid at all costs. What a bad business plan!

As it's done today, discovery is too often a game: a cat and mouse game. The cat lays out a maze to chase the mouse through by drafting a series of highly formalized questions—"interrogatories"—and a series of detailed document—"production"—requests. Together, they are a tome. The requests begin with several pages of definitions that define the scope of what is sought until they embrace matters of microscopic significance.

One frequently used offending phrase is "related to." It may be defined as something like "consisting of, referring to, reflecting or arising out of, evidencing, or in any way legally, logically, or factually connected with the matter discussed, directly or indirectly." When the parties want to know about a thing, it isn't enough to ask about the thing; they ask about everything "related to" the thing.

And so, with these words, the chase begins. Next, the mouse tries to scamper away. "May I have more time?"

"I'm frightfully busy."

"I really am looking for the cheese you want."

"Another sixty days perhaps?"

"I'd do the same for you."

Months later, when the mouse at last enters the maze, it's merely to put up more walls—the ritual continues. After the long wait, the discovery responses finally arrive. The mouse objects to every definition, every question, every document request. The objections are usually as inscrutable as the definitions. They often look like this: "The request is vague, overly broad, unduly burdensome, and not reasonably calculated to lead to the discovery of admissible evidence."

Sometimes, the mouse hands over some of its cheese after all these objections by saying: "Notwithstanding the foregoing," followed by a bit of a response. The other side ends up wondering: Was that all the cheese? Was it just a crumb? What's hiding behind the objection? Something? Nothing? Everything?!

The chase accelerates. In emails and telephone calls, the lawyers scamper and scurry back and forth. "There aren't any relevant documents. Why are you bothering? Trust me." "What do you really mean by 'related to'? My client looked up Bob's number in a company directory before calling him about this. Are you saying you want the phone directory?" "Do you want every copy of every draft of every scrap of paper associated with the meeting, the people who attended it, and the companies they work for?" And so on.

This sort of exchange is an inevitable consequence of over-drafting responded to by overthinking. It doesn't work. The mouse races into its hole, and the cat paws away at it from the outside. The chase has usually eaten up at least four or five months of back-and-forth as the lawyers lavish attention on building written proof of the detailed attempts they made to resolve this weighty disagreement.

The cat then asks for human intervention—from the judge. The cat chases the mouse down Mount Motion Practice. The cat crafts a needlessly complicated motion to compel, laying out for the judge rules and case law and repeating every definition, question, and request, along with the objections, generic and specific, and lengthy exhibits documenting just how hard the cat worked to compromise with the mouse.

The mouse asks for more time—so busy, so much to do to respond—a distant relative has surgery scheduled, or what have you. After a few months, the response is filed. The whole thing is gone through again, one whisker at a time, line by line, objection by objection, with extensions of time for reply briefs and trouble scheduling oral argument.

They argue before the judge or magistrate judge at last—the judge listens to the squeaking and yowling, head in hands, downcast of eye—for an hour or so before handing the whole thing over to a merciful law clerk. Four months or a year or two later, the court issues a written opinion—the cat will get the cheese—most of it anyway. It's been years since the chase began. A lot of the cheese has spoiled.

For a look at a chase scene, see the court's decision on a motion to compel in the California federal case *Ingram v. Quintana*.[1] The case was filed in 2011. The disputed discovery was sought in 2012 and 2013. The parties finally began moving to compel in January 2014. Other filings to compel came in as late as March, and the court resolved the motion at the end of May 2014, three years after the beginning of the case. The court in that case was relatively quick by many standards.

Decisions like this, with far longer delays, may be found in the thousands on judicial websites or search engines like Westlaw and LEXIS.

Anyway, when an order finally comes, mouse strategy number two kicks in. In response to the judge's order, a flood of documents covering the whole dairy industry swamps the cat: "You asked for documents, and boy are you going to get them." Something about the cheese is in there somewhere, but beginning lawyers will have to search and search for it—these days almost always electronically, but still laboriously.

This chase takes up most of the case and is repeated by both sides. There will be other rounds out of fear there is more to be found. There is sworn testimony to be taken at "depositions," and there are fights to be had about the questions that may be asked and the documents that may be used during the depositions. And so it goes. Civilizations grow and are ground into dust. The light from a distant and dying star reaches earth after its one-thousand-year journey.

The expense of it all is killing business for law firms and giving life to the unfair view that judges are feckless bystanders when it comes to managing a case—that they allow form to swallow substance.

There is no need for the profession to injure itself this way. There is no reason for the courts to be seen as enabling this. Many courts have adopted form discovery for cases like personal injury lawsuits. The federal system uses—and should expand—automatic disclosure rules. In rules or case-management orders, judges can bar boilerplate discovery objections—they can require parties to say why something is vague and so on.

More importantly, discovery could be a main topic of the first scheduling conference with a judge. The judge can set up a discovery session with the judge or magistrate for a nearby date or, better still, order specific disclosures at the first hearing.

Whenever the discovery conference takes place, the judge should ask the parties what things they want. All drafts of the contract. All emails that mention the contract. All emails that contain any part of the contract. Receipts for losses. Time records. And so on.

The judge can make a list. The list can go in an order in the judge's name. Because the parties have already discussed with the judge what's going into the order, they will have a hard time wiggling out of it. They will be reluctant to make frivolous, time-wasting distinctions about language written by the judge.

Even when the parties to a lawsuit draft their own discovery requests, courts should simplify how they resolve disputes about what potential evidence a party must produce. Within days of a dispute arising, the parties can join a video conference with a judge or magistrate judge, and the dispute can be resolved the same day with an order from the bench and without briefing.

The judge should not read and respond to each question or request. It saves hours of work to simply ask what the party wants. What documents? What information? Usually, a single thing a party wants is addressed in a half dozen or more questions—"interrogatories"—and documents demanded—"production requests." So, where a judge hasn't drafted the discovery in an order, discussing these in detail is almost always a waste of time. Defining what is wanted, determining whether it's due, and turning what is due into a court order is most efficient.

This is good news for judges as well as the clients paying for all this. By drafting the order or by eliminating written motion practice, judges save time. At worst, they will only have to talk to the lawyers without wading through mountains of documents. At best, with a judge having written the discovery order or with the parties immediately facing a judge rather than each other, parties misusing discovery will realize how foolish they will look telling a judge the comically persnickety things they tell each other. It works. Time spent on discovery plummets.

Let's take a couple of sample orders a court might issue at the first conference in a case, one from a contract case and one from a divorce. They follow a court's order barring the service of standard discovery requests.

A court in a contract case should first decide if discovery is needed at all. Where written contracts contain all the contract terms—where they are "fully integrated"—and where those terms have a plain meaning, all the court should do is read it and enforce it.[2] No discovery is needed, except perhaps on the damage caused by the breach. But where the meaning of the contract is unclear, an initial discovery order might look like this:

ORDER

No later than January 5, 2024, [giving the parties a month to comply is usually enough] the parties will produce to each other the following documents in their possession or under their control:

All drafts of the contract;

All written communications created prior to this lawsuit addressing proposed contract terms or the breach of any of these terms;

All documents created prior to this lawsuit addressing proposed contract terms or the breach of those terms;

All documents that support your calculation of damages.

There will be other documents of interest, of course. The parties may spell them out at the conference, or they may be added later. The important thing is that when a judge orders these disclosures, the parties don't have to wait for objections, negotiations, motion practice, a hearing, and a decision. The parties usually won't pretend they can't understand the judge's order. Things get moving. More orders can be issued by request.

Now let's look at an order in a divorce case. What's needed is painfully routine. Some courts have mandatory-disclosure rules. Sometimes, divorce cases are about children. But they are always about money—when there is any, at least. What's wanted in a divorce case, like much other discovery, is now easier to get than ever. Electronic records, accessible on the web, give the parties quick access to virtually everything they need. An initial discovery order in a divorce might look like this:

ORDER

No later than January 5, 2024, [giving the parties a month to comply is usually enough] the parties will produce to each other the following documents in their possession or under their control:

All statements of account from banks, credit card companies, investment firms, and employee-benefit plans generated from two years prior to the case being filed to the present with respect to personal, business, or trust accounts that they own, control, or may benefit from.

A complete financial affidavit in the form provided under the court rules.

All tax returns filed in their name or in the name of any nonpublic entity they own a majority share of or otherwise control generated from two years prior to the case being filed to the present.

All profit and loss statements generated by any nonpublic entity they own a majority share of or otherwise control generated from two years prior to the case being filed to the present.

Often, discovery in family cases becomes more complicated when there is a dispute over the value of the family home or other real estate or—most troubling—a dispute about the value of a privately owned small business. For those matters, the court may order more detailed discovery from the outset about books of account and the like. The court will also have to ride herd over the inevitable clash of experts about property value.

Finally, there is another technique some courts have used with success. It isn't an early intervention, but it makes for quick decision-making. It's called "baseball arbitration." There is, apparently, in some matters related to baseball, an occasion where each party makes a best offer and the arbitrator simply picks one version over the other. No splitting down the middle. When judges use it in discovery, this means that each party has to craft a proposed order for the judge that the judge is likely to deem the more reasonable. The judge picks just one version. It's fast; no writing is required, and it puts the parties' incentives in the right place.

This technique is useful to solve other disputes too. A good example is when a divorcing couple is fighting over personal household possessions. When a judge tells the parties that the one with the most reasonable list wins, first, they usually cut a deal and, second, if they don't, the judge doesn't have to consider the fate of each Hummel figurine or George Foreman appliance, nor does the matter have to be submitted to some form of later arbitration that may cost more than the possessions being fought over.

8 : CREATIVELY MANAGE COMPLEX CASES; NO CASE SHOULD BE TOO BIG TO TRY

Courts legitimately use legal doctrines to keep some complex disputes out of court. Some disputes are political questions so firmly assigned to another branch of government that courts may not review them. A good example is the power of impeachment, over which the Constitution grants the Senate "sole power." In some cases, individuals can't bring broad public issues into court. For instance, a citizen may not bring a lawsuit to stop a war or mandate new laws about climate change.

But there are cases that require more nuanced sorting out. Some of the parties bringing the lawsuit have the right to sue, but they are joined by many others with more questionable rights. The number of parties suing may mount into the thousands. They have sued everyone connected with the issue. They sue dozens or even hundreds.

Classic examples of these complex cases are the many lawsuits filed over the harm caused from tobacco and opioids. Lawsuits over both these issues have been like major weather events. The tobacco lawsuits resulted in a tsunami of money that broke over cities, states, lawyers, and even a small number of people who smoked and suffered for it. After the tobacco lawsuits, lawyers and governments with budget shortfalls had every incentive to consider similar lawsuits. Opioid-related lawsuits became the next hard-to-handle litigation.

This is not necessarily bad. Court proceedings revealed that tobacco and opioid lawsuits belonged in court. Tobacco companies and opioid manufacturers were repeatedly shown to have lied to the public when advertising and watched with open eyes while their products killed people. The companies ultimately admitted that real people were misled, became sick, and died.[1]

But the cases quickly became hard to handle. They became increasingly broad by expanding into related claims beyond the suffering center of the controversies.

Some courts treated these cases as too big to try. In federal courts, rules on multi-district litigation can rake claims like these into one court to deal with. Not a bad idea—in theory. But problems can follow. Cases in situations like this get joined in the name of a common topic, like tobacco or opioids, but they often involve parties with disparities in their connection to that topic.

Let's take opioids for example. The most complex litigation hasn't been about one addict at a time coming to the court for compensation. It hasn't been about government seeking to put the wrongdoers out of business and fining them for their wrongdoing. It's been about American cities and states claiming they should get money for what the police and social work agencies spent in dealing with the mess.

The lawsuits were also made more complex because many of the opioid makers went bankrupt. Ultimately, the parties were left to sue doctors, wholesalers, pharmacies, hospitals, and others who had roles in providing pills to patients. Lawsuits like these were filed in dozens of federal courts and in many state courts across the country. They left thousands of parties to sort out.

The response by some courts in cases like these can be concerning. Some treat cases like these as too big to try. Many courts responsible for cases like these start by trying to force settlements rather than by sorting out who has a claim and who doesn't. Massive settlement negotiations typically ensue.

When this happens, courts may be tempted to focus on how much money the defendants have rather than how much responsibility they have. Directly or indirectly, they might suggest to the parties: "Nobody leaves the room until they contribute." So they contribute even when guiltless.

We can't say what happened behind the scenes in the opioid lawsuits, but the pressure must have been enormous. The stakes certainly were. Some $32 billion has been raised so far to settle the opioid cases.[2] Was it all paid by the responsible parties? Did it all go to genuine victims? Have these lawsuits increased respect for the legal process or decreased it? In any cases like these, we should be sure we are satisfied with the answers to these and other questions.

We could consider handling cases like these another way. To begin with, we might use the very thing the courts sometimes overuse in other contexts—the requirement of standing. Many complex cases—many mass-tort cases—cry out for a legitimate application of this prolific doctrine.

In cases of indirect harm, the problem for many of the parties suing can be significant. Did they have a direct enough stake to sue? The amount of money lost on police and social agencies in some cases may be too speculative to say that they are directly caused by a wrong done to citizens. Picture the states and cities calling experts to say that, in the first year, a given social or medical problem absorbed 5.36 percent of police expenditures and 10.11 percent of social service expenditures and that, in the second year, the numbers were 6.12 percent and 12.034 percent.

There may be experts willing to give such testimony, but the work is troubling. It would have to be closely scrutinized by a judge before being allowed. Courts are meant to draw the line at points that strain credulity and common sense. If they don't, then experts can always find and measure some ripple effect from almost anything anyone else does. Yes, we affect each other, but we can't sue about every effect. That's what legitimate-standing analysis is supposed to be about. A person upset by a neighbor kicking the neighbor's own dog can't sue him. He can call the police.

If standing analysis showed that cities and towns suing for damage to their budgets in a given case lacked sufficiently direct stakes to justify suing, this eliminates over 19,500 real and potential plaintiffs.

Next, courts in cases like these could consider categories of defendants as candidates for summary judgment. Proximate cause would be a good thing for a court to focus on in some cases.

Did the doctors, pharmacies, distributors, and advertisers contribute substantially enough to be liable for a given medical problem? Would a reasonable person in their position have foreseen that their conduct would substantially contribute to the opioid crisis or something like it? Can we require pharmacies to investigate medicines ap-

FIGURE 8.1. *"Actually 48.7% of statistics are made-up."*

proved by the FDA and prescribed by a doctor to be sure it was safe and given to the right person in the right dose?

Doubtless, there are circumstances where some in this category may not deserve a summary judgment, but many defendants may share common factors that might be affected by a summary judgment in favor of one or two parties in the same category. A ruling on some might become legally a ruling on all. This could eliminate dozens or hundreds more parties or at least shape the settlement negotiations by liability rather than financial ability.

Where cases can't be pared down by summary judgments, the courts can order test trials. Indeed, this has been done in some opioid cases, and verdicts were given against CVS, Walgreens, and Walmart.[3] This reflects parties with characteristics in common with many other parties trying test cases. If not legally binding on every similar defendant, a few test trials can be deeply informative when, at last, those whose cases must go to trial get down to appropriate settlement negotiations.

For the most direct victims—tobacco and opioid addicts—thousands of lawsuits like these may benefit from test trials too. In product liability cases and elsewhere, courts often use test trials as bellwethers to guide settlement talks.

The 3M earplug case is a good example. Some 270,000 veterans sued the company over defective earplugs that failed to shield their ears from damage caused by battlefield noises. By the end of 2021, 3M won five cases and lost five cases.[4] It may not be true in the 3M cases, but often, cases with results of this type may be good cases for compromise.

The 3M cases appear mostly focused on the direct victims. The tobacco litigation was questioned as to whether it was adequately concerned with addicts. Many found the government promises that they would take care of the victims from their winnings hollow, and it appears very little of the giant tobacco settlement went to victims.[5] As of this writing, most of the opioid money will go to governments to support public programs linked to opioid abuse, but we may fear that the lines will become blurred during implementation and governments will use too much of their settlement money to prop themselves up rather than prop up anyone slumped over from addiction.[6]

Concern over who can sue doesn't by any means suggest that the guilty should go unpunished. Besides the actual victims, lawsuits by the federal government and the states acting in their roles as sovereigns have always been justified for mass wrongs. They vindicate the public interest, a matter distinct from local governments claiming they were directly injured themselves.

Federal and state governments can sue under trade laws. These laws give them the power to crush unfair trade practices—lying in advertising—and they permit government to fine and even pursue criminally the transgressing companies and in some cases their individual owners.[7] This is, in fact, exactly what the federal and state governments have done in many cases of this kind.

Cases truly too big to try don't belong in court. If the cases belong in court, courts must find a way to try them and yield money to the humans directly harmed. It's a matter of judicial credibility.

9 : MEDIATE, BUT DON'T DELAY THE CASE FOR IT

Settling a case can save you money. It might not be the money you would pay because you lose. It might be simply the money you would have to pay your lawyer. Courts often impose mediation of disputes to try to limit this damage.

Mediation is a good thing, but sometimes there is too much of this good thing. It's unwise for courts to build periods for mediation into schedules regardless of whether the mediation has any chance. It merely adds one more bubble to an already bloated schedule.

In fact, parties tend to settle more when they are under time pressure.

That doesn't mean they should be under unrelenting pressure to settle. As noted, sometimes settlements are forced for purely financial reasons. The parties aren't getting any closer to trial. Expenses are mounting, particularly from a brutal twelve rounds of discovery. So rather than get something that looks like justice, exhausted litigators limp out of court with a forced result. A perfectly innocent party often pays something just because it's less than the cost of further defense. This is a familiar reality to lawyers. Many have profited from that extra sum called the cost of defense. It gets added to the more appropriate calculation about the risk of loss.

Who can blame lawyers for making this calculation? The real responsibility for this factor is needless complexity in court. It simply takes too long and costs too much to litigate. This reality turns into cash. The judiciary should reflect on its responsibility for this extra cost because the judiciary is in the best position to eliminate it. Cases that should settle on their merits should settle. People shouldn't leave courthouses pointing to an incompetent judicial system as the reason they settled.

Mediation should happen first, before substantial expense starts. Right after the initial conference—or even before it—a magistrate or other judge could have a remote meeting with the parties to gauge the possibilities. Many times, there aren't any—yet. Many times, the parties aren't ready to gauge their chances of winning. The preliminary round of discovery the court orders may be a necessary prerequisite. If the parties haven't found any smoking guns—or if they have—their views about what the case is worth will likely change. If the court has managed discovery efficiently, the parties won't be bankrupted, and when appropriate, serious settlement discussions are best at this point. By the end of discovery and more obviously after the defeat of a summary judgment motion, the parties should be staring a trial in the face. Like the prospect of hanging, the expectation of an immediate trial tends to concentrate the mind.

10 : STREAMLINE TRIALS; THEY'LL BE MORE FINAL, MORE CREDIBLE

Like bad weather, everyone complains about the vanishing trial, but nobody does anything about it.

Often, trials don't happen because some party or another is penniless when they finally get a chance for a trial. They have spent all their money on the preliminary skirmishing so that by the time they get to trial, they simply cannot respond favorably to news from their lawyers that a large deposit of fees into an escrow account is now needed.

Some lawyers are fine with this. They have done a lot of chest-beating and skirmishing during motion practice and discovery. Then when it comes time for the combat that counts, stern warnings about the risk of loss and the enormous expense too often leave a party little real choice but to quit the field with a fraction of their goals met. The case is settled and withdrawn. The lawyer has gotten paid and hasn't "lost" the case.

If the focus of case management were to sweep obstacles to a trial out of the way rather than erect more of them, there would be more trials and fewer tribulations. Too many of us take for granted the idea that both parties settling and leaving angry means that justice has been done—nobody clearly won, nobody clearly lost. But that's often a mistake. It may only mean that the parties are dissatisfied with the result and the process that brought them there; the process is the main reason they settle. The judiciary gains no greater legitimacy by people thinking, "It could have been worse."

Not to disparage settlements in doubtful cases, but cases that ought to have clear winners and clear losers—or at least a decision by a judge or jury—usually don't yield them. It's too expensive. And some lawyers and mediators in settlement talks inflate the risks.

Don't blame crowded court dockets for the pressure. Courts in many places have fewer cases, and courts everywhere have fewer trials than they did thirty years ago.[1] It's the money that's creating the pressure.

Courts could order a six-month march to trial in even relatively complex cases. Courts could order briefs—b-r-i-e-f-s, as in the opposite of long—on the key legal issues. When the lawyers write them, they might remember that there are about two or three useful pages in the typical forty-page brief. Really. It's true.

The parties could spend an hour or so on the record crafting a custom discovery order with the judge. The parties could get help carrying it out through a quick hearing quickly arranged with a judge or magistrate. Summary judgment could be briefed, argued, and decided, and if it is denied, the case could be brought to trial within six months.

Are courts and lawyers too busy to move a single case so quickly? It's hardly likely. Remember, many courts aren't as busy as they once were. It's the same for commercial litigators. They aren't so busy either. And for those who work in a great personal injury mill on either side of litigation, standard, well-supervised discovery and speedy trials will make the mill work more smoothly and reduce the backlog more quickly.

Besides, most of what the lawyers and courts say they are so busy with is the very stuff we are talking here about eliminating.

Now let's consider some specific ways to make trials simple.

11 : DIRECTLY INVOLVE JUDGES IN JURY SELECTION

Federal courts select juries from a large group of potential jurors with a judge on the bench. Where judges don't oversee the process, it often becomes a fight for the affection of each juror by each lawyer as the lawyers smile and ask flattering questions and try to indoctrinate the jurors into being comfortable with awarding large sums of money—or, when the other side is asking questions, awarding claimants nothing. It's insulting to jurors. The biggest thing they complain about is that courts waste their time and insult their intelligence. Process dominates jury selection when jurors should.

Judges should consider overseeing jury selection in person. They could start by asking questions of the panel as a whole, and then they could whittle down the group—eliminating those who have genuine scheduling conflicts, illnesses, relationships with the participants, and the like. The court could also ask the questions counsel would inevitably ask. The remaining jurors might then be questioned individually by lawyers when needed—with a judge overseeing the questions. Jury selections that take weeks in some places can almost always be done in a day or two.

The selection process—needlessly called *voir dire*—might look something like this:

PANEL JURY SELECTION
1. The clerk administers the oath to the potential jurors. There might be anywhere between twenty and forty of them, depending on the length of the case and the issues in it.
2. The court gives a brief, neutral explanation of the case: This case is a dispute between the real estate–development team of Topco Builders and the City of Pynchon.

Pynchon hired the development team to build a soccer stadium in Pynchon for the Pynchon Pirates minor league soccer team. The stadium was to be the beginning of a new neighborhood to be built by the development team, including homes, businesses, and shops just north of Interstate 12.

But the development ran into trouble in the spring of 2022. The team wanted to play, but the stadium wasn't finished. The team missed its season. Pynchon fired the development team. An insurance company completed the job and then sued the development team for its expenses.

The development team and the city blame each other for all this. Your job is to decide who is right.

1. The lawyers identify themselves, their firms, the parties, and their witnesses.

2. The potential jurors will have already filled out questionnaires with basic information about their employment, family, and affiliations. They will then review a written questionnaire composed by the judge with input from the lawyers in the specific case. If they answer yes to any of the questions on it, they should stand after the judge has read all the questions. Those answering yes will wait for further questions in another room.

   a. Do you know or recognize any of the parties, the lawyers, or anyone associated with the lawyers or any of the potential witnesses in this case?

   b. Are you familiar with the Pynchon Pirates team in a way that might influence your decision in this case?

   c. Have you or anyone close to you been involved with the legal system where the experience left you with feelings that would make it hard for you to be a juror in this case?

   d. Do you have any important commitments that conflict with the anticipated trial schedule covering the next two weeks?

   e. The party suing is a government. Is there anything about this that would make it hard for you to be a juror in this case?

   f. The parties being sued are in the construction industry. Is there anything about this that would make it hard for you to be a juror in this case?

3. Potential jurors answering yes to any question are taken to another room to await further questioning if needed. Ultimately, they might be made to wait if the court is short on potential jurors, but if the prospects look good, they may be released at any time.

4. Under the watchful eye of the judge, the lawyers will then question the potential jurors left in the room one at a time in the witness box. The lawyers will have the potential jurors' information sheets in hand and may ask questions raised by the information. The parties should have already given their generic questions to the judge to be included in the written questionnaire, so the lawyers should have far fewer questions.

5. After the questions, the parties may then challenge each potential juror for bias or other good cause or use one of the parties' limited challenges that don't require cause—a "peremptory challenge."

6. The judge gives those selected instructions about what will happen next, the need to keep an open mind, and the requirement that they discuss the case with nobody and read nothing about it in the media.

Courts using this method preserve the lawyers' right to ask individual questions, but with the judge participating, the process takes a fraction of the time that unsupervised jury selection does. The trial moves ahead faster. The jurors are spared the cloying and prying of some lawyers. The federal courts have been doing this for a long time.

12 : INCREASE JUROR NUMBERS AND DIVERSITY WITH REMOTE JURY TRIALS

When it works smoothly, jury duty affirms democracy and strengthens the justice system. It reminds us that our system doesn't entrust your life to an elite, but to your neighbors.

Still, most people who serve on juries complain about the process. They hate being called. They are humiliated by the cattle calls at the courthouse. They are moved from here to there, made to wait, and treated like a number. Usually, they wait around the courthouse all day and aren't chosen. But when they are chosen—when they get to the substance of the job—they love deliberating about and doing justice. It affirms their faith in the actual decisions that get made in court. So, if we improve the process, we might improve the prospects of democracy itself.

We can start with broader-reaching, more detailed databases from which we might draw jurors. We can electronically choose them for service based on the parties and the case. Much cross matching of juror characteristics—race, gender, and so forth—could be done where that is a priority. Questions could then be asked of potential jurors, but they would be more focused.

More importantly, the outrageous idea of internet-based jury trials will ultimately find favor. The cries against this are illogical. Jurors are easier to observe on a screen. Clerks, judges, and attorneys can see them close-up. And they can't talk with each other during breaks. Yes, they may talk with people at home despite being told not to—but we can't stop them from doing that any better now.

Getting the right mix of races, backgrounds, and so forth will be easier with a large data base. And juror service will be easier when it doesn't involve commuting to and hanging around a courthouse. Jurors will be less intimidated when deliberating.

And we can't say the technology is impossible. With few exceptions, even the poorest people today have cellphones with cameras even if they don't own a car. This will allow them to participate in greater numbers than ever before. Where service is a problem, incentives can be given. After a certain number or days of service, a person might be granted a free device of some kind, or one might be loaned to them.

With legions of baby boomer retirees at home resting on their wisdom, convenient jury service might add new meaning to their lives. Retirees might volunteer to be summoned to remote jury service on days when it's convenient. They can give back without leaving home. They can turn the availability light on their profile to green, and courthouses can put them into the mix for that day's selection. People with no quiet place at home can use rooms at the courthouse or their local library. Making jury service easier will expand rather than contract juror pools. It can also expand the number of people who are stakeholders in the system and who will defend it to their friends. And the technology is only going to get better.

Not everyone waited for a pandemic to test online courts. According to National Public Radio, Australia, Canada, China, Denmark, the United Kingdom, and Singapore all used online courts before the pandemic. During the pandemic, jury trials went remote in at least eight states—Arizona, California, Florida, Georgia, New Jersey, Oregon, Texas, and Washington—with every state using remote proceedings for at least limited purposes.[1]

Some of us remember many years ago sniggering at emails, sneering at the internet, and laughing at the iPad. Someday, we will remember with equal chagrin scoffing at online jury trials.

13 : QUESTION THE NUMBER OF MOTIONS *IN LIMINE*

The trial will start in days. Particularly with a jury trial, lawyers worry that things that get said or shown in court—a graphic photograph, a far-fetched expert opinion—should be stopped before the trial starts so the jury won't suffer prejudice from exposure to them. In these cases, use a motion *in limine*—a motion metaphorically made on the threshold of the courthouse as the parties arrive for trial.

Yet a simple trial too often generates a half dozen of these eve-of-trial requests to preclude evidence. Eager associates can rack up billable hours toward their annual quotas churning them out. Too often the motions ask the court to prejudge hotly disputed issues or simply stake out ground for lawyers who know they are premature.

Where the party suing is planning for a trial that wanders far outside the bounds of what the party originally sued for and the evidence the party discovered, a motion *in limine* can be useful. For example, where a party is suing about leg pain and, at the last minute, claims a neck injury, a motion *in limine* can keep the case on track. This would also be true where the party wants to use an expert but never told the other side what the expert's opinion is.

This last one is surprisingly common. It's a classic form-over-substance mistake. Because they aren't ready to do anything else, many lawyers meet expert-disclosure deadlines by revealing only the subject on which the expert will testify—aerodynamics for instance. Later, once they have finally decided what they want the expert to say, they forget to provide the information to the other side. They never disclose the expert's opinion: a helicopter is particularly susceptible to rolling over when close to the ground, for instance.

In limine procedures used only when needed can save time—especially when we expect to take up citizens' time serving on a jury.

Used as part of some pretrial taunting, they needlessly delay trials because they take days to wade through. Good uses include considering whether an expert is competent to testify, whether an issue is in the case, whether a large block of evidence is relevant.

But often, lawyers are better off focusing on what facts they must prove, how they will prove them, and how they will forge these facts into a victory.

The lawyer is trying to prove a disputed point. How are they going to do it? They should plan every question they will ask a witness on direct or cross. They should refine each of these questions as they ask themselves whether it is a hammer on the anvil of their theme. They should discard those that aren't. And they should prepare themselves for where a witness's answer takes them. They should be prepared for the answer they don't want to hear, or they shouldn't ask the question in the first place.

The wastefulness of what usually happens has been noted before. As Judge Randy Wilson put it in the Texas *Advocate*, "When I was a young lawyer trying cases I was frequently tasked with drafting and arguing motions in limine . . . During my first few years on the bench, I listened patiently to motions in limine and soon realized that I was hearing these same boilerplate motions that I had inflicted on judges in the past. I now see motions in limine in an entirely different light and I suspect, based on my conversations with other judges, that I'm not alone." According to Judge Wilson, the motions are usually generic and often sweeping. Most importantly, "they waste time and damage the credibility of the lawyers filing them."[1]

An example of motions *in limine* can be seen in the case of the school with a leaking HVAC system. The case generated seventeen motions *in limine*, six of which the court granted. They ranged through every aspect of the evidence, from challenging virtually every expert's opinion to clarifying the relationships of the parties. Some were useful, but had the court treated them in the ordinary course rather than summarily hearing them on oral argument, the trial might have been delayed months. More importantly, this was a trial to the court, and the vast majority of the motions could have been ruled on in the ordinary course of evidence with no prejudice to any party.[2]

14 : MOST EXHIBITS PROVE UNDISPUTED FACTS; WE DON'T NEED THEM

Most cases yield pallets of exhibits—evidence that comes mostly in the form of documents. They might be medical records, emails between the parties, bank account records, deed copies, contract documents, receipts, or what have you. They come in large stacks even in small cases. They usually establish something no one is contesting, and when they arrive, we can hear the lawyers cry as they are craned or clicked into place: "They are unopposed, your honor and for the record."

But when no one opposes a document being admitted as evidence, should it tell us something? The document probably isn't needed because what's in it isn't contested.

And why all this worry about "the record"? Is it a record for the judge? The jury? Why would judges or jurors bother about a document that proves something nobody disputes? Lawyers should consider that an undisputed fact hidden within a document could simply be recorded on a list of admitted facts rather than left buried in the hope someone will needlessly dig it out of a pile of paper. But some lawyers will still insist it's for "the record."

Do they mean the court of appeals? That would be another mistake. If they already know this mountain of paperwork isn't needed and won't be reviewed in the lower court, why should they deceive themselves about the court of appeals? Courts of appeal are even less inclined to look at a mountain of undisputed exhibits.

Courts of appeal usually look for important mistakes about the applicable law. They also care about *disputed* facts that reveal what looks like a serious injustice. But lawyers shouldn't be fooled by their occasionally ruling that something could have been in the record but

FIGURE 14.1. *"As precedent your honor I offer the entire legal history of Western civilization on CD-ROM."*

wasn't. The ruling means the lawyer forgot something important. It doesn't mean that the lawyer didn't submit enough unimportant things.

The volume of exhibits about undisputed things is too often the product of indiscriminate preparation—it's easier to add a few more stalks to the granary than it is to sort the wheat from the chaff. When they offer too many exhibits, lawyers suggest they have been productive when they haven't. Most exhibits document admitted facts. Admitted facts don't need support. They should be listed and given to the trier of fact.

What conclusion did a doctor reach? Will a thousand typed forms or pages of illegible scrawl in an unrecognizable language help support this? No. The conclusion translated into English would help. The parties and the court can sort this out. They can use a series of conclusions labelled "admitted" or "undisputed" facts.

A written admission submitted to the jury might say: "On January 12, 2023, the doctor saw blood collecting between the skull and brain." This is better than saying during a closing argument: "Ladies and gentlemen, you will find on page 1,033 of the medical record that the doctor concludes—I know it's hard to understand—'observed subdural hematoma/CAT.' This means the doctor saw blood collecting between the skull and brain on a CAT scan."

Who needs the original document when the court can deem it established and allow the lawyer to assert it in front of the jury rather than take precious trial time to prove the uncontested point?

What a doctor writes on a form usually isn't disputed. *It's what to make of what they write that's disputed*. Lawyers should focus on the latter. They should get their opponent to admit the former. Judges should ensure that opponents respond in good faith.

And lawyers needn't worry about the "best-evidence" rule that says the original document is the best evidence of what it says. This is true, but it doesn't apply to admitted facts. Lawyers and judges should remember that a list of admitted facts that a fact finder can hold and read would be far more helpful than a pile of documents in which these things are hiding.

Most cases need few exhibits. Most evidence rules allow the parties to submit summaries of voluminous documents. Submitting them as part of the admissions should be the minimum, not the exception. But better yet, lawyers should obtain an admission of the fact they want drawn from the summary. "Bob charged a total of $212,000 on the company credit card between January 1, 2023, and March 1, 2023."

"Demonstrative" exhibits—those that depict evidence but are not evidence themselves—can bring a case to life: pictures, diagrams, lists of established facts. Physical objects are good. Summaries of damages are quite useful. Jurors say these things help.

Judges and jurors ignore most exhibits because there is nothing particularly important in them. Sometimes they ignore the few important ones too because the lawyers have buried the wheat under a mountain of chaff. And that's the lawyers' fault, not the judges' or jurors'.

Eliminating exhibits will help lawyers prepare for trial. Rather than asking a subordinate to gather every document related to the case and list them all as exhibits, the lawyers can try it this way. At the earliest possible point in the litigation, lawyers should ask themselves what facts they must prove at trial. For each fact, they should consider whether it's likely to be disputed. If it's not, lawyers should ask their opponents to admit it. "On January 2, 2020, Smith emailed Jones and said 'the deal is off.'" The email isn't needed. What the email *says* won't be disputed. What it *means* often will.

Cases are piled with emails. That they were sent and what they say is virtually never disputed. And usually only a sentence or two from a string of emails is important. That sentence or two could be on a list of admitted facts: "On September 10, 2022, Wadsworth wrote Bulkeley saying that he would pay 'the $10,000 I owe you' by the end of the year."

Courts should require and police these admissions at the earliest possible point in the case—starting with the case management process and all through discovery. Instead of legal skirmishing, parties preparing for trial should be fine-tuning a list of admitted facts for the jury and themselves and integrating it with their planned questions for witnesses. When the trial starts, they should be trying to win the *dispute*, not prove the undisputed.

Family law cases don't need mounds of financial records. Family lawyers should ask themselves, "What am I trying to prove?" The husband's 2020 tax return reports $250,000 in wages. The bank account had $1 million on January 1, 2020, and $30 on January 15, 2020. Lawyers who need these facts should provide opponents the documents and ask them to admit their content—not their import, just their content. Then there's no need for the document. The lawyers can weave these already-established facts into their questions for witnesses.

The admitted facts help lawyers prepare for trial. They shorten trials. They tighten the focus of witness testimony. They eliminate whole swathes of witnesses. Lawyers can get to what counts by *asserting* the long part that is undisputed fact (set in bold below) and *asking the real question*, which is usually the short part:

- "**Doctor, on January 12, 2023, you noted seeing blood collecting between the skull and brain.** Did that affect your opinion of the patient's condition?"
- "**The bank account had $1 million on January 1, 2020, and $30 on January 15, 2020. You wrote a check to your mother for $999,970 on January 15.** What for?"

- "You were driving down Main Street. It was a clear day. You reached its intersection with Elm. There's a traffic light there. Did you see it as you approached?"
- "You were a lab tech at Hemlock for twenty-three years. You had three promotions. You put in your retirement papers in May. Why did you choose May?"
- "You had the formulas on your laptop. You took the laptop home every night. The formulas were downloaded to a removable disk at 11:00 p.m. on April 2, 2022. Did you download them?"
- "Your tax returns show you had $500,000 in taxable income in 2021 and only $100,000 in taxable income in 2022. Can you explain this big drop in your income?"

Two examples will show the scope of the problem and the value of the solution. The first case was a challenge to the adequacy of Connecticut's public schools. The parties marked over 5,000 exhibits. All of them could easily have been waived into evidence without objection and collected dust somewhere. But the court ordered the parties to work on stipulations. They reduced the number to 826, and, with more effort, they could have offered only a fraction of this number—most of them were undisputed statistics, test scores, budget figures, demographics, and the like.[1]

The second case was a contested divorce. The exhibits were principally the usual account statements, tax returns, messages, and so on. The parties listed 173 exhibits. After evidentiary rulings and the elimination of undisputed facts, 173 exhibits became 7 exhibits.[2]

More time is wasted in most trials trying to establish the routine. Trials should focus on the extraordinary—the things that make or break a party's case. The rest is needless complexity.

15 : ACTIVELY OPPOSE CUMULATIVE AND TIME-WASTING TESTIMONY

Like exhibits, much testimony is often meant to establish some undisputed point. A witness is asked to authenticate a document, to show it's really what it appears to be—even when its authenticity isn't disputed—or to establish that a thing was said—even when it's undisputed that it was said. These things should be included in a list of things the parties admit and used as assumptions in questions like those above in chapter 14.

Trials can also be shortened by eliminating testimony peppered with objections to establish some preliminary or uncontested point. "You went to Harvard, doctor?" "Objection, leading the witness." The judge should say "overruled." This is both preliminary and presumably uncontested. Leading is permitted for such questions. You can put words in a witness's mouth when those words don't go to the heart of the matter and when the answer is undisputed.

The exchange with the expert could go something like this: "Doctor, you went to Harvard, Yale, and Southwest Texas Teacher's College. You studied epidemiology at Yale. Can you tell us what epidemiology is?"

Judges and lawyers should keep asking themselves: "What is the heart of this case and how do we get at it?" The idea isn't to knock the life out of a trial—it's to knock the stuffing out of it—and today's trial is mostly stuffing.

For lawyers having trouble imagining the heart of a trial, Hollywood can help. Because movies are supposed to be interesting, the lawyers in them don't spend much time offering needless testimony. You can see the heart of a trial in *Witness for the Prosecution, Anatomy of a Murder, The Caine Mutiny, A Few Good Men,* or any episode of *Rumpole of the Bailey*. For obvious reasons, these depictions never feature the small stuff. Judges and lawyers should wonder why they spend most of their time on the small stuff rather than what matters most.

Let's look at one example from *A Few Good Men*. This 1992 film is about the court martial of two marines, Dawson and Downey, for killing Santiago, one of their own, while punishing him for being weak. A Navy defense lawyer, Lieutenant Daniel Kaffee, played by Tom Cruise, cross-examines the base commander, Marine Corps Colonel Nathan Jessup, played by Jack Nicolson. Did Jessup try to whisk the picked-on marine away to safety or did he actually order the "code red" punishment? The Colonel's claims start to come apart as Lieutenant Kaffee asks why the young marine, supposedly leaving forever, didn't make any preparations:

> Kaffee: You flew here today, didn't you? You're wearing your dress uniform.
> Jessup: As are you.
> Kaffee: Did you wear it on the plane? . . .
> Jessup: I wore utilities on the plane.
> Kaffee: Toothbrush, shaving kit, underwear? . . .
> Jessup: I brought a change of clothes and some personal items.
> Kaffee: After Dawson and Downey's arrest . . . Santiago's barracks room . . . was inventoried. Four pairs of camouflage pants, three khaki shirts, boots . . . Why hadn't Santiago packed?
> Jessup: [silent]
> Kaffee: We'll get back to that. This is a record of phone calls from the base. You've made three calls. Do you recognize the numbers?
> Jessup: I called Colonel Fitzhugh to tell him I'd be in town. The second was to arrange a meeting with Congressman Richman. And the third was to my sister.
> Kaffee: Why did you call her?
> Jessup: I invited her to dinner tonight. . . .
> Kaffee: These are the phone records for September. And these are the letters Santiago wrote for nine months begging for a transfer. But when he finally got it, how many people did he call?

Zero! Nobody. Not one call to his parents or his friends to say he was coming. He was asleep at midnight and you say he had a flight in six hours. Yet everything he owned was in his closet or his footlocker. For one day, you packed and made three calls. Santiago was leaving for the rest of his life. And he hadn't called a soul or packed a thing. Can you explain that?

Jessup: [silent]

Kaffee: There was no transfer order was there? . . .

Kaffee: Do you have an answer?

Jessup: Absolutely. I don't have a clue. Maybe he was an early riser. Maybe he didn't have any friends. I'm an educated man, but I don't know the travel habits of Santiago. What I do know is that he was set to leave. . . . Are these really the questions I was called here to answer?[1]

This examination works, and fans of the movie will remember that Jessup ultimately unravels, railing at Kaffee that he "can't handle the truth." But what we should remember for now is that Kaffee could handle preparing his examination of a witness.

Notice how he dealt with the documents—the room inventory and the telephone records. Whatever had to be done to authenticate them and establish what they said was already done. It would be particularly admirable if what was in them had been stipulated before the trial even started.

That would have saved us the awkward half an hour or so usually eaten up by such mundanities in real trials. Here is what the precursor might have looked like in a real courtroom almost anywhere in the United States:

Kaffee: Lieutenant Fuzz, are you currently employed?

Fuzz: Yes.

Kaffee: How are you employed?

Fuzz: I am the office administrator at Camp Swampy.

Kaffee: How long have you been so employed?

Fuzz: Eleven years.

Kaffee: So, you were there at the time of Santiago's murder.

Kendrick: Objection. Leading.

Court: Sustained.

Kaffee: What years did your eleven years span?

Fuzz: 1983 to 1994.

Kaffee: Do you recognize the name William Santiago?

Fuzz: Yes.

Kaffee: Why do you recognize that name?

Fuzz: I remember he died while I was there.

Kaffee: While Santiago was there and you were office administrator, what were your duties?

Fuzz: I kept the office records, including all of the phone logs.

Kaffee: I am showing you now what has been previously marked as defense exhibit AAA. Do you recognize it?

Fuzz: Yes.

Kaffee: What is it?

Fuzz: This is the September 1991 phone log for Camp Swampy.

Kaffee: Is this a record you maintain?

Kendrick: Objection. Leading.

Court: Overruled. You may answer.

Fuzz: Yes.

Kaffee: Is it part of the ordinary course of your duty to keep this record?

Fuzz: Yes.

Kaffee: Was this record made at or near the time of the telephone calls recorded?

Fuzz: Yes.

Kaffee: Was it a regular practice to maintain these records?

Fuzz: Yes.

Kaffee: Your honor, I move to admit exhibit AAA as a full exhibit.

Kendrick: No objection, your honor.

Court: [sighing] Very well, exhibit AAA is a full exhibit. We'll break for lunch now.

And this assumes Kaffee knows the right questions to ask to admit a record in this way. Too many lawyers don't. In any case, it's only a shame that when this tedious exercise started, the judge couldn't have shouted: "Cut!"

This sequence is longer than the dramatic and effective exchange

FIGURE 15.1. *"Can you please identify which hand was mistakenly amputated?"*

quoted earlier. Worse still, that effort only got the phone logs in. The same thing would have had to have been done with a different witness to get the inventory of Santiago's belongings in. This is needless complexity.

Maybe it wasn't the lawyer's fault. The lawyer may have asked opposing counsel to agree to the exhibits, but opposing counsel refused. Instead, it should be the judge's responsibility. Judges traditionally think that interfering in such matters is none of their business. It's an adversarial system, and if an experienced lawyer can trip up an inexperienced lawyer during this process, that's why the experienced lawyer gets paid more.

But judges should rethink this assumption. Is the game worth the damage it's doing to the credibility and effectiveness of the justice system? It isn't too much to ask that parties cooperate in good faith to stipulate things that will wind up being uncontested anyway. Without such stipulations, we waste jurors' time; we waste the court's time, and—what should matter most—the life of the trial is sucked out, leaving a dead sea of the obvious and needless.

Considering what's disputed should lead lawyers not only to stipulate around the undisputed; it should give them the idea that much of what they were planning is needless. No points scored. No drama achieved. Once they realize this, they should have the courage to offer only what matters most. Yes, lawyers can let the fact finder get to know the party a bit with pertinent background. Otherwise, lawyers should spend their time preparing important testimony and closing arguments.

As with *A Few Good Men*, most cases have some human drama. Injuries, broken promises, stolen secrets, predatory trade practices, broken homes. If the public could understand how courts sort out these dramas peacefully, they might have more respect for the judicial system. It might also help people see how to solve problems in life. Watching well-done courtroom proceedings can help people in ordinary life learn to focus on the important facts, to weigh evidence when searching for the truth, and to make practical decisions with regard for those affected. This is becoming a lost art. With more trials run more efficiently, courts could remind people how to do it.

When lawyers realize that their cases rest chiefly on undisputed facts, they should ask the court to extend the time for argument and then make it a good one. No lawyer should be ashamed. A trial doesn't have to be long to be won.

16 : TOO MUCH EXPERT TESTIMONY IS DISCREDITING EXPERTS

Needless expert testimony may also be dragging cases down. Indeed, we should worry that the entire idea of expertise is undercut when matters of common sense or matters impossible to calculate are calculated with pseudoscientific assurances. Unnecessary fights over experts waste time.

We need experts in some cases. Courts often must rely on medical experts about the standard of medical care. In sophisticated commercial cases, experts in technical fields are often pivotal. But lawyers shouldn't think their cases weaker because they aren't calling experts or have fewer experts than their opponents. In many cases involving psychological harm, judges and jurors already have the tools to tell how mental suffering affects us. We have all been through it. Yes, there are cases where the harm is particularly distinct and experts are required. But we don't need much from an expert to know that physical harm causes emotional harm, that fighting parents upset children, and that a speeding car on a narrow road is a dangerous thing.

Some accident-reconstruction experts can be comical. In cases with unusual forensic evidence, they help. But sometimes, an expert for a party uses the same measurements and methods as the opposing expert and then leaps to the opposite conclusion. Their views aren't science at all. They are needlessly opining on something fact finders can better decide by themselves.

Take the example of a hypothetical motorcycle accident. It happened on a side street. A pedestrian was struck and sued the motorcyclist. The motorcyclist said the pedestrian was in the middle of the road. The pedestrian said he had pinned himself to the side of

93

a parked camper when he saw the motorcycle roaring up the street. Both sides had experts. The bike fell over after the collision. Parts of it were bent. There were skid marks in the road. The pedestrian's reconstructionist measured the location and length of the skid marks. They seemed to move from left to right on the road. He noticed that the right handlebar on the bike was bent. He concluded that the accident happened on the left side of the road, arguing that the marks show he turned toward the middle just after the accident and that the bent right brake handle shows that the bike was moving to the right after clipping the pedestrian and therefore fell over on that side.

The motorcyclist's expert concluded the opposite from the same evidence. The skid marks showed that the pedestrian was in the middle of the road before the accident and that the cyclist was trying to maneuver around the pedestrian when he was hit. The broken brake handle on the right side showed a frantic effort to avoid the pedestrian that failed because the pedestrian was too far out in the road.

The jury ignored them. They focused on better evidence. A neighbor testified to seeing the pedestrian in the middle of the road as she was going out to pick up her newspaper seconds before the collision. Another neighbor testified that the pedestrian lived on the street and was head of a neighborhood protest against motorcycles speeding on his street. She had seen him four times in the last month running into the middle of the road and waving down motorcycles he perceived to be speeding. Verdict for the motorcyclist.

Jurors' ordinary understanding usually triumphs over trumped-up expertise. Lawyers should rethink using experts for matters of common sense. Experts should tell us something we don't already know or can't perceive in other ways ourselves. Otherwise, they are wasting our time. They should never tell us they can do the impossible. The trouble is that sometimes they try—like the accident reconstructionist whose calculations showed that a woman ran over her husband, backed over him, and then drove frontwards over him again, all by accident.

The profession's tendency to call experts on every side of every issue in every case may even be undermining our trust in experts as a whole. Where they were once viewed as disinterested sages, they are too often seen today as for sale rather than salient.

FIGURE 16.1. *"I didn't hire a lawyer, but I found a neuroscientist who can explain why it wasn't my fault."*

To keep them credible, we should consider using them sparingly.

Here's how it might be handled in a divorce case. Let's take a hypothetical. One spouse was a realtor and the other was a heart surgeon in Manhattan. The surgeon reported just $125,000 of income. His wife reported that she had seen now-missing bank account statements around the house with large balances. She hired an expert to show that the earning capacity of a heart surgeon in Manhattan was more than $125,000 a year.

The court barred the expert under the rules for being unnecessary. As soon as the surgeon was cross examined on the witness stand, he was confronted with the obvious question: "Heart surgeons in Manhattan typically earn far more than $125,000 a year, don't they?" The surgeon answered, "Yes, of course." No need for the expert. Indeed, the witness admitted that they typically made $500,000 or more. Government statistics showed that surgeons of any type anywhere in the country made $250,000 or more. The expert testimony cost over $50,000 and wasn't needed.

The same parties disputed the value of the marital residence in a tony town during the great COVID real estate boom in the Manhattan suburbs. Both sides had an expert. One said the house was worth $1.2 million. One said the house was worth $750,000. The house had been purchased for $1.1 million eight years earlier. Both sides admitted in testimony that the number was most likely around $1 million.

The court held that given the undisputed rapid rise in property values in the area, the property was at least worth what they paid for it— $1.1 million. Besides, in the grand scheme of things, the house was awarded to the wife. There were no proceeds to be split. The value number—in rough form—was only needed to consider how to divide what was left.

Courts can play an active and helpful role when they discourage parties from using needless experts. They are wasting time with them and often bankrupting their clients with needless expense and complexity. Experts shouldn't complain. Right now, they are mostly seen as little better than hired guns. If they were only used when they have something useful to say, they might be better respected—and the respect they receive is their only stock in trade.

17 : CONSIDER COMMON SENSE FIRST IN FAMILY COURT

Particularly in family courts, an army of experts and helpers stand between the judge and the parties—and not just testifying experts.

The parties have lawyers. Matters are referred to family court support staff for screening, investigation, evaluation, and mediation. Courts frequently appoint Guardians *ad litem*, and the parties pay them to consider the best interests of their children in ways similar to what the court's staff does.

Child-protection agencies are often brought in. Protective-order applications may sail back and forth to bar one parent from annoying the other or the children. Lawyers may be appointed for the children. Courts increasingly appoint custody evaluators to opine on custody decisions reserved for judges.

Sometimes, the whole family is sent for psychological evaluations, therapy, and reunification interventions, and expert witnesses are hired to advocate for competing forms of custody.

All this can take years. By the time the process is completed, the facts on the ground have often changed, or the matter has been decided without any help from the courts.

Let's take a familiar hypothetical custody dispute. A husband and wife had three children aged between ten and fifteen. Both parents had jobs. He made significantly more than she did. The case lasted three years. The docket showed over 120 entries for motions, rulings, and other filings. A guardian was appointed at the father's expense. He was ordered to pay alimony and child support during the litigation. On top of paying all of this, he was ordered to pay tens of thousands of dollars in attorneys' fees for both himself and—by order of the court—his wife.

Both sides agreed that the other parent was a fit parent. They were battling only over where the children would sleep most nights. They both had clean, adequate homes to house the children. Still, the battle raged. Experts were hired for trial. Reunification therapists were hired. Individual counselors were retained.

By the time of trial, both parties were broke. The mortgage on their home was in default. The couple's retirement funds were raided. The children were on food stamps. At trial, the parents spent almost the entire time trading barbs about who yelled at the other the most and which one shoved the other the most and generally sought to convince the court that they were good and the other parent bad. The trial took twelve days despite the judge trying to shorten it.

Three hundred and fifty thousand dollars in fees later, the court entered orders that the parties should get equal access to the children but defer to the children's informed preferences. Because she earned less, the wife received alimony without opposition. The court ordered child support by applying a court-created formula. Meanwhile, the children voted with their feet. Two of them stayed with their father and one with their mother.

In too many cases, this scenario is destroying families in the name of saving them. For what? This is often the wrong result, but us census statistics show that in three out of five child-custody cases, this convoluted system still produces the same result every time: young children make their primary residence with their mother, and the father gets a schedule of parenting time centered around the weekend that looks remarkably similar in most cases.[1]

Judges should play a stronger role in ending the confusion and poisonous delays caused by the system overworking these cases. The expense and delay have ruined lives, discredited courts, and spawned demented conspiracy theories like those that have infected public dialogue about the other two branches of government.

Another hypothetical custody example can illustrate how it might be done. A couple with three children came to court for an initial conference and interim orders. Both parents said they had an adequate home for the children but that they didn't trust the other parent. The judge ordered family-court staff to examine the two homes, meet the children, check court and child-protection records, and report back orally on the facts in three weeks.

FIGURE 17.1. *"Such have been the delays in this case,
I fear custody of this child is no longer an issue."*

Three weeks later the court held a trial. The court staff reported that the mother's home was suitable, but so was the father's home. Both parties had difficulties with issues, but no agency had found them unfit. The mother testified that her mother lives with her and helps with the children every day. The father testified that he had a gainfully employed uncle who lived with him and that he didn't work because of a disability that didn't prevent him from caring for the children.

The court ordered joint legal and physical custody and rotated the children week by week between the parents. They squabbled about pickup and drop-off, but neither side appealed, and they carried out the schedule. This hotly contested case went to judgment three weeks after the first date the couple appeared in court.

It's the judges' job to listen to the parties in custody cases and decide the best interests of the children. Sometimes a judge needs expert help. Mediation is good. Agreements are good, but often the best way to get agreements is to ensure a swift, fair hearing of the parties' divergent views without battalions of experts who might produce the same commonsense rulings as an experienced or well-trained judge.

18 : INTRODUCE TIME CLOCKS TO ENCOURAGE EFFICIENT TRIALS

Speaking of not wasting time, a chess clock in a trial is a splendid thing. To use them, lawyers and judges agree in advance that during a trial each side gets so many minutes on the clock. Whenever lawyers speak, including to object, the clerks slap the button on their side of the clock, and the lawyer starts losing time.

Lawyers are usually surprised at how well it works. Jurors are quietly grateful. The trick, of course, is for a judge to fairly allocate the time. But it's the fairness of the allocation, not whether to set a time limit, that should be the central focus.

Courts can benefit from time clocks because trials illustrate Parkinson's Law: work expands to fill the time allotted to it. If lawyers have no end point for a trial, it drags. If lawyers have only a rough end point, it will be exceeded. When you have a clock ticking, the lawyers are less likely to challenge it. They've taken exams. They know when it's time for pencils down.

Consider an example of efficiency with a time clock at its center. Judge William Alsup of the federal Northern District of California managed the case, *Mathews v. Chevron*. The case was little more than a claim for negligent misrepresentation. Because it was brought under the Employee Retirement Income Security Act (ERISA), it became complex—because of confused case law.

Judge Alsup focused on the facts, the parties, and a trial. He resolved discovery disputes using baseball arbitration. He ruled quickly on the pretrial motions. Most importantly, he took the time before trial to work with the parties to eliminate exhibits and impose a time clock. The trial was to the judge—no juries are allowed in ERISA cases.

Each party was allocated its minutes. The clock ran against the party whenever its lawyers spoke. So they spoke less. They made fewer frivolous and disorienting objections. They called only those witnesses they needed to call, and counsel actively sought each other out to stipulate facts or at least exhibits. The case was about whether company representatives misled employees into retiring early by denying rumored retirement-benefit enhancements that were adopted shortly after they retired. The trial took only a few days. The judge took just five days to make his sixty-page decision. The basic result was upheld on appeal.[1]

Now let's consider the alternative, all too common, scenario. A teacher sued parents, students, and school board members, claiming they had cost him his job by defaming him. While battling for years over discovery, the defense claimed the statements were protected by an absolute privilege because they were made to the state board of education during a license-revocation procedure. The claim was important because if teachers could sue children for complaining about them, then who would dare complain about even the worst teacher? The privilege was absolute. No repleading would save the complaint. It was a rare example where the law mattered more than the facts.

The judge decided it was easier to have the jury hear the case than to decide the motion. Jury selection took weeks as the lawyers, without court supervision, wrestled for the jurors' affection, flattering and complimenting them with their questions and asking them things like, "If you could be a monkey, an owl, or a short-haired pointer, which would you be?"

The trial was a nightmare. There were no time limits. Every objection was a speaking objection. The lawyers battled each other sometimes for an hour over any number of them. The judge thought it was his duty to mostly stay out of the way and let things unfold in front of the jury without cutting the lawyers off when they were arguing objections—even when the objections were simply designed to disrupt the trial. Even when some mysterious person pulled the fire alarm in the courthouse, the judge made no inquiries or imprecations. He believed the adversarial system would take care of itself.

This continued for three months. Finally, after a week of deliberation, the jury returned a nominal verdict against two of the nine

defendants. Again, the trial judge refused to consider the legal argument about absolute privilege. Finally, after another several years,
the state supreme court overturned the two verdicts—on the grounds
that the statements were absolutely privileged. The nearly ten-year
saga cost parents and the school board hundreds of thousands of dollars to end up where it should have in the first place if the judge had
placed the idea of justice over devotion to an unfettered adversarial
system.[2] It's usually about the facts, but sometimes it's about the law,
and time is always money in court. So, judges must use judgment.

19 : NEEDLESS OBJECTIONS ANNOY JUDGES AND JURORS

Finally, a witness gets to the heart of her testimony. It's damaging. It's specific. It's persuasive. And it's immediately interrupted. The lawyer for the damaged party leaps up, wailing, "Objection, objection!" But objection to what? Why?

An objection is supposed to be a lawyer's way of stopping someone from giving prohibited testimony—testimony that is precluded under the rules of evidence—usually because what's being offered isn't reliable enough to be called evidence. But too often, objections have nothing to do with that. It's just that the testimony is hurting, and the lawyer will do anything to disrupt it—even calling attention to its importance by shouting, "Objection! Objection!"

The rules of evidence are beautiful things. We can understand most of them. They have useful purposes. They usually keep out unreliable testimony, like hearsay. "Bob said that Carol told him. . . ." They ensure that witnesses, not their lawyers, testify by generally barring lawyers from asking their witnesses leading questions on disputed issues. "And when you approached the light, you were being particularly careful, weren't you?" Evidentiary objections have short names lawyers can raise and judges can swiftly rule on: "Objection. Relevance." "Objection. Vague."

Still, most objections in court today actually annoy the judge and jury and waste time. With trials few and far between, too many lawyers don't know the rules of evidence well enough to make a proper objection. It's surprising how many judges don't know the rules either. What results is frantic lawyers objecting whenever their opponents finally get around to asking an important question.

Beyond the shouted word, there are at least two variations of this phenomenon. Often, counsel makes a speaking objection: "I object.

FIGURE 19.1. *"Your Honor, I object! This line of questioning*
is making my client look really bad."

The witness was obviously trying to deny she was at the beach house
that night, and counsel won't let her do it." An outraged response may
then ensue, and the judge has to ask the jury to leave the room. A half
an hour is burned up while the lawyers exchange accusations. Sufficiently lathered up, the lawyers simply rinse and repeat.

The second version, equally prevalent, is the kitchen-sink phenomenon: "Objection, foundation, leading, assumes facts not in evidence,
the rule in Shelley's case, perpetuities, the rule of thirds. . . ." These
kinds of objections tend to say more about the lawyer than about the
evidence. Lawyers who want jurors to respect rather than revile them
and the process should learn the rules and apply them sparingly and
skillfully.

In the interest of time and clarity, judges should strictly police objections. Objections have names: "leading," "calls for hearsay," "assumes facts not in evidence" (better called a "loaded question"). Once
the objection is named, the judge rules. When the judge needs more,
the judge asks. Most judges and lawyers know this is how it's supposed to be done. But too many lawyers don't do it, and too many
judges don't stop them. Waste and confusion result. Jurors look down
on the lawyers responsible for it and the judges who don't stop them.

20 : MAKE A POINT, NOT A MUDDLE, WITH PRIOR TESTIMONY

Lawyers often use witnesses' prior testimony to discredit them. In another court hearing or in an evidence-gathering question-and-answer session—a "deposition"—witnesses sometimes give different answers than they give at trial.

Prior contradictory testimony can expose when witnesses aren't telling the truth. But too many lawyers lose the essence of the contradiction and waste time by fumbling through the process of pointing it out.

Many times, lawyers start by asking the witness, "Did you give a deposition?" only to hear: "I'm not sure."

"Didn't we have a question-and-answer session in my office?"

"Oh yeah, that. Sure."

"Didn't you swear to tell the truth?"

"I don't remember much about it. It was two years ago."

"I am showing you now your oath. You took that oath, didn't you?"

"It says so, so I guess I did."

"Didn't I ask you if you had ever been to the beach house before?"

"I don't remember." And on and on.

Now let's consider an alternative: "Your honor, I questioned Ms. DeVito under oath when I was searching for evidence in this case. She says now she had not been to the beach house before. But in earlier testimony, she swore she had been there before. I would like to read to the jury my question and her answer from her earlier testimony." The judge lets the lawyer proceed, and the lawyer says: "I am reading from Ms. DeVito's November 11, 2022, deposition on page 12, line 1. Question: 'Were you ever at the beach house before?' Answer: 'Yes.'"

This can be powerful in front of a jury. It can be followed up with a question to the witness. "Here today you swore in front of this jury that you had never been to the beach house before. Three months ago, you swore you had been there before. When you gave that denial a few minutes ago to the ladies and gentlemen of the jury, you were lying, weren't you?"—passionate denial—"In fact, you knew you were lying because you knew that there are dated photographs of you at the beach house that prove you were lying?"

It might be helpful to do this in front of a judge because the witness might break and the truth might be revealed. Alternatively, the earlier testimony could go on a list of undisputed facts. It all depends on whether the drama might be fruitful.

21 : PUNISH MISCONDUCT WHEN IT HAPPENS RATHER THAN IN A SEPARATE PROCEEDING

Sanctioning someone a few thousand dollars for lying under oath or destroying evidence is no problem to the perpetrators so long as covering up the truth is worth more than the money sanction. And separate proceedings before ethics boards or criminal courts just multiply rather than simplify litigation.

Parties are better off asking the judge for an adverse inference of some type in the case where the misconduct took place. This means that if someone destroys their computer, you ask the judge to instruct the jury to assume the computer contained evidence establishing something the offending party doesn't want to be known. "Ladies and gentleman, you should assume that the computer that was destroyed contained trade secret information that Mr. Jones was prohibited from taking." For perjury, one can say something like this: "Mr. Smith lied to you. You may assume that this wasn't the only thing he has lied to you about. It's up to you what that may be. But you know he has lied to you under oath, and you may consider that lie when you consider whether to believe the other things he told you."

Prior to trial, judges should consider taking a more active role in curbing discovery abuses. One of the areas of greatest abuse happens outside the view of the court at depositions. Because no judge is present, the parties in depositions typically waive most objections about everything except the form of the question—for instance, loaded questions, such as, "When did you stop beating your wife?" or compound (two-part) questions, such as, "Did you turn left and then start speeding? Yes or no?" The practice is merely to say "objection form" to preserve the claim that the question itself is so hopelessly flawed that it and the answer should be entirely disallowed. Once the objection is made, the witness is supposed to answer, and the matter gets sorted out with the judge later, at trial.

Still, most bars have a few lawyers notorious for their hedgehog approach to depositions. They interrupt every question with an objection. Many of them are speaking: "You can't ask her that. How is she supposed to answer a question like that?" "Can't you see she was trying to tell you she wasn't there?" And on and on. Judges hate slogging through transcripts to sort out this behavior, and lawyers are loath to burden judges with these matters.

But judges should think about at least taking up the worst of them, and doing it themselves rather than sending the matters for years of proceedings before ethics boards. Take the example of the lawyer who had been sanctioned six times for her frivolous, insulting, degrading, delaying, and endless objections at depositions. After a report of several failed attempts at deposing a medical witness, a personal injury plaintiff's lawyer finally got fed up and brought the issue to the court. Seeing the belligerent response of the accused lawyer, the court decided the deposition should proceed in court, figuring no lawyer would be foolish enough to behave that way in front of a judge.

That turned out to be wrong. The lawyer went right back at it, objecting to every question. Objecting to where she was asked to sit. Objecting to her opponent's facial expressions—pacing, grimacing, thrusting her hands on her hips, criticizing the court. After around eight warnings, and two attempted sessions about the deposition, the court took up the other side's motion for sanctions. At the hearing, it turned out the lawyer was caught on a hot mic during the deposition advising her co-counsel in obscene language that she was deliberately giving her opponent—or possibly the judge—a hard time. After a hearing, the court imposed a seventh sanction. While the prior sanctions had been mere warnings or financial penalties, this time the court suspended the lawyer.[1] She was promptly replaced in the case by other counsel and substitute counsel carried on in a professional way.

Not dealing with a problem on the spot means the case must drag on with the misconduct continuing while ethics matters pend in another place. It seems obvious, but surprisingly, that is how things often proceed—it keeps a judge from having to shoulder the responsibility for the ugly business of disciplining a lawyer.

When misconduct happens in front of judges, judges should conduct themselves accordingly. They are the makers of manners in court. They must see that the manners made are observed.

22 : CROSS-EXAMINE CRISPLY, CRUSHINGLY, OR NOT AT ALL

Time spent on cross-examination is usually most effective when it is a series of forced concessions. The old saw about never asking a question you don't know the answer to is mostly right. The answers should be inescapable—so much so that the attempt to escape only makes things worse:

Q: So, you had been to the boathouse before 2020?
A: No.
Q: I'm showing you a photograph in evidence as Exhibit 3. That's you in the photograph, isn't it?
A: Yes.
Q: That's your handwriting under the picture, isn't it?
A: Yes.
Q: And you wrote, "My boathouse visit, 2018"?
A: Yes.
Q: So, you visited the boathouse before 2020, didn't you?
A: Yes.

While more skillful lawyers can seize a spontaneous opportunity, in the main, it's best to refrain unless you can reign.

Now let's see the final part of the cross-examination in *A Few Good Men* as an example of seizing the opportunity while still pinning the witness in with the inescapable. Remember, the issue is whether the top brass intended to protect the murdered marine by transferring him or whether the colonel in charge actually ordered the "code-red" punishment that led to his death. The colonel insisted he had ordered his subordinate to protect the young marine:

Kaffee: Can he have ignored the order? Or forgot it?

Jessup: No.

Kaffee: Could he have thought, "the old man is wrong." When Lt. Kendrick talked to the men, any chance they ignored him?

Jessup: Ever been in the infantry son? Ever served in a forward area? Ever put your life in another man's hands, and his in yours? We follow orders, son. Otherwise, people die. It's that simple. Are we clear? Are we clear?

Kaffee: Crystal. One last question before I call Airmen O'Malley and Rodriguez. If you ordered that Santiago wasn't to be touched—and your orders are always followed—then why was Santiago in danger? Why would it be necessary to transfer him off base?

Jessup: He was a substandard Marine.

Kaffee: You said he was transferred because he was in danger . . . Then why the two orders?

Jessup: Men can do things on their own.

Kaffee: But your men never did. Your men obey orders. So Santiago wasn't in danger, right?

Jessup: You snotty little bastard.

Kaffee: If Lt. Kendrick gave an order that Santiago wasn't to be touched, why did he have to be transferred? Kendrick ordered a code red because you told him to! And when it went bad, you signed a phony transfer and fixed the logs. You coerced the doctor, colonel! Jessup did you order the code red? . . .

Jessup: You want answers?

Kaffee: I want the truth!

Jessup: You can't handle the truth! Son, we live in a world with walls that must be guarded. Who's gonna do it? You? You, Lt. Weinberg? I have more responsibility than you can fathom. You weep for Santiago and curse the Marines. You don't know what I know. Santiago's tragic death saved lives. And my existence, while grotesque to you, saves lives! But deep down, in places you don't talk about at parties—you need me on that wall. We use words like honor, code, loyalty. They're the backbone of our lives. You use them as a punchline! I haven't the time or inclination to explain myself to a man who needs my protection—but questions

the way I do it. Better just thank me. Or pick up a gun and stand
a post. But I don't give a damn what you think you are entitled to!
   Kaffee: Did you order the code red!?
   Jessup: You're goddam right I did![1]

Drama in court is not a bad thing. It's the lack of drama that's killing us. But remember the drama in this cross-examination centers on
an inescapable point around which the whole interchange pivoted.
Jessup had made the dangerous move of speaking in the absolute—
his Marines *always* obeyed orders. Once he had done that, it was a
simple matter of hanging him with his own words.

This cross-examination involved what many would say was arguing with the witness. Of course, they were heated, but it's cross-
examination. Cross-examination is naturally adversarial. Judges
should rule a lawyer is merely arguing with the witness not when
there is a sharp point and counterpoint between the examiner and
the examined, but when—as it so often does among the unskilled—it
merely amounts to pointless contradiction or ridicule. If all the examination amounts to is a lawyer scorning the witness, the lawyer
shouldn't bother cross-examining at all. In fact, this can be powerful.
The lawyer dismissively announces they have no questions for a witness whose deficiencies speak for themselves. Judges and jurors will
be grateful. The lawyer will win respect. The trial will be shorter and
more focused.

23 : HUMANIZE OVERSTUFFED, BEWILDERING JURY CHARGES AND INTERROGATORIES

After every witness has testified and every document has been admitted into evidence, after the lawyers have made their arguments, it's time for the judge to explain to the jury that it's their job to decide the facts and apply to them certain legal rules to decide who wins. The jury charge is when the judge explains these rules to the jury.

The parties to a lawsuit often fight over what the judge should put in the jury instructions. They might propose cut-and-paste blurbs they think favor their client or that at least make them look diligent or even aggressive. Jurors hate them because they are often too long, contain too much jargon, and are badly organized.

The fastest way to address a jury charge is for the judge to propose a draft to counsel at the outset of the trial and ask for redlined proposals about that charge. Many judges do the same types of trials all the time—think auto-accident cases—it shouldn't take much time to assemble a template from experience.

Judges can help jurors by developing human-centered—juror-centered—model instructions. Most courts have model instructions. Many miss the mark. They seem crafted with everybody but the jury in mind—a little for the plaintiff, a little for the defendant, but most of it for the appellate courts. Formalism triumphs.

With fear of being overturned by an upper court in mind, many of those drafting jury instructions quote either exactly or too closely the legalese from the upper courts rather than explain the law in words jurors can understand. A favorite violator of this is the instruction about proximate cause. Here is what it might look like:

By proximate cause, I refer to a cause that in a natural and continuous sequence produces the accident/incident/event and resulting injury/loss/harm and without which the resulting accident/incident/event or injury/loss/harm would not have occurred. A person who is negligent is held responsible for any accident/incident/event or injury/loss/harm that results in the ordinary course of events from his/her/its negligence. This means that you must find that the resulting accident/incident/event or injury/loss/harm to [name of plaintiff or other party] would not have occurred but for the negligent conduct of [name of defendant or other party].

To find proximate cause, you must first find that [name of defendant or party]'s negligence was a cause of the accident/incident/event. If you find that [name of defendant or other party]'s negligence is not a cause of the accident/incident/event, then you must find no proximate cause.

Second, you must find that [name of defendant or other party]'s negligence was a substantial factor that singly, or in combination with other causes, brought about the injury/loss/harm claimed by [name of plaintiff]. By substantial, it is meant that it was not a remote, trivial, or inconsequential cause. Nor is it necessary for the negligence of [name of the defendant or other party] to be the sole cause of [name of plaintiff]'s injury/loss/harm. However, you must find that [name of defendant or other party]'s negligence was a substantial factor in bringing about injury/loss/harm.

Third, you must find that some injury/loss/harm to [name of plaintiff] must have been foreseeable. For the injury/loss/harm to be foreseeable, it is not necessary that the precise injury/loss/harm that occurred here was foreseeable by [name of defendant or other party]. Rather, a reasonable person should have anticipated the risk that [name of defendant or other party]'s conduct [omission] could cause some injury/loss/harm suffered by [name of plaintiff]. In other words, if some injury/loss/harm from [name of defendant or other part]'s negligence was within the realm of foreseeability, then the injury/loss/harm is considered foreseeable. On the other hand, if the risk of injury/

loss/harm was so remote as not to be in the realm of reasonable foreseeability, you must find no proximate cause.

In sum, in order to find proximate cause, you must find that the negligence of [name of defendant or other party] was a substantial factor in bringing about the injury/loss/harm that occurred and that some harm to [name of plaintiff] was foreseeable from [name of defendant or other party]'s negligence.

This is just one section of the civil charge that a judge might give following the case law in an ordinary personal injury case.

But jurors don't ever have to hear the words "proximate cause" to decide a case. Instead, the concept could be put into useful English. This will save time drafting, reading, and—for jurors—puzzling over the jury charge. Here is a first step that works for a single defendant:

You can't make people pay for damage they didn't cause. The law requires proof of three things before you can say one person's wrongdoing caused someone else's injury. To cause an injury, the wrongdoing must be indispensable, foreseeable, and substantial in bringing about the harm at issue.

A wrong is an "indispensable" cause of the harm if the harm would never have happened without the wrong happening first.

A wrong is a "foreseeable" cause of a harm if the average person could have foreseen that what they were doing might actually cause harm similar to the one suffered.

Where multiple things contribute to someone being harmed, a wrong has to be a "substantial" enough cause to blame the person who is alleged to have committed the wrong. If the wrong had only a small role in causing the harm compared with other things, then it isn't enough of a cause for blame.

This covers the key elements most case law requires. Still, why we need both the substantial factor part and the "indispensable" or "but-for" element isn't clear. These topics could be combined. We'll talk more about multiple causes later, but for now, assuming the party suing isn't mostly responsible, everything useful the but-for instruction might have covered is included in the notion of being substantial.

So, let's drill the single defendant causation charge down a little further:

> You can't make people pay for harm they didn't cause, shouldn't expect, or when they only played a tiny role in causing the harm.

> The law makes a person responsible for harm when the person suing isn't mostly responsible for the harm, when the harm wouldn't have happened without a substantial contribution from the person sued, and when the person sued should have seen the harm or something like it coming.

This would be a bridge too far under some of the case law. We could try to stare down the contradictory decisions surrounding proximate cause, but we would do better to avert our eyes and try to put the basic values in the cases into words jurors can understand.

Is something still missing that a jury might need? Does it really help to say the same thing twice? Or multiple times in different ways? It's probably best to leave the jury to focus on a simpler sentence than try to parse the nuances among varying versions. The only other thing that might help is an example:

> Let's say you hit a ball with an aluminum bat in a crowded neighborhood. If the ball breaks a window, we can fairly say you broke the window and you should have seen it coming. You should have to pay for the window.

> But let's say the sun reflects off the bat while you're swinging and blinds a driver on the street who runs off the road and destroys a neighbor's fence. You had no reason to see that coming, so you shouldn't have to pay for the fence.

> Or let's say there were two balls headed for the same window. Your ball missed but the ball that broke the window was hit by someone who said they were hitting the ball the way they did because they saw you doing it. The window wouldn't have been broken without you, but you might reasonably think your contribution to breaking it was too small to make you pay for any part of the window.

If judges and lawyers focused on jurors when considering jury in-structions, the instructions would be easier to write, faster to read,

© Mike Baldwin / Cornered

FIGURE 23.1. *"Maybe this wouldn't happen if you
didn't allow the trial to drag on so long."*

and more easily digested. The jurors wouldn't have to ask many questions about it or—as doubtless happens—simply ignore the instruction entirely. Trials would likely end sooner if jurors had a better idea of what they were supposed to decide.

Jury instructions need no technical terms to accurately explain the law. They should be in plain English. They should be brief. And each juror should have a set of them in the jury room during deliberations. Fortunately, many jurisdictions are starting to catch on to the need for plain language, but overcharging remains a serious problem.

Jury interrogatories are written questions the jury is told to answer and return along with their verdict form. The questions have proliferated unwisely over the years.

It's understandable to think that if judges make jurors walk me-
thodically through the legal thickets of the case, they are more likely
to get them to follow the law. But this takes inadequate account of the
fact that the jury's job is to decide the facts and the judge's job is to
decide the law.

Take a complicated contract case as an example. Courts are likely
asking too much of jurors when they give the jurors the contract and
ask them if the defendant violated its duties under paragraphs 10 (c)
(2)(iii), 12 (b)(4), 23, 25, and 28 and addendum 5, paragraph 6 (b).

As an alternative, a questionnaire could reduce the issues for the
jury to fact-finding with the court then entering judgment based
upon the legal effect of the facts found.

So, if the issue is fault for late performance, the judge should ask
the jury to decide whether "the general contractor BobCo. was at
fault for late completion or whether the late completion was the fault
of the electrical subcontractor, Electro-Bilge." If there are multiple
parties to judge, let the jury assign a percentage of responsibility to
each—including zero.

If the issue is "best efforts," ask the jury if the contractor did its best
to get the job done on time. If it's "reasonable notice," ask whether the
developer gave the contractor fair warning about its defective work
and enough time to fix it. Get the answer, and the court can decide
what judgment the answer requires based upon the plain language of
the contract. If the language isn't plain, either the court or the jury
will have to decide what, if anything, was agreed.

24 : SAVE TIME IN COURT TRIALS BY SUBSTITUTING LONGER CLOSING ARGUMENTS FOR POSTTRIAL BRIEFING

In trials where the judge, rather than a jury, is the fact finder, courts can make efficient use of closing arguments. There are no juries in most family courts. Cases seeking court orders rather than money awards also usually involve no jury.

A closing argument to the court is best when it takes place at the same time it would during a jury trial—immediately after the end of evidence, when everything is fresh. Because they sum up the evidence and argue why the law favors a given side, closing arguments are the lawyers' last chance to convince the judge why their client should win.

Judges and lawyers can discuss basic legal precepts before and during the trial, and, if they do, many times everyone will agree on the basic applicable principles before the closing argument. When everyone doesn't agree, closing argument is a good time to debate gaps in the standard with everyone having a copy of the cases and sharing their ideas. Five-page memos listing each side's key legal principles can be handy—sometimes.

Long oral arguments are usually better than posttrial briefing. Posttrial briefing substitutes paper for people. It can waste time and understanding. In many places, the parties will ask for about forty-five days to get a trial transcript, and the plaintiff will ask for thirty or sixty days after that to write the brief. The defense will then want thirty or sixty days to respond; and the plaintiff, another fourteen days or so to reply. Courts often then schedule the oral argument for some time after that. This results in the argument sometimes taking place four to six months after the trial—after everyone has forgotten it. The court and the lawyers find themselves crawling through the transcript and sifting through the exhibits all over again. It's like retrying the case.

A robust and immediate closing argument can be more direct, more dynamic, and, therefore, more effective. It's best when it's a vigorous exchange of ideas between the judge and the lawyers. Judges shouldn't be afraid—when the trial is over—to suggest what's on their minds. They should share the questions they are struggling to answer about the facts and the law. They should confess the impressions they have formed and give the lawyers a chance to talk them out of them.

Lawyers should assume judges aren't playing devil's advocate with their questions. Usually, judges are actually signaling lawyers about some aspect of their intended ruling, and lawyers should jump at the chance to influence this. The last thing closing argument should be is a speech, but judges should be sure to give lawyers a chance to address topics they haven't covered during their exchanges with the bench.

After a thorough discussion with the lawyers, judges should begin writing their opinions immediately. Judges will almost always know at that point the side they favor and why. They should write this down before they forget—even if it's only a few sentences. They start writing from their gut what they decided and why. Nothing else is needed— for starters, anyway. "Jones wins because he promised to deliver the cow no later than July, and even though the contract said time was of the essence, he delivered the cow in November."

That explanation can be the centerpiece of the opinion. Presumably this took the applicable legal principles into account—the principles should be fresh too at that point—and any quotation from controlling authority can be written into the opinion as the next step. A good decision should include the principles that must be applied— and just those—not every related concept. The court should be seen applying them. It should explain in plain terms what result followed and why. We'll talk more about this later.

25 : KEEP CASES IN THE HANDS OF A SINGLE JUDGE FROM START TO FINISH

Judges who finish hearing cases are usually in the best position to decide them when they have overseen the cases from the start. Experience over time makes a dispute familiar and permits a judge to decide a case from a deep understanding of it.

Keeping cases in the hands of a single judge is usually more efficient too. When no particular judge is assigned to handle a case, no judge feels strong responsibility for it. It may be easy for the judge to deny motions, continue hearings, give in to lawyer agreements, and move the matter from one judge's desk to another.

Most times, individual oversight by a single judge can move a case along more quickly. It can start with a management conference. Judges can use these conferences to set a schedule. Judges can also use them to tailor orders requiring the parties to answer specific questions about claims and defenses and produce specific documents pertinent to the case. In family cases, a judge might issue temporary orders. The conference can be set for a realistic but fixed period of time—it concentrates the mind.

A judge familiar with and solely responsible for a case can usually decide things easier while being accountable for unreasonable delays. Because in many places judges rotate where they sit and what they sit on, this won't work perfectly, but judges die too, and when they do, their in-boxes are usually full.

Associated with this question is the issue of specialization. Many state courts have assignments by category—family cases, civil cases, complex cases, criminal cases, juvenile cases, administrative cases, and the like. Judges skilled in particular areas often develop techniques for moving cases faster and are readily familiar with the issues that recur. This is a legitimate consideration, but many of the techniques that work in one area of the law work in other areas of the law too, and there are other things court administrators have to consider. Judges get burned out. The terrible grind in family and juvenile courts is particularly noteworthy. Some judges are more affected by the agonizing stories about children and families then they are about crime. Many times, it simply hits closer to home and can wear a judge down.

Judges also become set in their ways. They might be less open to new ideas in an area they have worked exclusively in for years. They can also form opinions about the lawyers who appear in front of them. Some might play favorites. Some might merely reflect the skepticism that comes when a particular lawyer makes a habit of poor performance or—worse yet—of misrepresenting facts or law to the court. It can be hard to put experience aside, but sometimes it's necessary.

In the US district courts, judges are usually generalists. They handle everything from the most complex criminal cases to medium-sized personal injury cases between citizens of different states. It requires a judge to be nimble, but at least it's harder to get stuck in a rut.[1]

26 : SPEED CASES TO TRIAL WITH JUDICIAL ADMINISTRATION INSTEAD OF SLOWING THEM DOWN

Inefficiency in the courts can be a weapon in the hands of the wealthy and other entrenched interests. Trial procedures and motion practice aren't the only things slowing cases down. Institutional characteristics can slow things down too.

Court systems are not known for being particularly nimble. While many lawyers and judges don't realize it, there is massive administration behind the scenes in most judicial branches. The ratio of judges to total staff is high. For example, there are around nineteen thousand judicial-branch employees in California and two thousand judges—a ratio of almost ten to one.[1]

Judicial employees usually operate in silos with often-unclear connections to the other silos. The judges have one silo. Their court clerks—as opposed to law clerks—often don't really report to them. Naturally they cooperate with judges, but they report up the chain of the clerk's silo. Court reporters have their own silo. There are law clerk silos. There are facilities silos. Family services silos. Technology silos. Human resources silos. Secretary silos. Education silos. Bar-relations silos. Branch-legal-staff silos. Ethics silos. Marshal silos.

Judges are often nominally at the head of agglomerations of these organizations for geographic locations and ultimately for larger areas—districts, circuits, and up to the top of the whole state or federal branch. But there is usually a parallel structure of other permanent people who—depending on the leadership—more or less do the same thing as the judges who nominally lead things. Many states layer other functions on top of all of this, including operating some prisons, probation systems, and the like.

The difficulty is that some judicial organizations have trouble deciding how they work. Are they run by the judges? In former days in many places, this was the way it was. The lines of authority were clear. Yet, it was also often unprofessional. Jobs in many systems were doled out by patronage. Scandals ensued. Jobs were professionalized. The silos were erected.

There isn't a beautiful solution to this. The most important thing is for any jurisdiction to at least know what it is. Who in a given courthouse really has the final say over clerks, secretaries, court reporters, legal researchers, court protection services, and marshals? The top judge? Will the judge be obeyed, or will the nominal subordinates climb the ladder within their own silos to someone who can reach a higher judge who can overrule the local judge? Without this being clear, it may mean less gets asked. Less gets done. Business may crawl. Innovation may be stifled. Judges, lawyers, and the public may be forced to lower their expectations about the system.

To give you an idea of the relative complexity of judicial administration, let's look at one version of the organizational chart of New York State's court system: [2]

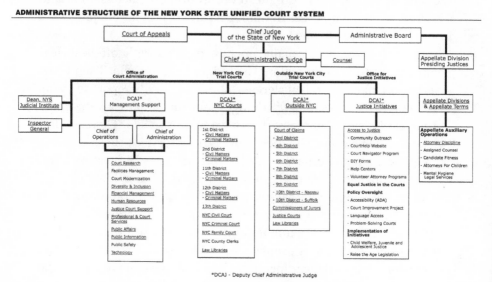

FIGURE 26.1. *Administrative structure of the New York State Unified Court System.*

It isn't a small matter to run a system like this. As you can see, the chief justice is the nominal head of the system, but there are two powerful positions below—the chief court administrator, who is also a judge, and the office of court administration. If you look at the office of court administration, you will see an organization representing thousands of employees, many of whom never see a judge in a courtroom. In most systems, there is a senior manager who is not a judge but wields enormous power over the workings of the system.

This is likely necessary. Judges come and go. Remember, they are usually older and don't have twenty or thirty years to learn the system. The real point is that to make a system work smoothly, the nominal organization of judges should be able to influence policy within the enormous parallel structures that operate behind the scenes. Those seeking to reform a specific court system must first inform themselves of this system along with its mysteries and machinations.

27 : ACCELERATE AND SIMPLIFY JUSTICE WITH TECHNOLOGY

Technology is one part of judicial administration with good reason to expand. It is changing the way courts do business, and it might as well be for good rather than ill.

Yet, incredibly, with all that has happened with electronic filings and remote hearings, poorly justified security concerns have left many courthouses with no Wi-Fi connections for the public or lawyers.

This is only the tip of the technology iceberg. Technology inadequacies can be found at the center of many contemporary courtrooms, particularly with respect to the role of court reporters and monitors.

These roles are ripe for change. It's hard to justify traditional court reporters or monitors today—stenographers who produce transcripts of court proceedings from shorthand key strokes or recordings. A good case can be made that we can create a record with sophisticated recording instruments alone. As of 2019, at least fourteen states relied on audio or video recordings rather than the traditional system.[1] There is good reason that this number is and should be growing.

Court proceedings can easily be recorded on video and played back in a word-searchable format. Proceedings can be live streamed over the internet for all to see for all time. Many courts are doing this now. You can go to many court system's websites and find a link to their live streaming system. Much of this progress followed the closure of the courts during the COVID-19 pandemic, when judges, clerks, parties, witnesses, and the public first began meeting online.[2]

Do courts really need court stenographers or court monitors to do what can be done with video or even audio technology? With current searchable video and audio technology, why do we need written transcripts? With current high-quality video technology, we can skip around and easily search for words and see the context, tone, and demeanor with which something has been said.

Good microphone systems are essential. It's a fine example of formalism that in many courthouses the microphones are solely for the benefit of the court reporter or monitor. Many times, they are the only ones who can hear in a large courtroom because the microphones don't amplify much; they feed into the headset worn by the reporter or monitor. The parties and the judge, by contrast, are left constantly asking people to speak louder. The simplest of amplifying microphones could fix this.

Changing the transcription system wouldn't be good for the professionals who create written transcripts. They are often among the kindest and hardest working people in a courthouse, but everything must evolve, and people who might have gone into that job, and some in it, might develop video expertise instead while court reporters and audio monitors are phased out. Courts have much to gain from people

FIGURE 27.1. *"It's clear from the replay that it was a leading question."*

with new technical skills. Technology in court must change, but technical workers are one group within the court system with a good case for growth.

Technology can help overworked clerk's offices too. It can mean that hearings don't have to be postponed because a clerk may not be physically available in every courtroom. For short hearings, a clerk available from anywhere in the system can electronically monitor the proceeding and enter the brief orders that typically come from a brief proceeding.

For longer proceedings where exhibits are offered, electronic documents can mean that the exhibits can be handled from anywhere in the judicial system. In some places, it already sounds quaint to suggest otherwise. Photographs of most—certainly not all—physical objects will do. Even for these proceedings, clerks could be in an electronic queue. When a hearing is ready, a clerk who is somewhere— anywhere really—and is listed as available may be engaged to handle entering the electronic exhibits into the system. The other details of this courtroom function can be worked out. Of course, all of this is being done increasingly online, so it already matters less where any of the participants are.

Every court system could have a searchable database of judicial decisions. When a court cites a case or an exhibit in a decision—or most everything else—the online reader might reach it instantly with a hypertext link. This doesn't have to interfere with companies in the business of selling legal research capability given that the links could be through their services. But innovation in these services should be encouraged. These companies should adopt easier ways to access their products and less formal ways for searching for cases on point. Legal search engines are more vital now than ever. They should continue to innovate.

28 : VIRTUAL PROCEEDINGS SHOULD BE THE RULE

It took many courts until the 2020s to convert to electronic filings and to electronic exhibits. A few likely still haven't gotten there. And the country's first significant use of remote hearings and trials happened in 2020, in response to the COVID-19 pandemic.[1]

The connections were a bit buggy for a time. But they worked. In a remote trial, electronic exhibits have proved much easier to deal with. In a remote courtroom, everyone has an amplifying microphone in front of them at all times. It's easy to hear. Judges can look the lawyers in the face the whole time. Better still, they get a front view and even a close up of witnesses—they can see every blink, twitch, and smirk.

With remote proceedings, no expert has to travel across the country. Witnesses have far fewer excuses for not showing up. And all of them can be given standardized courtroom background photos to use, so we aren't snooping around people's homes and offices. If we use them, it will help us remember we are in court. We don't have to abandon the ceremonies of courtesy and respect that symbolize the seriousness of court proceedings.

There are countervailing considerations. The physicality of pacing the room, looming in front of the jurors, approaching the witness will be lost, but the trade-off is that everyone can zoom in on a witness or a juror and the judge and can gauge exactly what they're up to. Remote proceedings mean people can't use travel schedules as an excuse to postpone a hearing. And jurors are sometimes more honest when an alleged victim and their twenty-seven supporters aren't ten feet away from them making cow eyes in their direction.

Like them or not, remote proceedings aren't going away.

29 : AS A JUDGE,
PREFER THE MODEL OF
A VILLAGE ELDER

The simplest bits of humanity and common sense actually govern the largest number of cases. Small-claims proceedings often involve enforcement of a basic promise or a protest over some small imposition. The hospital bill. The unpaid credit card debt.

Evictions are usually about people not paying their rent and when they will get out with the minimum of fuss. The largest number of family law cases are between angry people with much to fight over emotionally and not so much otherwise.

These aren't meant to be cold-hearted observations. They merely reflect experience with dockets. And it is not to say that small claims, evictions, and family cases are not sometimes complicated. This is only to suggest that the vast majority of cases in the vast majority of places are not.

In many of these cases, there are no lawyers involved at all. This makes it the last place where judges and lawyers should be formalists. An effective judge in cases like these is more like a village elder, dispensing homespun wisdom and trying to get everyone leaving with the feeling that they have been fairly dealt with.

The job is chiefly forward looking. In small claims, maybe it's about recognizing a debt but giving some time to pay. In evictions, a judge might ask tenants who haven't paid their rent what they are asking the court to do. Are they suggesting that they shouldn't have to pay their rent? Usually, tenants concede they aren't entitled to free housing from their landlords and ask for a little more time to get out. A court can enter a judgment for a specific agreed-upon day with a

FIGURE 29.1. *"Oh, he's pretty wise—I clerked for him."*

few compromises about the circumstances. Sometimes a referral for rental assistance solves the whole thing.

In family cases, directing the parties toward the future is especially important. What obstacles are in the path of raising the children? How does the party think they can be resolved? Solutions often come from focusing on the parties' solutions rather than their grievances. Judges shouldn't sit idly by while parties assail each other's character in ways that have nothing to do with caring for children. Family cases should look to what happens next with the human beings who once formed an intact family. They both trust the ex-husband's sister. Perhaps she can oversee the father's next visit with the children. Would that be okay with both of them? Many times, so long as the idea is someone else's, that's enough.

When equal treatment of each parent is possible, it's often best. Why pick a winner between parents when it can be avoided? Labelling one the "better" parent only makes the other parent want to prove through future dealings that this isn't so.

The idea that judges might make suggestions and steer the parties to a fair result is admittedly contrary to the views of many judges and lawyers. There is certainly an alternate view. It is that the judge reacts but does not interact. Yet with two unrepresented parties before the bench, it's hard for people to see a fair system when the judge makes them try to guess what the rules of practice say about filing a timely motion or asking for an extension of time. It suggests that formalism should triumph over humanism.

Yes, the more formalist view makes more sense when both sides have lawyers. In such cases, traditional thinking holds that we have an adversarial system where the skill of the lawyer triumphs. We can hope that this also yields justice, but too often it doesn't. Of course, judges may not become advocates for the side with the weaker lawyer, but judges can still use judgment. When they can see a large injustice being perpetrated in the name of a small formality, they should consider speaking up. When they don't, they risk the credibility of the system. The overworked public defender or the overwhelmed free-legal-services lawyer is far from a match for well-funded lawyers for a large employer or corporate landlord. If the matter boils down to a forgotten section of the applicable rules, a judge might inquire about its significance under the circumstances without threatening to destroy the adversarial system.

The rule of law is strongest when people who come before justice see justice being done and leave court convinced that it was attempted and likely achieved—especially when they lose their case. Judges are not stone gods. They should be respected leaders of the community who are neither automatons nor busybodies. The village elder is a pretty good model: a listener, a questioner, and an admittedly flawed but sincere seeker of wisdom.

30 : CASES ARE BETTER RESOLVED ON THEIR FACTS THAN ON THE LAW

Do legal rules solve most problems in court? Or are problems solved by judging facts against those rules? No matter how hard we try to make them sound specific and complex, most legal duties are—and should be—spelled out only in broad terms, and usually the facts should and do resolve the case.

Rules require us to do things, like to behave as a "reasonable person under the circumstances." We must honor our agreements. We must respect property rights. We must not "materially mislead." We must not act with "malice." These are common values. The rest of the job is to put them to work.

Cases are usually easier to decide when lawyers and judges identify and apply the most basic principles that govern a case. The more complicated they make the standard appear—the more legal layers they add to the analysis—the less likely the parties in court are to be satisfied that they found justice rather than confusion.

Some people take on legal duties voluntarily—in contract for instance. Others have legal duties thrust upon them by legislation or by judge-made law—"the common law." Regardless of the source, there is usually a core of principle we can identify. After that, it's best to focus the lawsuit on the facts.

Let's take three examples. In a breach of contract lawsuit, the basic legal principle is simple. The courts enforce most freely made bargains. So, the problem may be approached from there in steps with the help of a few subsidiary legal principles. First, was there a bargain? Was there an offer? Was it accepted? Was something of value to be exchanged? Did the parties agree voluntarily? Second, what are its terms? The law enforces the plain words of a written agreement rather than what might be gleaned about the agreement from hearing testimony about unwritten intentions. Third, did the party accused fail to do as promised? Fourth, if so, how do we give the nonbreaching party what it expected to get?

In complex cases, there are more principles to draw on, but the parties to a lawsuit and the judge writing about it should start with the basic principles and apply them to the facts without clouding the discussion with needless legal throat clearing, irrelevant factual background, and principles that might apply in some other contract case but not in this one. Humans. Not forms.

Courts should resist the temptation to hear evidence outside of the written terms in a contract for the sake of a "complete" record. They needlessly complicate matters if they give in too easily to lawyers' requests for testimony based on their imaginative discovery of ambiguities. In most contracts, judges know what the parties meant. It's wasteful to give in to small doubts.

In a claim for trade secret theft, the Uniform Trade Secret Act covers three basic things that must be established to have a trade secret—there must be a something not generally known, it must have independent value, and its owner must have taken reasonable steps to protect it from disclosure.[1] Judges and lawyers should focus on these three things, not case law that needlessly regurgitates them or jiggles them a tiny bit this way or that. This allows them to get to the facts and discuss at length what should be made of them in light of the human conduct shown on the record.

The common-law background, the law in other jurisdictions, and, usually, the legislative history should be avoided whenever possible. The basic concepts in the statute will do nicely.

In family law cases, this is true of most custody and alimony statutes. The statutes list specific criteria. Judges can directly apply them. It's more effective than wasting time on case law that adds little to them or belabors the court's discretion to apply them equitably. Besides, the criteria are usually flexible and unweighted. They amount to asking a judge to do what's fair—they tell the court to consider the parties' contributions to the marriage, their contributions to its failure, their needs, their skills and future prospects, and the like.[2]

In a personal injury case, lawyers needn't make the thing look more complicated than it is. Most cases boil down to whether the person being sued acted like a reasonable person under the circumstances—including where the circumstances make the defendant a surgeon—thus whether this person was a reasonable driver, a reasonable property owner, a reasonable surgeon, or what have you.[3] It doesn't add much complexity to consider cases that involve well-defined notions of reckless or intentional misconduct either.

Yes, whether any duty at all is owed takes up time in some cases, but many times cases get tied up in knots by confusing what a person has to do to fulfill a duty with the limits of a duty. A "no-duty" result can often seem unfair. Of course, cases exist where this is so and where finding no duty is a fair result, but justice isn't served by unfairly stretching the notion of "no duty" to avoid a trial. Justice is better served—on summary judgment or at trial where a judge or a jury finds the behavior reasonable.

Consider the kind of cases that dominate most dockets. They pose questions like, Was this self-defense? Would a reasonable surgeon have snipped that artery? Was that driver following too close? Was he driving too fast for conditions? These questions are best answered by exploring the facts more and almost never the law. It might be self-defense if she had good reason to fear harm. A reasonable surgeon might snip an artery if that was required to insert a stent in it. Was it raining? Was the road straight? Was he an experienced driver? Was it a high-performance car? These kinds of questions are most of the courts' work. And despite what too many people fear, a group of people who assemble as jurors usually come to consensus answers to these questions once they are allowed to focus on the facts.

31 : DEPLOY CANONS OF CONSTRUCTION SPARINGLY— ONLY WHEN THEY HAVE A COMPELLING REASON TO EXIST

Canons of construction—rules governing the interpretation of statutes and contracts—can be useful where they reflect ordinary human experience about how people say what they mean.

But sometimes, canons are more like a grab bag of sayings. Judges and lawyers pull out of these bags whatever saying suits their purpose at the moment while grabbing the opposite saying on the same subject on other occasions when they find themselves on the other side of the issue.

Textualists are fond of selected canons. Justice Antonin Scalia thoroughly examined them along with Bryan Garner in *Reading Law: The Interpretation of Legal Texts*.[1] For textualists, when the words aren't plain enough, they will turn to a canon here and there to fill in the gaps—or, at other times, to originalist history.

By contrast, Justice Stephen Breyer saw the job not as focusing on words and canons about those words or on historical records selected by a judge. Justice Breyer saw the job as determining the general purposes and consequences of a law. As he explained in his book *Making Our Democracy Work*, Justice Breyer believed judges struggling over the meaning of a statute should ask: What would Congress want us to do?[2] For this, he would turn frequently to legislative history. More about that later.

For now, it's enough to say that both views may be questioned because both views can be seen as camouflaging the fact that the judge is exercising judgment. Justice Scalia may have been trying to judge what those who wrote the law were concerned about when they wrote it and apply it as they would have in their time. But Justice Breyer says that what the drafters were concerned about must be judged not against the drafter's own time and its needs, but against our time and its needs.

If we believe that judges should apply law in light of the values in it and the people before them, then Justice Breyer has the better argument. But, as we will see when we talk about legislative history, guessing what Congress would do is too much like asking, "What would Jesus do?" Like Justice Scalia's method, it can be influenced by where you look. What history book or original historic writing? What part of the legislative history? Can either approach really convince us that it's objective?

Perhaps we would be more convincing if we stopped trying to channel the Founding Fathers or "what Congress would want" and say instead: "This is a law against unreasonable searches. Was this search of this person by these searchers reasonable in light of the facts involved and its implications for those who might be affected by this law in the future?" These humans. This humanity. A judge's judgment of what's reasonable. Canons of construction often can't help us decide what "reasonable" search means or what "undue" burden means or what process "due" means. Only facts will, and those facts should be from our time if we are to convince the public—as we need to— that we have a justice system that is just.

But now, let's get back to the limits of legal canons.

A judge recently asked a law clerk to sort out the meaning of a statute that listed limited grounds on which a case might be reopened and whether that limited list was exclusive or might be added to by grounds stated in another statute. The clerk said the second statute couldn't add to the first one, invoking the principle embodied in the Latin maxim *expressio unius est exclusio alterius*—"the expression of one thing means the exclusion of others."

But having found one saying, the clerk forgot about another—*in pari materia*. Statutes covering the same subject must be read in harmony with one another. This saying—this canon of construction— applied best. It applied best because, while both applied, only one of them made sense.

Perhaps searching for a practical view would have been better than

FIGURE 31.1. *"Your sign expressly excludes dogs: It does not exclude any other animals, thus 'expressio unius est exclusio alterius.'"*

searching for an applicable canon. When there are two things that are both law, courts must try to make them both work. So, call it choosing a canon or applying common sense, reading two laws as in harmony offends neither of them.

Some canons make no sense because they have nothing to do with how legislatures express themselves. For instance, courts have held that when legislation conflicts with judge-made "common law," judges should read the legislation narrowly—it should be applied as little as possible.[3] This canon is used by judges who don't like the legislation. Judges who like the legislation resort to the canon that says remedial legislation should be construed broadly—it should be applied as much as possible.[4] Because these canons are aimed at each other, they should be fired.[5]

We don't have to resort to canons when the words are clear. But sometimes judges find ambiguity where it doesn't exist. Sometimes, it's easier for a judge to find something unclear, point to a canon, and then blame the canon rather than human judgment for the outcome. Is this convincing?

Still, some canons embody common sense and reflect human experience. They can prove useful if legislative language is unclear. When a rule addresses a topic specifically, it trumps a mere general reference: Language in a statute that says, "Arts grants will be distributed by the Arts Council reasonably," must yield to the more specific language saying, "The Garde Arts Center will receive 2 percent of all grants distributed by the Arts Council."[6]

The absurdity doctrine is a useful canon.[7] If a statute says, "all tax payments must be made in person at the tax collector's office on the fifteenth of the month," a court won't interpret it to mean that if the fifteenth is on a Sunday, the hapless taxpayers must appear before a closed office, nor would a court likely punish a taxpayer for paying the tax early. Is this a canon or good human judgment?

There are a few rules of thumb outside of statutory construction that are useful in resolving ambiguities too. It seems only fair to resolve doubts against the person who wrote a piece of language. It seems especially fair to resolve doubts against the drafter when the contract is one-sided—where only one party had any input into the language—in consumer contracts and the like—in what we call "contracts of adhesion."[8]

The Scalia and Garner book covering canons is thorough and thoughtful. Justice Scalia's view of the use of canons and his textualist approach in general are thoughtfully critiqued by Charlie D. Stewart in "The Rhetorical Canons of Construction: New Textualism's Rhetoric Problem."[9]

32 : RARELY RESORT
TO LEGISLATIVE HISTORY;
IT'S OFTEN UNRELIABLE

Most people with legislative experience will tell you not to assume that what is said about a bill on the record is a good indication of why it was passed or what it means when the words used aren't clear. A key vote might be garnered for a wide variety of reasons—many of them never expressed.

Just as Justice Breyer got it right when he poked holes in textualism and originalism, Justice Scalia rightly exposed Justice Breyer's pragmatism as equally flawed when, in *Reading Law*, he exposed the subjectivity of reading the tea leaves of legislative history. Let's consider this much the way Justice Scalia did.

Senator Rene Milhous might say she favors a bill to license homeopathic medicine providers in exchange for requiring additional consumer disclosures and a signed consent form thirty days prior to treatment. She might explain on the floor of the Senate that the bill is intended to condition the license on written disclosure and consent for *every* treatment. The bill itself might say only that "homeopathic treatment providers must disclose the nature of their work to their patients and obtain a written consent to treat no later than thirty days prior to treatment." The unexpressed reason for what Senator Milhous said might be any of the following:

- The senator believes what she says is true. Five other senators agree with her. Five senators disagree with her, and none of the other senators are paying attention.
- In the crush of business, the senator is the only one who spoke about the bill. Every senator with an opinion agrees with her

view. Every house member with an opinion disagrees with her. The president signs the bill with a different view of what it requires altogether.

- The senator is actually opposed to homeopathic medicine and couldn't get what she wanted in the language, so she read a statement into the record prepared by a medical society to make it harder to provide homeopathic treatments.
- The senator couldn't care less about the bill but was asked by another senator, a constituent, a doctor, or a lobbyist to read the statement, and—owing a favor—she read the statement on the floor.
- The senator meant exactly what she said but was reading from a synopsis of an earlier draft of the bill.

Too often, legislative history is an unreliable guide. We don't need it when we can see the meaning of a law without it. We should only use legislative history when (1) there is no other choice and when (2) there is a repeated and clear consensus from start to finish about what the bill was designed to do.

Turning to legislative history can be little more than another way for the judiciary to appear objective when it is really using human judgment. The mistake is to believe that merely complicating the inquiry makes it more convincing. But informed readers know that judges can often read the history and make it point to whatever outcome they want while they disclaim responsibility for the result.

The battle over legislative history reflects the willingness of progressive jurists to reach into questionable realms the same way textualist/originalists reach into questionable realms when they maintain that words like *equal protection* and *due process* don't require different things in different centuries.

The classic modern example of this issue was *United Steelworkers of America v. Weber*. In that case, steelworkers imposed a quota favoring minorities for certain training, and this ran squarely into a civil rights law prohibiting employers from granting employment opportunities based on race. Admitting that the practice was prohibited by the statute, Justice Brennan, quoting an earlier case, wrote for the majority that "it is a 'familiar rule, that a thing may be within the letter of the statute and yet not within the statute, because not within its spirit, nor within the intention of its makers.'"[1]

It's easy for many people to agree with the result, but we should be uneasy about how it was reached. Over the years the debate on the usefulness of legislative history has continued. Justice Breyer addressed it in his 1992 law review article, "On the Uses of Legislative History in Interpreting Statutes."[2] To his credit, he appeared to recognize its limitations, arguing that it is "sometimes" useful, but the truth is closer to rarely than sometimes. *Rarely* should mean that legislative history should be resorted to only when a court is faced with impenetrable language and can find an impeccable answer.

Again, Justice Scalia's alternative suffers from the same flaws. Faced with impenetrable language, he would likely have looked to canons like the fixed-meaning canon, which would have led to a jog through the history books and selected primary sources. But as we already know, most canons point anywhere you aim them—like legislative history can—and the history books depend too often on who wrote them and which primary sources you choose.

The first thing to do is avoid canons and legislative history absent any alternative. They needlessly complicate explanations that could focus on the judge's reasoning in light of the basic value at stake and the consequences for humans and humanity.

Canons and histories can pose as objective ways to justify decisions when they are more often masking a judge's inadequately explained view of the right result. When faced with impenetrable language, the best thing to do is to decide from the words the legislature used; the surrounding law; and, if all else fails, the legislative history to determine the statute's basic goal. This is likely easier to discern than to find what the legislature meant by specific words. In those rare instances in which the words are impenetrable, the court should interpret them to meet the legislature's basic goal in light of current realities. If the legislature disagrees, it can amend the law.

Let's look at an example of needless resort to legislative history. Justice Breyer wrote the majority decision in *Varity Corp. v. Howe*. The case involved a federal statute that made employee-benefit-plan administrators—the people who run company pension plans, medical plans, and the like—"fiduciaries." To interpret this word, Justice

Breyer resorted to legislative history to justify using common-law notions of the term against the backdrop of employee benefits.[3]

But there is nothing impenetrable about the term "fiduciary." The statute itself mandated that these fiduciaries administer their benefit plans "solely in the interest of plan participants and beneficiaries." Any dictionary tells us that a fiduciary owes precisely this high duty—putting the beneficiary's interest first. The common law—courtesy of Judge, later Justice, Benjamin Cardozo—recorded in 1928 that fiduciary duty requires the "very punctilio of an honor most sensitive."[4]

The rest of *Varity* was about the facts and didn't require resorting to legislative history. The issue was whether, when company representatives lied to employees, they were lying about the company's general business prospects or lying about the benefit plans concerning which the company owed the fiduciary duty.

Once Justice Breyer got to the facts, it was easy for the court majority to see that this discussion was plan related and thus fiduciary. It was equally easy to decide that fiduciaries aren't supposed to cheat the people they are required to protect.

The case is a good example of the foibles of textualism too. Needlessly, the other legal issue in the case was whether employees injured by the company's breach of this high duty could do anything about it or whether the company could cheat them with impunity. This turned on what the law meant when it allowed benefit-plan participants to sue for "appropriate equitable relief." The majority let stand a decision granting relief but left several things about that relief unsettled.

In a dissent, Justice Scalia skipped over a straightforward reading of this language to suggest a counterintuitive result—a wrong without a remedy. First, he rightly ignored the legislative history and then, more questionably, examined the words in other sections of the statute—in ways we might think subjective—to conclude that Congress wanted only relief for the benefit plan itself. In doing so, he recognized that Congress prohibited cheating individual participants but then assumed that Congress would want cheated plan participants to be helpless when it came to making good their losses. His view seemed to prevail in a later case and was only rebuffed many years later when Justice Breyer found an opportunity to end it with the support of five other justices.[5] As Judge Posner might have said, go figure!

33 : REDUCE DISTRACTIONS BY IDENTIFYING FALLACIES

Justice Oliver Wendell Holmes rightly began his practical survey, *The Common Law*, saying that "the life of the law has not been logic: it has been experience."[1] But Holmes was complaining about formal logic, the resolution of conflicts from formalist first principles rather than from problem-solving experience.

Logic of the informal variety has been forged in the light of human experience. Judges and lawyers who understand the informal fallacies can spot weak arguments, point to them by name, and defeat them. They can keep a case focused rather than diverted.

Some fallacies crop up again and again in court. Neither the courts nor the parties should waste time using them:

- The bandwagon—"The majority view of courts is . . .
- The strawman—where you lose an argument you never made.
- The false equivalent—"You can have a knife, so why can't I have a tank?"
- The slippery slope—"If women can vote, horses will demand it next."
- The circular argument—"You are wrong because what you are saying isn't right."
- Cherry picking—where you ignore all but the evidence that favors you.
- Argument against the person—"You can't believe him; he's a communist."
- The red herring—"Sure we have to raise taxes. Don't you like children?"
- Poisoning the well—"Let's hear from Bob, the man with the death's head tattoo."

- Appeals to emotion—"He must be guilty. Think how the victim has suffered."

In cases with no binding authority on a question, the bandwagon may be the most common fallacy courts fall for. The appeal in essence is this: "Jump on, the music's playing and we're rolling down the road!"

This phenomenon usually appears in connection with the words "we adopt the majority view." Indeed, a search of these words quickly yielded 550 uses of this phrase in the federal courts alone. You might wonder: What's wrong with that? Don't we want uniform laws?

We do, of course. The problem is that most of us would also like them to be just, and there isn't much justice in a court merely hewing to the "majority view" and "the courts have repeatedly held"—merely quoting *those* court's conclusions while ignoring the minority view and giving no explanation why the court chose one over the other. This is formalism: another unconvincing way judges bury their judgments.

We can see a typical example in the Northern District of New York's decision in *United States v. Deyoe*. The court in that case dealt with the question of whether a sex offender–registration statute applied to a person who was convicted of a sex crime before the registration

FIGURE 33.1. *"Well, heck! If all you smart cookies agree, who am I to dissent?"*

statute was enacted. Deyoe argued that the registration requirement was a punishment for his crime, that he had already been punished, and that government couldn't punish him again by forcing him to register because Article I, Section 9 of the Constitution forbids substantive laws being applied retroactively—ex post facto.

Rather than explore *whether* the registration was a retroactive punishment or some lesser administrative imposition—not a substantive change—the court turned to what other courts had said. The court explained: "Defendant's argument has been raised several times by other convicted sex offenders in this district and across the country and has universally been rejected." The court rested its reasoning on the observation that "the courts in this district have held that prosecuting a sex offender under [the registration statute] is not retrospective as [the registration law] does not punish the individual for previously being convicted of a sex crime." It concludes: "This Court adopts the majority view and finds that because defendant is charged with violating [the registration law] for conduct that occurred after [it] was enacted, there is no ex post facto violation."[2]

Too many court opinions fail to convince us justice was done because they leave us asking the two-year-old's question: "Yes. But why?!"

Deyoe is an example. If there is a minority view, the court didn't discuss and distinguish it. The pivot of the opinion appears to be little more than that the defendant's view—which is barely explained—has been rejected by "the majority" or "universally"—we can't be sure which. Relying on the number of other courts that have ruled on a topic rather than exploring their reasoning and explaining why they agree with it is a classic example of the bandwagon effect at work.

But we can find other fallacious reasoning at work in *Deyoe* too. When the court stated as its justification that "prosecuting a sex offender under [the registration statute] is not retrospective as [the registration law] does not punish the individual for previously being convicted of a sex crime," the court used circular reasoning.

What the court said was no different than saying, "the law is not retrospective because it only looks forward." We end up back where we started without any treatment of the real issue—*why* isn't registration a new punishment for an old crime? The registration is a bad thing without a new bad act to justify it. Deyoe committed a crime and was punished for it. Then the authorities reached out after his time was served and whacked him again without his doing anything and without any new trial. Why wasn't that punishment? On this question, we get no answer.

The absence of explanation on the key issue in the case may leave us wondering if more fallacies were at work here. The court noted at the beginning of its decision that Deyoe was convicted of raping a fourteen-year-old girl. This is pretty powerful poison into the well. The government, perhaps without needing to say it out loud, made an argument "against the man" that made disagreeing with the government view awkward. Who wanted to be seen siding with Deyoe? He was a sex offender.

If you would like more reading about the informal fallacies at work in legal decisions, many have been compiled in Kevin Saunders's 1992–1993 *University of South Carolina Law Review* article, "Informal Fallacies in Legal Argumentation."[3]

34 : DON'T BLUR LAWS
TO CONQUER FACTS

Not all duties are created equal. Some are harder to comply with than others.

One example is the spectrum running from fraud to fiduciary duty. Refraining from fraud is a duty we owe to strangers. It is one of the lowest duties known to law. It only stops us from intentionally misleading people into harm.

Fiduciary duties are at the opposite end of the spectrum. The fiduciary duty is the highest duty known to law. We shouldn't impose it lightly, but once we do, we should stick to deciding the facts and avoid perverting the principle when we don't like the outcome it produces. If we give in, we risk destroying the character of a legal duty, and that character counts—it tells people what they can and can't do.

And yes, well-defined legal duties are warped all the time. In federal courts involving pension fiduciaries, some courts favoring employers over employees have occasionally turned the highest duty known to law into the lowest duty known to law.

A good example of this was the Seventh Circuit's 2004 opinion in *Beach v. Commonwealth Edison*. In that case, after a trial, the Northern District of Illinois found that Commonwealth Edison employee-benefits officials had used false information to mislead an employee named Beach into an early retirement.

The federal ERISA law that applied said that employers are the fiduciaries of their benefit plans and must put their employees first when administering them. A trial judge had found that instead of telling the truth, company officials in the case had misled a beneficiary into retiring and missing out on a benefit enhancement. The lower court recognized that fiduciaries misleading beneficiaries breach their duties.[1]

The Seventh Circuit overturned the trial decision. Perhaps the court majority was uncomfortable with the result. After all, we don't normally make employers put their employees' best interests first. Instead of expressing this belief and saying—unlike every other court— that there was no fiduciary duty about benefits information, the court recognized that there was a fiduciary duty but ground the duty into dust over a protesting and eloquent dissent.

The majority held that the fiduciary duty only prevented the company from engaging in fraud and that the ERISA fiduciary duty imposed nothing else.[2] Mercifully, the court in later cases backed away from this dangerous line blurring, but it remains a worrying reminder that, whatever their philosophy about how to deal with unclear concepts, judges shouldn't simply see what they want in the law when it's clear.[3] Sometimes the law requires no interpretation, and what matters is how it applies to the facts.

Courts that don't like the facts should focus on what they don't like about them. Labelling a horse a duck is a different and dangerous thing. The law builds a set of expectations in those governed by it—they benefit from a high duty, for instance. To tell those subject to a law that a thing declared to be a high duty actually imposes the lowest possible duty invites cynicism. It undercuts public confidence in the courts.

Other places where duties frequently lose their meaning are in cases dealing with concepts like recklessness, bad faith, malice, and intent. Starting in 2020, words like *emergency* seemed at risk too. If everything is an emergency, then nothing is—the concept loses its meaning.

Complex, contradictory rules yield complex and contradictory decisions. They invite appeals. They invite new lawsuits with new allegations. They tie the system up in knots.

35 : ENDLESS CONSUMER DISCLOSURES AREN'T DOING US ANY GOOD; THEY ARE JUST LOW-HANGING FRUIT

One of the most tangled bargains lawyers make with legislatures and the courts is about disclosures—warning labels, consent forms, and the like. Do they work, or are they merely encouraging wasteful litigation and mocking the law in our daily lives? Here are some examples drawn from life:

- A home exercise mat says not to jump from a very high place and land on it. It says not to use it without a doctor's advice and supervision. It says not to exercise when you are in delicate health.
- Stadiums, ski resorts, amusement rides, restaurants, parking garages, carnivals, and a host of other places consumers visit want consumers to know that the owners and operators of these facilities aren't responsible for what happens to consumers and their property during their visits and that by being present consumers agree that the owners and operators can be as careless as they wish.
- Most prescription drug ads are dominated by beautiful sunrises, walks on the beach, and warnings that among the consequences of using this drug may be death, disability, insanity, and a nasty rash.
- Summary-plan descriptions about employee benefits often contain so much useless information that their readers miss all the important things—hardest to find are the benefits' limitations, exclusions, and the like.

FIGURE 35.1. *"Caution: This drug causes dizziness in mice, gastrointestinal problems in rabbits, headaches in chickens, photosensitivity in monkeys, drowsiness in hamsters . . ."*

- Financial documents are often so long that what gets signed only incorporates by reference far longer documents we might find somewhere on some website—but by signing, we agree to them.
- Internet consent forms for routine purchases and upgrades are a load of nonnegotiable guff that nobody bothers to read. Most companies no longer even make us scroll to the end of the terms before clicking that we agree to them.

The root of these embarrassments may be that ordering more disclosure is low-hanging fruit. In legislatures, in agencies, and in courtrooms, it's easier to resort to them than it is to decide whether something is actually dangerous. The result is a needlessly complex and discrediting tangle of disclosures and disclosure rules.

Useless disclosures may have been readily accepted by some of those who are required to give them because they think they can easily be rendered inert by those who draft them: "They want information; we'll give it to them alright—until they beg us to stop."

Litigation resulting in overcomplicated and useless disclosures is a waste of time—at least it is if we care about consumers.

There are two potential ways around this problem. If a safety issue is important enough, we could consider regulating the thing or feature, not merely the information about it. Short of that, we could require—and, more importantly, enforce—rules that require short, plain statements of things that the vast majority of users need to know and shield companies from responsibility for failing to disclose with *equal* prominence things that one-tenth of 1 percent of all users need to know.

In fact, we could consider holding companies responsible for needlessly over disclosing. We might think about disclosures in a hierarchy. Section 1: what most users need to know. Section 2: rare cases. In television ads, the most frequent side effects suffered could be disclosed, and then the ad can say, "For less frequent side effects, please see our website." Where likely risks are spelled out on television or on the website, the disclosure could include a rough approximation of the chance of something happening: "Among our trial group of 1,200 people: nausea (10 percent), rash (5 percent), discolored urine (1 percent)."

The reason for this is that when someone gives us too much information, there is a real risk we won't process it. And with consent forms, when consumers can't engage in a reasonable activity without giving nominal consent about risks and rights, they have no meaningful alternative but to check the box and "enter at their own risk." By allowing this, we are complicating life rather than simplifying it and mocking regulation rather than imposing it.

Sometimes, this yields the thing we seek to avoid. A 1996 study in the *Journal of Experimental Psychology* showed that warning labels about violence on television programs didn't steer people away from watching the violent shows; instead, they created a "forbidden fruit" attraction to the shows.[1] For some, the phrase "don't step on this part of the ladder" only dares them to do it.

36 : REDUCE JUDICIAL TESTINESS; USE MULTIPOINT TESTS ONLY WHEN EACH POINT HAS MEANING

Does the legal profession too often mistake testiness for thoughtfulness? It seems like courts that create multifactor tests to decide issues are partly trying to increase our impression that they are being deliberative. The tests may have been used by other courts. The process looks objective, almost scientific. But when the points are pointless, the proliferation of multipoint tests is nothing but high formalism.

The truth is that too many traditional multipoint tests can be challenged as consuming time with little to show for it. Let's consider a few examples from this vast field:

- The appropriately named "lemon test" for determining if a law violates the rules against establishing or interfering with religious practices. Each piece of it simply restates the same question:
  - Does it have a secular, or nonreligious, purpose? (Is it about religion?)
  - Does not advance or inhibit a religion (restates the thing to be decided).
  - Does not promote an extreme entanglement with religion on the government's part. (Does it establish or interfere with religion? This is another way of restating the thing to be decided).[1]
- Factors used to test the fairness of an attorneys' fee award calculated on the basis of a "lodestar"—that is, *after* the fee has been determined based upon a reasonable hourly rate times

a reasonable number of hours. These factors merely restate
things that should have gone into determining the lodestar in
the first place:

- The time and labor required (restates the issue — a fair rate
  for a fair amount of time);
- the nature and difficulty of the responsibility assumed
  (already subsumed in deciding if the time spent was
  reasonable);
- the amount involved and the results obtained (irrelevant,
  especially in small consumer cases where we subsidize
  lawyers to take them);
- the fees customarily charged for similar legal services
  (subsumed within finding a reasonable rate × reasonable
  hours);
- the experience, reputation, and ability of counsel (this
  is subsumed in whether the rate the lawyer charges is
  reasonable);
- and the fee arrangement existing between counsel and the
  client (irrelevant to what's fair — utterly manipulable).[2]

- Factors to determine the distinction between the mandatory
  and the directory in a statute either restate the problem or
  are irrelevant to the inquiry at issue — whether a thing *must*
  be done or is simply a procedure to accomplish the thing that
  must be done:
  - Whether the statute expressly invalidates actions that fail to
    comply with its requirements, or, in the alternative, whether
    the statute by its terms imposes a different penalty. (Must
    the thing be done?)
  - Whether the requirement is stated in affirmative terms,
    unaccompanied by negative language. (Irrelevant given the
    variants that could be imagined — i.e., "licenses will be issued
    once the fee is paid." Is the fee optional or do we have to
    torture *once* into being "negative language"?)
  - Whether the requirement at issue relates to a matter of
    substance or one of convenience. (Must the thing be done?)
  - Whether the legislative history, the circumstances
    surrounding the statute's enactment and amendment, and

the full legislative scheme evince an intent to impose a mandatory requirement. (Must the thing be done?)

- Whether holding the requirement to be mandatory would result in an unjust windfall for the party seeking to enforce the duty, or in the alternative, whether holding it to be directory would deprive that party of any legal recourse. (Circular—if the legislature mandated this result, it isn't an "unjust windfall," and are there such things as "just windfalls"?)
- Whether compliance is reasonably within the control of the party that bears the obligation (assumes an unexpressed legislative intent).[3]
- The McDonnell Douglas test for whether an adverse employment decision was based upon prohibited discrimination (race, sex, etc.):
  - A prima facie case (in practice always met by virtue of claiming discrimination);
  - A nondiscriminatory explanation (always present—performance, behavior, routine layoff, etc.);
  - Proof of pretext (restates the only real issue—whether the decision was made for discriminatory reasons).[4]
- Judge Posner's test from *Heard v. Sheahan* for tolling the statute of limitations based upon a continuing course of conduct is too subjective to be of any use.
  - A continuing course exists when a series of events has a cumulative impact.[5]

The doctrine of continuing course of conduct reflects that an event that isn't yet complete shouldn't trigger a deadline to file a lawsuit about it. The problem is knowing when several actions should be deemed part of the same event.

Whether a thing is a series of events or a single event is subjective. Some courts have held that a series of paychecks in the wrong amount is a series of events, and others have held it is a single event—the original miscalculation.[6]

In 2000, in *Bodner v. Banque*, the Eastern District of New York held that a bank's persistent refusal to pay compensation owed to claimants was a series of events tolling the limitation period.[7] It could just as easily have held there was one event—the bank said no. Its refusal to change its mind is hard to see as a series of events if we are to take that notion seriously. It would toll the limitations period for any wrong not righted.

The real reason courts apply this doctrine appears from the case law to be a common core of facts, a claim of serious wrong, and a defendant who is a person with a substantial duty to the person suing —a fiduciary, for example.[8]

Giving people more time to sue in these cases is a judgment call about fairness. The tests developed about these decisions give little more than the appearance of objectivity that misses the real issue and leaves people wrestling over rhetoric rather than right or wrong. Formalism over humanism. Why did the *Bodner* court allow the lawsuit? Because the French bank in the case was holding money in trust for Jewish customers during World War II. The bank stole their money when the Nazis arrested them. A very big duty coupled with a very bad act.

37 : SIMILAR-SOUNDING CASES
AREN'T PRECEDENT

Despite the importance of each case's unique facts, many times the legal profession leans too heavily toward making fact decisions seem like legal decisions. Again, when this happens, we raise form over substance. Anonymity over accountability. Fact decisions require human judgment, and decisions about facts that try to appear to be about law needlessly deflect those judgments away from the judge.

This is often accomplished when we treat the outcome of a similar-sounding case as a kind of "factual precedent."

Courts would be better off without factual precedents. Properly understood, precedent is a legal principle that guides a case. It's the thing that the doctrine of *stare decisis* says we should follow. Precedent creates the duties courts enforce as "judge-made law," as opposed to duties arising from contract, statute, or regulation. An example of such judge-made law is the requirement that "the operator of an automobile must use reasonable care at all times."

Factual precedent isn't so much a legal concept as it is the by-product of herd mentality—the "bandwagon" fallacy illustrated earlier with cases about the "majority view." In non-jury cases, lawyers sometimes try to convince judges—and judges sometimes try to convince each other—that there is value in observing that another case with similar-sounding facts came out the way they want the current case to come out.

This leaves lawyers and law clerks devoting countless hours to looking anywhere they can to find some case somewhere that sounds like this one and came out the desired way.

"This is a case about a dog. There was a case in California about a dog. It must be on all fours." But rightly viewed, these analogies have no legal force. And we shouldn't see them as justifying an identical

157

result merely because they involved similar facts to the case we're working on.

The first problem is that no case is ever exactly the same as another unless they are cases involving the same events and parties. Each case is unique. Citing a supposedly similar one only leads to furious counter-briefing, with either party pointing out how the cases are different and pointing to cases that really are like this one—and this only encourages another round of briefing in which the parties insist the first case really was saliently similar and the others weren't.

If the judge accepts this approach, instead of deciding the facts of the pending case, the judge ends up deciding whether this case is most like the one where the plaintiff won or most like the case where the plaintiff lost. The judge then follows the outcome in that case.

Consider how a dispute between a spaniel owner and a pedestrian bitten by the dog can illustrate this folly. Many states have statutes making dog owners liable in most circumstances for the dog's biting. A few consider the owner's negligence—whether the owner failed to restrain the dog when the owner knew or should have known the dog was dangerous.

Such a case should be about the facts related to the dog. Is the breed known to bite? What was this dog's prior behavior? Had it bitten before? Was it aggressive? What did the owner know?

Instead, in too many cases the briefing revolves around the outcome of other cases. A court may have once granted a summary judgment in favor of a sheepdog owner. Another court held against the owner of a collie. The pedestrian seizes on the collie case. The owner cites the sheepdog dispute.

Briefing ensues as to which case should control the outcome. At oral argument the bewildered parties listen as the lawyers fight for their analogy. "You should find for the spaniel owner here, your honor. The sheepdog whose owner won a summary judgment was just like our spaniel here. Spaniels and sheepdogs are playful, loveable, heartwarming. And just like the spaniel here, the sheepdog there gave its owner no warning signs. No wonder the judge threw that case out of court, which is why you must do the same here, your honor.

"And remember, your honor, this case is nothing like the collie case. That collie was obviously a biter. He'd bitten before, and the spaniel in this case never did. Besides, collies look menacing with their long, strong muzzles, bristling with teeth. Collies are bigger, longer, faster, meaner. Collie owners must be on their guard. No wonder the Collie owner lost. He knew he had a dangerous dog on his hands and did nothing to stop it."

The pedestrian's lawyer disagrees: "That collie and this spaniel are birds of a feather. They were both raised on the same dog food. They both lived in a suburban neighborhood. Neither of them had obedience training. And the collie having bitten before hardly matters. He bit a burglar. That's what they're supposed to do. Besides, the sheepdog analogy is no good at all. That sheepdog had only three legs. It was a near-sighted twelve-year old, and its hair was hanging so low over its face it probably didn't even know the difference between a man and a chunk of wood. No wonder the judge let the poor owner off the hook. But the spaniel in this case is a menace to society. The collie's colleague in crime. Its owner should pay."

Rather than simply having a brief trial about *this* dog, the poor judge feels stuck between the Scylla of the sheepdog and the Charybdis of the collie: "What to do? Find cases involving other dogs? It would give the law clerks something to do. On the other hand, that collie did bite, burglar or not. Okay. We'll follow the sheepdog. *Bloom v. Sheepdog Owner* is the appropriate analogy. We'll cite it. Judgment for the dog owner. But wait, an upper court might overturn me. Summary judgment denied. It's a question of fact: is the spaniel more like the sheepdog or the collie?"

It is doggone frustrating. First, isn't the case about this dog and this pedestrian? Why retry two other cases instead of trying this one? Besides, the *fact* that another judge ruled for a dog owner over a pedestrian in a given case is not evidence that the decision was correct. The judge's reasoning may matter but no one even told us what it was. All we got were a few facts and the outcome. This is the fallacy of the bandwagon at work—we're just rolling along, following the herd.

And it's not just about safety in numbers. Lawyers and judges taking this approach try to suggest the outcome is *legally* compelled: "Of the fifteen cases involving dogs attacking horses, the horse owners have won thirteen out of fifteen; therefore, the weight of authority favors horses, and I am thus compelled to find for the horse owner."

FIGURE 37.1. *"I'll have what everyone else is having."*

But this isn't law—it's horsing around with facts to make them look like law. Judges in such cases suggest they are powerless because some kind of precedent decided the case, not them. "Blame them, not me, if you don't like the ruling." Slavish obedience to misperceived precedent is the sin of substituting mimicry for judgment.

There are many theories on how judges judge. Most of the studies, like too much of law, are an attempt at appearing to be a science—even a social science—rather than an art. In his book *How Judges Think*, Judge Posner argues that sometimes judges are simply legislating—using a kind of pragmatism that focuses on the consequences for the future of adopting one rule over another. But when he says judges legislate, he sounds more like a realist. He suggests that judges can't get in touch with the basic value in the law and apply it but simply impose their own values instead.

Realists like Judge Jerome Frank in 1930 went so far as to suggest that judges decide cases based on their own views and simply backfill the law into the decision to look like a justification. This thinking suggests that even when written statements of the law are clear, it hardly matters what they say. Precedent and legal principles are largely irrelevant to decision-making. So, we should pay careful attention to what judges eat and whether they are well rested. This goes too far. It's more relativist than realist.

This kind of junk psychology won't help us win respect for the rule of law, and it won't help us understand what really goes on either. What really goes on is more disappointing than judges imposing their own values. Too often, judges are simply trying to look like other judges. The bandwagon is one reason for this of course, but it goes deeper. Pointing to another judge's decision is to seek anonymity in the appearance of objectivity. It's formalism at work.

Thus, in such a view, a case that sounds like the one we have must be assumed to represent a first principle about how to decide the case we have in front of us. It's what goes into the equation and dictates the outcome. We suggest we are taking this "rule" and applying it to the facts to spit out an inevitable outcome. It has the convenience of making its author look reasonable, but it adopts a legal view responsible for needless complexity. This process implies that the right ruling must be discovered by process or precedent, that it is not crafted by a flawed human being.

This approach is usefully explored in Timothy Capurso's "How Judges Judge: Theories on Judicial Decision Making," in the *University of Baltimore Law Forum*.[1] It brings us back to the idea of resolving cases formulaically even by applying mere aphorisms. "The law will not aid a wrongdoer," says the judge refusing to enforce an immoral contract. "The employer is liable for the acts of the employee." "The sovereign can do no wrong." This thinking might suggest that one need only consult books like the eighteenth century's *Blackstone's Commentaries* for definitive answers or the nineteenth century's *Broom's Legal Maxims*—a seemingly endless catalogue of maxims and canons.[2] This is formalism: the answer is in there somewhere, not in us.

We see "factual-precedent" cases most when a court is dealing with the frayed edges of the law. In many cases, there is a basic rule with a frayed edge. For example, a statute allows injured persons to recover double damages if they prove the person who injured them violated the traffic laws with "reckless" disregard. No upper court has addressed the issue, and the lower courts are split over whether the law creates its own standard of recklessness or whether the injured party has to prove common-law recklessness. Here are two ways courts might deal with the issue:

FORMALISM: "The majority rule in the lower courts of this district is that the statute embodies its own standard of recklessness. Indeed, in *Smith v. Jones*, the court faced a violation of the same traffic law as the one at issue here, and the plaintiff prevailed without showing common-law recklessness."

AN ALTERNATIVE: "As the court reasoned in *Smith v. Jones*, the statute uses only the word *reckless*. It does not define the word. It does not say that a party may recover merely by alleging recklessness. Binding precedent requires us not to fashion new causes of action out of statutes that state none. Therefore, *recklessness* should be given its established common-law meaning rather than guessing that the legislature intended us to make up a new one."

What should appear above all is the judge's reasoning. When this reasoning is done correctly, we can see a judge who believes in giving the word *reckless* its familiar legal meaning. Another judge might search the soul of the legislation and find something broader. What matters is that judges give voice to their thoughts and reasons so they can be understood and judged. Merely pointing to the outcome of a similar case does nothing for us.

38 : THE BEST LEGAL WRITING IS LITERATURE, NOT FORMULA

Lawyers and judges are most convincing when they think about literature as they write. A good brief, a good decision, is a good story. That's how Jefferson conceived the Declaration of Independence: a people who freely associated themselves with a monarch who abused his power had the right to sever ties with him.

The Declaration of Independence had colonial heroes and a royal villain. But sometimes the heroes in a legal drama are only ideas—or, better yet, ideals.

Whoever the hero is, good legal writing can use literary devices to give life to ideas because readers absorb living ideas better than dead ones. A word should be, as Justice Holmes said, "the skin of a living thought," not, as he could have said, "an accurate reflection of the speaker's meaning."[1]

Lawyers and judges shouldn't fear literary devices as much as they do. Every time some judges consider metaphor or analogy, they fear they will be seen as joking about serious matters. But literary devices, even those that might use irony or other techniques, such as puns that flirt with humor, are powerful when they have a purpose.

Literary devices shine a light on meaning as with Holmes's "skin of a living thought" or Learned Hand's "Juries are not leaves swayed by every breath."[2] And yes, even light humor can bring light to a judge's view as this one did in 1855: "If the defendants were at fault in leaving an uncovered hole in the sidewalk of a public street, the intoxication of the plaintiff cannot excuse such gross negligence. A drunken man is as much entitled to a safe street as a sober one, and much more in need of it."[3] What better way to illustrate that a condition associated with an accident may have nothing to do with its cause? As with other things, it's a matter of judgment, but a key question is whether it sheds light on the point at issue, even about serious matters.

Nobody does this better or bolder, issue after issue, than the highly readable magazine the *Economist*. Its April 2, 2022, edition reported the European Union's opposition to sending armored vehicles to embattled Ukraine with the headline "No tanks, EU" and described Russian strategy as "the envelopment, please." In a later edition, it called the Supreme Court's contentious future after the *Dobbs* ruling "a gaveling storm." There are definite limits. Here's one from a court decision that fails because it illuminates nothing but some cringe-worthy rhyme:

> This case presents a vicious duel
> Between the U.S. of A. and defendant Ven-Fuel
> Seeking a license for oil importation,
> Ven-Fuel submitted its application.
> It failed to attach a relevant letter,
> And none can deny, it should have known better.
> Yet the only issue this case is about,
> Is whether a crime was committed
> beyond a reasonable doubt.[4]

A good rule of thumb: avoid anything that sounds like a limerick.

As for organization, what we learned in high school English works surprisingly well in court. Most arguments can be presented like a three-part thesis. "Jones isn't liable to Smith for three reasons. Jones doesn't own the property. Jones doesn't control the property, and Smith fell down because he was high, not because there was anything wrong with the property."

These three points tell the story. The rest of the brief in that case can be three sections, one for each point. It's surprising how much legal writing can have five sections like a high school essay: an introduction, three points, and a conclusion. Most of the time, it works.

Here is an example in a more complex field: "Smith should lose his trade secret–theft claim because, for three reasons, there was no secret to steal: the information was known by everyone in the industry, the information had no value, and Smith did nothing to keep it secret."

When three points don't work, lawyers should think again. Many times, they are needlessly complicating their claims.

Resisting this truth, many lawyers complained mightily when in 1998 the federal courts began limiting the number of words in briefs rather than the number of pages. Battle was joined again in 2016 when appellate rules lopped one thousand words off the fourteen-thousand-word limit and five hundred words off the seven-thousand-word limit for reply briefs. The *New York Times* and the *Wall Street Journal* quoted lawyers' complaints that complex cases require complex briefs and that lawyers were being needlessly punished for a few bad briefs.[5]

But complex cases don't necessarily require complex briefs. The path to victory is to place complex issues into arguments judges can understand and absorb, not to revel in the intricacy of the problem. More importantly, it is not the complex core of briefs in tough cases that make them too long. It's the *needless* complexity of the briefs.

It's logical to assume that if the information was meaningful—helpful even—judges likely wouldn't complain. And yet they do. In 2006 and 2007, the author and editor Bryan Garner interviewed eight of nine sitting US Supreme Court justices, and all of them complained about the length of briefs, but in ways that made clear that it was the needless material in the briefs, not their length.[6]

Judge Mary Beck Briscoe of the US Circuit Court of Appeals for the Tenth Circuit was quoted in the *New York Times* on the issue during the 2016 controversy. She summarized most judges' views effectively by noting—with emphasis on the key word—that many briefs are "*needlessly* lengthy." She believed lawyers would be better served "by excising tangential facts, secondary or tertiary arguments" on matters "on which a party is unlikely to prevail." She emphasized that this would "do the court and their clients a service by focusing the court's attention on the core facts and dispositive legal issues."[7]

When it comes to legal writing, the trouble between the bench and the bar is that they are talking past each other. So, let's try to be more specific about the *needless* parts that make up so much legal writing.

39 : DON'T PLOD THROUGH THE HISTORY OF THE CASE AND FAMILIAR STANDARDS

One reason many lawyers have trouble getting their points across is because they are caught up with the traditional throat-clearing exercises: "This action was commenced by writ, summons, and complaint on February 14, 2022. An answer was filed on April 15, 2024. The defendant, Anthony P. Jones (hereinafter 'Jones' or 'the defendant'), now moves for summary judgment under Federal Rules of Civil Procedure ('Fed.R.Civ. P.') § 56."

It sounds awfully serious, but who cares about the first part, and who doesn't know the second part? Think about a judge looking at the piece of paper. Unless it has something to do with the motion, who cares when the lawsuit was filed? And lawyers shouldn't trouble judges by telling them that Anthony P. Jones will be called "Jones."

Another thing on that score. Unless lawyers want to force judges to keep going back to see who the party is again and again, they shouldn't call a company named "Anthony P. Jones, Inc." by "APJI." Acronyms that aren't self-explanatory are just confusing. If it's a company, just call it "Jones" or, if you must, "Jones Inc." We can also refer to parties by the role they play in the case—"the consumer," "the manufacturer," "the employer." Alternating this with the actual name of the party gives the court something it can use—the name and the role.

Also, the document the judge is reading is likely called "Memorandum of Law in Support of Summary Judgment." So, we already know that the matter before the court is a motion for summary judgment. This is especially so if the writer works this idea into the topic sentence: "The court should grant BobCo. summary judgment for three reasons." While it isn't true of all rules, we can also assume the judge knows the rule number for summary judgment. Those nervous about leaving the rule number out should work it in later. We'll see how in a moment.

But first, you can likely do without the two or three pages of quotations from the rules and the case law about summary judgment. Readers will know it was lifted verbatim from your last motion. They also already know the standard for summary judgment and have the same cut-and-paste material about it. They may even take pride that theirs will be a longer summary of summary judgment than yours. But when part of the painfully familiar standard is needed for a particular reason, it works best when you work it in only when and where you need it.

Here is an example of what a lawyer might do if some of the case law about the standard matters later in a brief:

> A jury should decide if Jones owned or controlled the land.
> Jones had an equitable interest in the property. He has been seen
> helping people work on it. On the other hand, Jones claims he
> transferred his interest in the property, and the last time anyone
> saw Jones near the property was two years before the accident.
> Jones's interest is doubtful, and if the outcome is reasonably
> in doubt, the court should deny Smith's motion for summary
> judgment. As the Seventh Circuit in 2020 held in *McAvoy v.*
> *Pierce*: "Rule 56 requires the court when considering summary
> judgment to resolve all doubts in favor of the non-moving party."

This is also true for motions to dismiss and for similar motions courts see every day. Use what's needed about well-known rules only at the point where it's needed.

40 : JUNK THE JARGON

Most professions use stylistic conventions and insider language as a barrier to entry. Barriers to entry of this type mean that people off the street have no idea what we are talking about. Jargon is a small example of a barrier.

It isn't necessarily because the subject matter is so complicated that a doctor calls a bruise a "contusion" or a lawyer calls a self-represented person a "*pro se.*" It's because they learned these terms in school, and the terms created distance between lay people and experts.

This is not to say all jargon is useless. Just most of it. It's one reason why juries don't understand our arguments. It's one reason why the parties to a lawsuit can't read the judge's opinion when the case is over. It's part of what leaves them wondering why the judge threw them out of court. It forces legal stakeholders to consume enormous energy trying to figure what someone is saying. It is formalism. Formula. Form over substance.

Whatever it is, it costs the profession more than it's worth. Many times, lawyers can't understand what other lawyers say and why judges decide the way they do. Needlessly complex writing leads to meritless appeals. It leads to new litigation. More people would accept the results they receive in court if they understood those results.

But the problem isn't just about jargon. Sometimes, our complex and convoluted writing reflects disordered priorities. Too many lawyers write first to bill hours, second to avoid malpractice, third for the appellate court, and only last for the judge they wish to persuade.

Winning a case with a brief depends on persuading a judge. Winning a case leads to more business. It avoids malpractice, and it improves the odds of winning on appeal. Yet winning depends on the thing too many lawyers put last.

Cryptic writing is also sometimes camouflage for bad ideas. It may

FIGURE 40.1. *"Yes Peters, it is just legalese.*
It's all just legalese. We're a law firm."

be that the writer hasn't worked out the arguments well enough to express them. Or the argument is just fatally weak. They say that when the facts don't support you, argue the law. When the law doesn't support you, argue the facts. When neither of them supports you, pound the table.

Too much of legal writing is pounding the table. It's interference surrounding something important but hardly discussed. For a profession built on argument and persuasion, this reality should have us shaking our heads.

And it has only gotten worse. Computers make writing so much easier. Online research makes finding cases arguably on point a matter of a few clicks. This encourages lawyers and judges to pile on the case law, hoping it will give them gravitas. And, for appellate judges, the proliferation of eager and intelligent law clerks means they have to be given something to do, and too often this means filler. As we will discuss later, there are better uses for them than mere make-work.

Now, let's talk about what works and what doesn't in a series of steps.

41 : NEEDLESS DETAIL IS . . .

Too much legal writing complicates the obvious and trivializes the momentous.[1]

Too many briefs and opinions are attempts to appear scholarly, objective, or even mechanical. In reality, by volume, too much of what we find in briefs and opinions has form without function.

This is usually because of needless detail about the facts and the law. On the legal side, much of it has been cut and pasted. After saying too much about the case's procedural posture, after giving useless factual background about the parties and events, most lawyers and judges then work up the standard of review with multiple citations that they won't ever talk about again in the motion or decision. They are there because they are boilerplate.

Some flies get killed with sledgehammers. Once lawyers cite a recognized controlling legal authority for a legal principle, there is no point in them using string cites—lists of the twenty-seven times the controlling authority said the same thing. Of course, someone might be challenging whether something is still good law, but that's not the usual case.

Even in complex cases, there are usually just a few key issues, but judges and lawyers often find a way to make them more complicated. When simplified, they often come in threes. Someone overcharged, underperformed, and refused to repair. A driver wasn't paying attention and collided with your car. They could have avoided the collision by turning the wheel, stepping on the brake, or sounding their horn. The rest is filler.

In most personal injury cases, the last item really gets piled on, with the list going on for a dozen items saying little more than these three points but merely making them seem more substantial—especially to those who see how long the list is but don't read it—for instance, "she could have turned to the left; she could have turned to the right; she could have looked up; she could have looked down; she could have applied the brakes; she could have applied the gas . . ."

There are alternatives. Lawyers and judges seeking to eliminate the needless and marshal their arguments to good effect have many resources to turn to. The most transformative set of books on the subject were written by Bryan Garner. Two of his best are *Elements of Legal Style* and *The Winning Brief*.[2] Lawyers who want to win should take a cleansing retreat with books like these when they write their next briefs. They should lock the doors, ignore how most briefs are written, and reinvent themselves. Their clients—and judges—will thank them.

42 : THE BEST
APPELLATE DECISIONS
DEEPLY AND PLAINLY
EXPLAIN THE LAW

Needless to say, lawyers aren't the only legal professionals who could better express themselves. Remember, judges used to be lawyers. Many appellate judges used to be appellate lawyers. The bench boasts some fine writers, but what they produce is not the norm. Do we look forward to reading what most judges write?

Too many appellate decisions are a muddle, dominated by a history, decided by a footnote. They are thick with distracting information and often fail adequately to consider and explain the central legal rules they adopt, leaving lower courts with inadequate tools to apply them. This is formalism at work. The mechanical approach—the emphasis on mere process—fills in for the absence of an organizing principle about the judges' roles in deciding cases.

We can see needless complexity on display by reading a random appellate decision. We can stick a pin in a map and pick a random jurisdiction and a random opinion within it. They almost all suffer from the common flaw of being needlessly complex.

So, let's give it a try by randomly selecting a decision by the Indiana Supreme Court. There's nothing particularly bad about this court's work. We could easily find worse. Yet it suffers from the same basic flaws as the rest.

The case is *City of Marion v. London Witte Group*, LLC, from June 17, 2021.[1] It began with a summary of the decision. If we count the summary, there's at least one part of the decision that has the right length even if it lacks the right breadth.

Unlike many case summaries, this one is only two paragraphs. It's around 150 words, mostly a little bit about the facts—usefully written. Then it explains how the case got to the court—we hear too much about this in appellate decisions, including this one. But the main trouble with the summary is there are only 9 words about the legally important thing in the decision.

The second paragraph of the summary says that the court reversed a ruling that a claim was barred by the statute of limitations—that the claim was filed too late. We are told that this was because the court adopted the "adverse domination doctrine." But the summary doesn't tell us what the doctrine is or summarize why it was right to adopt it. Anyway, at least it contains the big news: Indiana recognized the adverse domination doctrine—whatever that is.

The next part of the decision probably is the first part that may have been written by a judge—or a law clerk. The summary isn't in the same style as the rest of the opinion, and many courts have people whose job it is to write these often-interminable summaries.

This next section is a painfully detailed "Facts and Procedural History," beginning with seven pages of "background" about the mayor of Marion, his successor, and a development project, replete with the precise dates of events, dollar amounts of financing, agreements, the names of everyone associated with the project, and a blow-by-blow account of every event associated with the project at issue, including shell games with money and favors for the mayor.

Unfortunately, readers have no idea as they wade through these details which facts in this section have any bearing on what the court had to decide and in what detail we should remember them. Will it really matter for what happens next that $63,400 was to be spent for the elevator and $60,000 for the HVAC?

This section includes over a dozen specific dates that have no subsequent significance and around thirty-nine distinct dollar amounts, many listed to the penny, whose use with such precision will remain a mystery as we try to keep on reading—as we try to keep these numbers in our heads—as we wait to see if these precise amounts matter again later—only to find out that they never do.

The next part of the opinion contains one of the most common

FIGURE 42.1. *"It's plotted out. I just have to write it."*

flaws of all decision writing. It's the incantation of the procedural history. Like many other decisions, this one starts with the filing date of the complaint. Is this needed?

It almost never is, but here it actually is because the question is whether the complaint was filed too late. But after all of the other useless dates, how are we to know? The decision doesn't tell us this date is important until much later. It just lumped this important date in with the unimportant dates in a disembodied recital of what happened before the case made it to the high court of Indiana. Why not give us only the important dates and give them to us only when they are important?

Finally, after almost three pages, we get to the point of why the case is here. The lower court held that the statute of limitations had expired and granted a summary judgment—judgment without a trial—in favor of an accomplice of the former mayor on two "counts"—parts—of the complaint. The reader takes note and again thinks: "When do we get to the court's *opinion*?"

Not yet. Next is almost a page of boilerplate recognizing that upper courts give no deference to lower courts' decisions to grant summary judgment and reciting the familiar summary judgment standard. Who cares at this stage? Again, courts should save such information for when it might matter.

Finally, nearly halfway through the decision, the court reached the discussion that mattered. The Indiana Supreme Court decided to adopt the equitable tolling doctrine of adverse domination. The decision described what the doctrine does: it "tolls"—halts—the statute of limitations running against a corporation that was controlled when the time to sue expired by the very wrongdoers the corporation now wants to sue.

The doctrine comes from the legal assumption that corporations only know what their agents know—agents like their company officers, lawyers, and so on. Deadlines for many lawsuits start running as soon as the person with the claim knows of the wrongdoing they wish to sue about. If the agents are the wrongdoers, it's unfair for courts to use their knowledge to stop the corporation from going after them. The doctrine applies to municipalities—they are in law "municipal corporations." It can be used against wrongdoers and those who conspire with them—like the company the city was suing in this case.

The court could have spent more time describing the doctrine in its own words and explained why it's a good idea to toll the limitation period against people who can block the discovery of wrongdoing. Instead, the court used most of its ruling, like so many other courts, to quote itself and other courts. It described the doctrine in just thirteen sentences. Only two of them are actually in the court's own words. But they aren't about why the doctrine is a good idea. They noted without saying why they did it that other courts have adopted the doctrine and that even an Indiana court used it once—so it must be good.

Yes, it's valuable to try to harmonize the common law across the country, but when most appellate courts write, they spend more time quoting other decisions than on anything else. We almost never hear the authentic voice of the court that is making the decision explaining and justifying its value judgments. This court's *opinion* mostly tried to look like it wasn't the opinion of the judges on the court, but the

opinion of some other judges on some other court—and we are supposed to assume they must have known what they were doing:

> "Adverse domination is an equitable doctrine that tolls statutes
> of limitations for claims by corporations against its officers,
> directors, lawyers and accountants for so long as the corporation
> is controlled by those acting against its interests." *Clark v. Milam,*
> 192 W.Va. 398, 452 S.E.2d 714, 718 (1994) (adopting the adverse
> domination doctrine). It "applies to causes of action against the
> wrongdoing directors . . . [and] against co-conspirators of the
> wrongdoers." *Indep. Tr. Corp. v. Stewart Info. Servs. Corp.,* 665
> F.3d 930, 936 (7th Cir. 2012) (citing *Lease Resol. Corp. v. Larney,*
> 308 Ill.App.3d 80, 241 Ill.Dec. 304, 719 N.E.2d 165, 172 (1999)).
>
> The doctrine has been adopted by many state and federal
> courts. See, e.g., *F.D.I.C. v. Smith,* 328 Or. 420, 980 P.2d 141, 148
> (1999) (adopting the doctrine); *Wilson v. Paine,* 288 S.W.3d 284,
> 289 (Ky. 2009) (same); *Resol. Tr. Corp. v. Scaletty,* 257 Kan. 348,
> 891 P.2d 1110, 1116 (1995) (same); *Farmers & Merchs. Nat'l Bank
> v. Bryan,* 902 F.2d 1520, 1522–23 (10th Cir. 1990) (adopting the
> doctrine as part of federal common law). And the doctrine "has
> been generally accepted by federal courts to be the law of states
> that have not yet explicitly ruled on the subject themselves."
> *Clark,* 452 S.E.2d at 718 (citing *Resol. Tr. Corp. v. Farmer,* 865
> F. Supp. 1143 (E.D. Pa. 1994)). Indeed, an Indiana federal court
> applied the doctrine nearly three decades ago, believing an
> Indiana court, if faced with the same facts, would have done
> so. *Resol. Tr. Corp. v. O'Bear, Overholser, Smith & Huffer,* 840 F.
> Supp. 1270, 1284 (N.D. Ind. 1993).[2]

Appellate courts have carried the practice of quoting other courts
too far. This hasn't so much convinced us that there is harmony
among the courts. It has suggested instead that the court that drafted
the opinion had nothing to say. In many courts, decisions simply leap
from one quotation of an earlier decision to another, no matter how
awkward it is for the reader. These gymnastics suggest that courts
avoid responsibility for their decisions, and it discourages original
thought by promoting the fallacy that if no one has ever said it before,
it can't be right.

Again, in many cases, it's because the judges don't have an organizing vision for what they are supposed to do or at least don't want to tell us what it is. Imposing their own views? Finding the majority view? Finding the one true view? Finding the historic or traditional view? The Indiana case could have discussed the values behind the rules limiting the time to sue. It could have noted our dislike of people profiting from their own wrongs and explained how these principles applied to the human conduct in this case.

Experienced opinion readers also know that they can find opinions on both sides of most major issues—even something like the doctrine of adverse domination. We could rewrite the Indiana opinion cutting and pasting from decisions that have rejected the doctrine. What really matters is *why* the court adopted rather than rejected the doctrine and how it worked in enough detail so that lower courts could apply it, but we got precious little discussion of that here—and all of it by other courts, not the court deciding the case.

After briefly focusing on the key issue, the Indiana opinion then returned to the periphery. It walked at length through the summary judgment process, duplicating the work of a trial court. Having spent just eight short paragraphs to adopt and explain this important point of law, it devoted sixteen long paragraphs to doing the trial court's job in considering a summary judgment. And, as we will see, it focused on fact-based minutiae the lower court would have to grapple with rather than a law-based explanation of how the doctrine worked.

Without saying whether anyone disputed it, the court also discussed at length how the defendants showed that on the face of the lawsuit—prima facie—the lawsuit was filed too late under the applicable statute of limitations. This was wasted space if everyone agreed this was true. And, indeed, there is no sign in the opinion that this was in the least way disputed.

The court then carried on being a trial court, reviewing the facts of the case and telling the trial judge to go about finding whether the mayor—in league with the defendant company—controlled whether the city might sue over the corruption.

Caught up with its trial court task, the court then undercut its too-brief explanation of how the standard worked. The court had explained that the doctrine is automatic. The limitation period would

toll so long as the wrongdoers were in control. Yet during its unnec-
essarily detailed discussion of the facts, the Indiana court suggested
that the trial court should consider whether "it is reasonable to infer
that Mayor Seybold would not pursue legal action that would uncover
his alleged wrongdoing."[3]

Given the court's weak explanation of what kind of "wrongdoing"
is needed, readers might think that the wrongdoing had to be an actual effort to stop the city from filing a lawsuit. But a second reading
shows this can't be what the court meant. It seems clear enough that
the wrongdoing had to be the underlying intentional wrong—the corruption that the lawsuit is about—not efforts to stop the city from
suing over it.

Still, given what the court said about the need for an inference that
the mayor wouldn't sue, the decision suggests that to toll the limitation period, the lower court had to infer that the mayor in fact would
have blocked the lawsuit rather than it being enough that he was in a
position to do so.

Because of its important role in shaping the law, making a clear
rule on this should have been the court's top priority. When it discussed the doctrine, the court should have fleshed it out enough to say
whether the doctrine applied only when a wrongdoer actually would
have blocked a lawsuit or whether it would be enough that the wrongdoer had the power to block a lawsuit. Perhaps the court didn't find
any case law it could quote on this topic, so—rather than speak with
its own voice on this important point—it simply skipped it.

The court might have usefully discussed a number of things. Should
courts extend the deadline only for active interference? How will this
rule work with other rules that extend limitation periods? Is there a
value in the predictability and stability of having an inflexible number
of years to bring a lawsuit? Is basic fairness what counts in tolling this
limitation period? Is it a matter of preventing people from shielding
their wrongdoings with the very power they are accused of abusing? If
the court discussed these matters, it might have helped lower courts
and other appellate courts grapple with the same issues.

Instead, the court avoided this more difficult task to focus again on
tangential matters. Many upper courts love burden shifting, and the
Indiana court proved no different. It held that if a prima facie case for

control by a wrongdoer is made, the burden shifts to the party being sued to show that someone else could have brought the lawsuit.

Of course, if someone else could have brought the lawsuit without the wrongdoer, then the alleged wrongdoer didn't have control. This is little different than saying that a party showing control wins unless the other party shows a lack of control.

As in discrimination cases, this kind of shifting *almost* never matters. It does sound rather analytical, and therefore its author might think it would make the ruling more credible. But they'd be wrong.

The Indiana decision is mercifully shorter than many but equally vague about what counts. Here's an alternative that seeks to save time and directly confront the principle adopted. The most important thing appellate courts do is settle the law. The Indiana opinion could have begun its opinion with this rule:

> To bring a lawsuit we first have to know we have been wronged. That's why many statutes of limitations don't start running until the party with a claim learns of the claim.
>
> But what about where a corporate officer commits a wrong but no one finds out about it? Does the corporation know of the wrong because its officer does? That's the normal rule.
>
> But this isn't the normal case. Like other courts, we aren't willing to let wrongdoers get away because they also happened to control the company they wronged. That's why we are adopting the "adverse domination" doctrine.
>
> This doctrine says that the time limit on when to sue won't start running—it will toll—for so long as the corporation is controlled by those who are said to have wronged it.

Many well-intentioned professionals might instinctively recoil from this approach. What about the facts? Where is the discussion of the procedure posture? The standard of review?

But there is no reason for alarm. Courts can work in those matters when they matter and only if they matter. For instance, just before overruling the lower court, the upper court might have said, "The trial court didn't apply the adverse domination doctrine. The appellate court didn't either. Both courts were wrong about the law on this point, and we don't defer to lower courts' rulings on the law because we are the final authority in this state on what the law says. Therefore, we reverse both lower court decisions and send the case back for a hearing on the merits of the claim."

This takes care of the procedural posture and standard of review without having them clogging the path to the discussion that matters most. Yes, you can cite a case on these points if you want.

The facts can wait too. They matter very little here. The upper court only had to decide if the parties disputed the claim that the mayor intentionally wronged the city while controlling the decision about filing a lawsuit over it.

It would have been enough to say that the city presented the lower court with evidence that the mayor extorted bribes from city contractors while controlling the filing of city lawsuits and that the former mayor insisted that the city council and others might have initiated a lawsuit without him. Thus, there was a fact dispute. The rest should have been left to the trial court—except for saying that a reasonable jury could find either way while citing a case for the proposition that this genuine dispute meant summary judgment would be wrong.

Instead, the Indiana court added to the earlier confusion by again suggesting that the inquiry is needed because "the reasonable inference would be that Mayor Sebold would not let an investigation into the bond fund be successful, which creates a genuine issue of material fact as to whether he would have allowed a suit to be filed."[4]

In twenty-three pages, we got more than we needed about the facts and less than we needed about the law. We are still left wondering if the question is whether the mayor controlled the filing of lawsuits in general or whether to apply the doctrine the fact finder would have had to conclude that under these specific facts, the mayor likely would have blocked the lawsuit. The court's initial description of the rule suggested one thing, and its discussion of the lower-court proceeding that would follow suggested another.

Again, Indiana deserves no special blame here. But it not only doesn't have to be this way, it wasn't *always* this way.

A random sample of three Indiana appellate decisions from 1935 shows they averaged 2,024 words.[5] The *City of Marion* case was 7,536 words—nearly four times as many. A random sample of three Connecticut Supreme Court decisions from 1935 shows an average of 1,889 words.[6] A sample of three cases from the same court in 2019 shows an average of 11,834 words, more than six times as many.[7]

Contemporary courts might consider a time when matters had to be written out in longhand before they got included in a court decision.

The pragmatic Justice Oliver Wendell Holmes usually gave us a few choice words and aimed them at the main legal question, explaining the court's ruling in ways intended to guide action. One of his most celebrated decisions was the 1919 case of *Schenck v. United States*.

In *Schenck*, Holmes reviewed briefly the criminal charges against Schenck and his compatriots for anti-war pamphlets they published. After noting the competing claims, Holmes dove deep into the human aspects of free speech in language an ordinary person could understand:

> We admit that in many places and in ordinary times the
> defendants in saying all that was said in the circular would have
> been within their constitutional rights. But the character of every
> act depends upon the circumstances in which it is done. The most
> stringent protection of free speech would not protect a man in
> falsely shouting fire in a theater and causing a panic. It does not
> even protect a man from an injunction against uttering words
> that may have all the effect of force. The question in every case is
> whether the words used are used in such circumstances and are of
> such a nature as to create a clear and present danger that they will
> bring about the substantive evils Congress has a right to prevent.[8]

We can all understand what might happen in response to false cries of fire in a crowded theater. Equally, a danger being "clear and present" instantly evokes a threat we would want to act on. One hundred years later, we can still hear people say: "That's like shouting fire in a crowded theater." And Holmes's image of a clear and present danger was colorful enough for Tom Clancy to use it as the title of a 1989 novel and for Paramount Studios to make a 1994 movie of the novel using the name. It tells us two things we must look for before acting. Vague possibilities don't count. The distant future isn't the court's concern.

Holmes is alive for us because we know from his ruling what limits will be imposed, and we agree with them because Holmes justified the rule with vivid imagery rooted in ordinary human experience.

By the way, Holmes reduced this famous decision down to just 1,680 words. Brilliant reduction, Holmes!

Now let's contrast some judicial writing styles. There are many examples to consider. As with any writing, the better it begins—the deeper it reaches into the key issues at the outset—the more likely a work is to persuade. And judges should be in the persuasion business: faith in the rule of law is the only thing between many of us and the block.

Here is how Judge Irving Kaufman of the us Second Circuit Court of Appeals began a 1985 opinion about freedom of association, one of the rights guaranteed by the First Amendment:

> Fascinated by the penchant of Americans to band together and gather strength from association, Alexis de Tocqueville wrote:
>> The most natural privilege of man, next to the right of acting for himself, is that of combining his exertions with those of his fellow creatures, and of acting in common with them. The right of association therefore appears to me almost as inalienable in its nature as the right of personal liberty. No legislator can attack it without impairing the foundations of society.   —A. de Tocqueville, 2 Democracy in America 203 (Bradley, ed. 1954).
> It is this ability and propensity of our citizenry to unite and pursue desired goals that form the foundation of American political thought. Indeed, the very existence of this nation stands as a testament to the efficacy of political organization.[9]

With his first words, Judge Kaufman perfumed his decision with the romance of history and invited us to consider the nation's highest ideals and achievements. We are eager for more.

Let's contrast this with a Third Circuit opinion on the equally precious First Amendment right of free speech:

> Plaintiffs, a collection of individuals and entities involved with various aspects of the adult media industry, brought this action challenging the constitutionality of 18 U.S.C. §§ 2257 and 2257A

(the "Statutes"), which are criminal laws imposing recordkeeping, labeling, and inspection requirements on producers of sexually explicit depictions. Plaintiffs also challenge the constitutionality of certain regulations promulgated pursuant to the Statutes. Plaintiffs claim that the Statutes and regulations violate, inter alia, various provisions of the First, Fourth, and Fifth Amendments to the U.S. Constitution—as applied and facially— and seek declaratory and injunctive relief.[10]

Like most opinions, this one encourages us to flip and skip until something important comes into view.

Here is how it might have begun:

In 1998, Congress passed a law requiring adult-film makers to keep records of the identity and ages of those who appear in their films. The law was called the Child Protection Obscenity Enforcement Act. Its stated purpose was to protect children from being physically exploited by pornographers.

The filmmakers are wrong to say this violates the First Amendment. The law doesn't automatically violate their right to free speech. It doesn't even regulate what they have to say. Because these are content-neutral regulations, the Constitution only requires that they protect a substantial government interest, impose no needless burdens, and leave open other ways to communicate for those regulated. Because the parties here haven't developed evidence on these three issues and the companion claims about illegal searches, we will return this case to the lower court to give them a chance to gather it.

For now, it's important to see that the law shows that Congress aimed at deterring deeds, not stifling speech. The statute, 18 U.S.C. § 2257, requires those who produce film of "actual sexually explicit conduct" to keep records of each person depicted and to attach a label to each film indicating who was keeping the records and how to reach that person.

No poetry here, but in this version, we at least know immediately what the claim is, what the court is doing with it, and why—all without formalist clutter.

Now let's see Judge Henry Friendly take wing in the opening lines of a simple breach of contract case about chickens in New York:

The issue is, what is chicken? Plaintiff says "chicken" means a young chicken, suitable for broiling and frying. Defendant says "chicken" means any bird of that genus that meets contract specifications on weight and quality, including what it calls "stewing chicken" and plaintiff pejoratively terms "fowl." Dictionaries give both meanings, as well as some others not relevant here. To support its, plaintiff sends a number of volleys over the net; defendant essays to return them and adds a few serves of its own. Assuming that both parties were acting in good faith, the case nicely illustrates Holmes' remark "that the making of a contract depends not on the agreement of two minds in one intention, but on the agreement of two sets of external signs—not on the parties' having meant the same thing but on their having said the same thing." *The Path of the Law*, in Collected Legal Papers, p. 178. I have concluded that plaintiff has not sustained its burden of persuasion that the contract used "chicken" in the narrower sense.[11]

Many find this opening amusing. Some serious-minded judges might even criticize it. Opinions don't begin this way. Judges shouldn't try to be funny. Was Judge Friendly trying to be funny? No. He was trying to be lucid, and perhaps some legal writers think there's something funny about that.

Let's look at another decision about chicken from the First Circuit. Here's how it lays an egg:

This appeal concerns a suit in the District of Maine by the insurer of a chicken products manufacturer to recoup the losses that it paid to the manufacturer for the losses that the manufacturer incurred when its products were recalled following a salmonella outbreak. Subrogated to the rights of the manufacturer, the insurer sought damages from the manufacturer's chicken supplier for claims under Maine law for breach of warranty and strict product liability. In support of those claims, the insurer's complaint alleged that the manufacturer received two truckloads of raw chicken from the supplier that was contaminated with Salmonella Enteritidis and was therefore "defective" under Maine law. The supplier filed a motion to dismiss, which the District Court granted as to all claims. The District Court did so after ruling that the complaint's allegations did not suffice to plausibly allege that the raw chicken that the supplier sent to the manufacturer was "defective." The District Court also concluded that the insurer's strict liability claim was independently barred by the economic loss doctrine. We affirm.[12]

Here is another way it might have begun:

What makes a chicken defective? Is it enough that it's riddled with salmonella? Apparently, not in Maine. Maine law recognizes that it is perfectly normal for chicken to be crawling with salmonella. That's why we cook it.

This is bad news for the insurance company in this case. It had to pay $10 million to a food processor it insured when federal regulators ordered nearly two million pounds of chicken destroyed. It hoped to recoup this money from the company that supplied the chicken.

But it can't. The trouble is that while it's undisputed that the processed chicken products somehow had salmonella hearty enough to survive cooking and infect consumers, the insurer hasn't alleged plausible facts that the offending salmonella was present before the processer started passing the formerly bare breasts off as "chicken cordon bleu" and "chicken Kiev."

It's a matter of warranty law—Maine warranty law because this is a lawsuit between citizens of different states about an incident that happened in Maine. Like other states, Maine's commercial code says that merchandise comes with certain binding—even if unspoken—assurances from sellers.

Too many decisions start by complicating things. Some complications need never be explained, and others are best sprung on us a little at a time. There was no need here to explain subrogation rights. They aren't in dispute and might be worked in later if we need them. The procedural posture—what the district court did—is another thing to leave until later. We are better off knowing immediately what the case turns on both legally and factually—what makes a chicken defective and its absence here.

43 : THERE IS A BETTER HOME FOR LAW CLERKS OUTSIDE OF BUSY WORK AND JUNIOR JUDGING

The decisions we have just reviewed are an excellent lead into another reason why some published opinions tell us so much about the facts, the procedural posture, the parties' claims, the rulings of the courts of Luxembourg, and every time the court has said, "the court reviews errors of law de novo."

It's likely because of the misuse of law clerks. There are more of them today than ever. They are usually intelligent, ambitious, diligent, and inexperienced in the practice of law. Yet these fledgling lawyers may be writing by sheer number of words most appellate judicial decisions today and a large percentage of lower court rulings.

Are we wasting their talents?

Judges finding work for law clerks may be one of the biggest reasons legal decisions have come to say more while meaning less. Law clerks are eager to help. It's easy to say yes to their willingness to write some or all of an opinion. But when it comes to the main thinking behind a decision, it's difficult for them to reflect their judge's view, not to mention the views of the other judges joining in an opinion.

In what voice should they speak about the core of the ruling. Textualist? Natural law? Realist? Pragmatist? After all, they aren't speaking for themselves. And many law clerks only serve for a year or two. They're just getting to know the person whose voice they are assuming, and we know they certainly don't want to offend them—or the other judges signing on. The easiest thing may be to make the ruling long but predominantly judgment free. In other words, formalism—the appearance of a deliberative process—is the easiest thing.

FIGURE 43.1. *"The ones just out of law school are especially frolicsome."*

Commentary on law clerks has consistently and increasingly pointed to their growing influence. From works like the 2006 book *Sorcerers' Apprentices* to the 2013 book *In Chambers*, the influence of law clerks has been documented and measured through leaks and ultimately scientific surveys of clerks and their role in creating the bones of decisions and even, in many instances, in writing the entire decision and influencing its outcome.

A 2014 symposium on the issue by the *Marquette Law Review* explored views about law clerks, expressing long-standing concerns that they add to needless complexity:

> Clerks not only facilitate an increase in the aggregate number
> of opinions simply by being available as a source of labor, they
> encourage proliferation by having an incentive to see their judge
> make a name for him or herself via separate opinions. Their role
> as primary authors likewise changes opinions' style in a way
> that increases length, footnoting, reliance on jargon, and the
> incorporation of multi-factor balancing tests, all of which [the
> Yale Professor Anthony] Kronman characterized as a product of

"the combination of hubris and self-doubt that is the mark of the culture of clerks."[1]

There may be disputes among clerks about the level of their influence, but it's fair to say that most appellate judges make their own decisions on the outcome of an appeal but usually write only a portion of their opinions and often none of them. Law clerks write them.

And this means they have to write them with care not to leave the judge out on a limb or suggest something other judges won't agree with. It's safer for the clerks to make the opinion look meaty, with extensive background about standards of review, rulings below, the detailed contentions of each side, and the applicable law and its history, and then to either minimize the explanation of the reason for the court's decision or leave it to the judge to write a brief bit on that part. The judge may also not want to go out on a limb or speak from a viewpoint not necessarily endorsed by the other judges signing on to the opinion. Either way, we too often get an enormous carcass of bones with only a little meat attached.

In the worst scenarios—a tiny minority, we hope—judges abandon their duties to law clerks altogether. There was a lazy trial court judge who spent most of his time in chambers telling war stories to his lawyer friends or sleeping off an extended lunch. When he asked his law clerk for a recommended ruling in a case, the clerk thought it best to give him versions going either way—one with the plaintiff winning, one with the defendant winning. Finding the decisions waiting on his desk after lunch, the judge signed them both without reading them and dropped them in the out basket.

Law clerks have good uses. But we are wasting their time using them to make decisions needlessly complex. Typically, law clerks are skilled at legal research. In a page or two, they can summarize for their judges the legal claims of the two sides. More importantly, the clerk can summarize what the law actually says. This is common already.

But perhaps the most useful thing they can do is ferret out contradictions in the court's prior statements of a legal rule and set the contradictions and ambiguities up for the court to resolve or provide additional guidance about unclear rules, like the adverse-domination ruling we saw in the Indiana case.

Many of us would be surprised at how many of a court's rulings are incomplete or contradict other rulings of the same court or an upper court. Law clerks freed from the tedium of cranking out pointless background could be assigned to look for areas like this in designated places, searching for points of law needing clarity, like the definition of proximate cause, strict liability, reasonable care, plain language, parol evidence, and the like. This scholarly work could then be used as issues come up.

Another good use of law clerks—perhaps best done in conjunction with rotating panels of semiretired judges—is summary-disposition spotting. The appellate courts—often because they are slow in processing cases—face mostly baseless appeals. The sheer volume of appeals can look daunting to appellate courts. But we all know that the reversal rate on appeal is less than 20 percent.[2] Of the 80 percent of appeals that fail, many of them are frivolous and shouldn't have to be squeezed in for twenty or some other number of minutes of oral argument.

Appeals for too many litigants—maybe even a majority—are a way to postpone a reckoning with reality or simply lash out at the system. Most judges and lawyers likely believe this but—in the name of process—may be afraid to admit it. Still, if they wanted to, appellate courts could develop more ways to decide a case on a fast track and without oral argument. Rotating teams of law clerks and judges screening new cases can spot these and dispose of them using expedited, truncated briefing that shortcuts normal procedural steps, such as waiting for transcripts and mediation.

This could free up time for the court. Perhaps 50 percent or more of appeals could end in five or six weeks with a one- or two-page opinion affirming the lower court—one or two pages sharply focused on the reason for the ruling. The reason is key. Summary rulings without any decent explanation of why they are summary and why they were ruled as they were would undercut the courts' legitimacy.

Still, the best use of law clerks is likely spotting and sorting out contradictions and ambiguities in the case law. Unlike most of what we have them doing, this work is profound and goes to the heart of what appellate courts should be doing.

44 : APPELLATE COURTS SHOULD REFORM RUSTY RULES

If they reduce needless complexity, appellate judges would have more time to do what they are best at: shaping and clarifying the law. It is remarkable how frayed some of our most basic concepts are. The tolling of limitation periods. Proximate cause. Unfair trade practices. Civil rights claims. The more we study appellate rulings, the more we can see that too many of them are inscrutable or contradictory.

Yet these loose ends of the law don't often get cleaned up because too many judges place precedent and process over substance. Upper courts too often quote themselves, or even argue about which of their prior sayings they should quote, rather than first seeking in any precedent they might cite not words from an earlier decision but an underlying governing principle that the court might then try to express plainly.

Here are a few examples to illustrate the potential for appellate courts to clean up rusty rules in ways that would help lower courts decide cases:

A. *Tortious interference with a contract*

In these cases, one party claims the other party has damaged them by interfering with their contract with a third party.[1]

Many courts have adopted the *Restatement of Torts'* definition of this claim. Like many products of its kind, this definition suggests that it was the work of a committee. Sometimes this means a long and confusing rule.

The *Restatement* takes eight separate points to express a relatively modest idea:

1. A defendant is subject to liability for interference with contract if:
   a. a valid contract existed between the plaintiff and a third party;
   b. the defendant knew of the contract;
   c. the defendant engaged in wrongful conduct as defined in Subsection (2);
   d. the defendant intended to cause a breach of the plaintiff's contract or disruption of its performance; and
   e. the defendant's wrongful conduct caused a breach of the contract or disruption of performance.
2. Conduct is wrongful for purposes of this Section if:
   a. the defendant acted for the purpose of appropriating the benefits of the plaintiff's contract;
   b. the defendant's conduct constituted an independent and intentional legal wrong; or
   c. the defendant engaged in the conduct for the sole purpose of causing harm to the plaintiff.[2]

There is a relatively straightforward principle here that could be expressed more plainly. Tortious interference with a contract is *an intentional interference with a contractual relationship, without justification, by someone not a party to it.*

If each of these words is given its obvious meaning, courts could easily apply the rule. It shouldn't be difficult to understand that if there isn't a contractual relationship, intent, or interference, or if there is justification, the claim fails. An invalid contract is not a contract. A contract that gets breached or disrupted or has its benefits misappropriated has been interfered with. An unjustified interference is wrongful.

B. *Unfair trade practices*

In many states, unfair trade practice decisions are among the most vexing. Statutes passed against unfair trade practices are aimed at promoting honesty in business, but they have also created much busyness in courts.[3]

The first question courts ask under the statutes is usually whether "trade or commerce" is involved. This is usually undisputed, and we might wonder why we bother saying "trade or commerce" anyway. The courts never distinguish one word from another. Isn't trade merely a subset of commerce?

The next step some courts take is traditional but obtuse. They apply a vestigial thing called the "cigarette rule" that originated from Federal Trade Commission (FTC) thinking about cigarette regulation. It has three blithering bits: "(1) whether the practice, without necessarily having been previously considered unlawful, offends public policy as it has been established by statutes, the common law, or otherwise—whether, in other words, it is within at least the penumbra of some common-law, statutory, or other established concept of unfairness; (2) whether it is immoral, unethical, oppressive, or unscrupulous; (3) whether it causes substantial injury to consumers (or competitors or other businessmen)."[4]

Faced with this gelatinous, monotonous list, most courts quote this language and then ignore most of it. After an extended explanation, many courts resort to something closer to what the FTC adopted. Paired down even more, courts could define an unfair trade practice as *"intentional conduct unjustified by some greater good to consumers or society that causes a consumer substantial harm of a type other consumers might suffer."*

This sheds most of the lard in the language. It relieves individual consumers of the burden of trying to prove that an unfair practice happens to everyone and yet focuses on things that might in fact affect everyone. It reveals that most unfair trade practice laws are loosely constructed and invite broad judgment calls about right and wrong. Legislatures made them this way, and courts can neither cover this up nor rewrite the laws.

c. *Causation*

Now, let's take a closer look at causation in general and proximate cause in particular.

This book is caused by a big bang. Without the beginnings of the universe, we could have been spared this book. But that's not how we think about causes in court. It would be unfair to rage against God and nature for something that is more directly the author's fault.

So, to be fair, a system with a narrower focus is required. After all, we look for causes for things so we can hold someone responsible for the damage that flows from them. Regardless of the confused case law, the sensible center to understanding the idea of causation is to think of a "legal" cause—a cause we hold someone responsible for in court. Indeed, legal cause is a better name for the whole concept of causation in court.

Most people think it's unfair to hold someone responsible for something they can't control. But that's really more about duty than consequence. Courts often confuse the two. In most cases, we don't have a duty to stop something over which we have no direct or indirect control. So, let's start by not confusing those two concepts.

More importantly, once we have a duty and have breached it, causation tries to identify what results a court should hold us responsible for—that is, what results a court should say we legally caused.

About this, lawyers and judges too often confuse the idea of something being a "substantial factor" in causing a harm with something being a "reasonably foreseeable" consequence of something a person has done.

This last part is the root of what we should call a "legal cause." Let's return for a moment to a more damaging version of the story we used in discussing jury charges.

If you hit a baseball toward a window, a broken window is reasonably foreseeable. It is even reasonably foreseeable that someone on the other side of the window might be hurt by broken glass. But if you swing your bat, the sun reflects off of it, a nearby driver is blinded, drives off the road, and explodes a gasoline storage tank, these things are not reasonably foreseeable from your swing, and you aren't responsible to the driver, the storage-tank owner, or anyone injured in the ensuing conflagration.

Really, that's almost all we need to say about ordinary causation, and yet appellate cases have written volumes on it.

In particular, they usually start with the big bang issue. They say a cause must be a but-for cause or a "cause in fact."[5] In other words, the thing would not have happened but for what the alleged wrong-doer did.

But as we discussed earlier, why talk about it separately? We can address this issue by what we consider a legally sufficient cause. And, of course, if there is no harm at all, there isn't anything to talk about anyway. The progress goes like this: (1) There is a duty. (2) That duty is breached. (3) Damage is legally caused by the breach.

What we haven't talked about is the genuine problem of multiple causes that combine to create a single injury. To allocate liability in such cases, many jurisdictions have adopted the sensible idea of comparative negligence. Where an injury is 50 percent or more caused by the person seeking to blame others, that person loses their claim. This means where the cause of the injury is between the party suing and the parties being sued or where it is mostly a consequence of the negligence of the party suing, the injury likely would have happened without anything the defendants did. So, this also addresses the but-for or cause in fact element so many courts awkwardly make into a separate issue.

But if the person suing is 30 percent at fault, and person A is 50 percent at fault, while person B is 20 percent at fault, person A pays 50 percent of the damages, and person B pays 20 percent of the damages.

But where a person is 1 percent responsible, that person should be seen as not a "substantial factor" in causing the injury. Anyway, to allocate blame among multiple wrongdoers, a jury would first have to decide the person sued was at least a substantial, as opposed to nominal, cause of the injury. Yes, this calls for judgment by the jury about what is insubstantial—but most things do, and it doesn't help to pretend they don't.

Courts have mixed these concepts and swapped labels around so much that no one can say there is just one correct answer, and we can't either.

Still, there is a principle we might recommend: people who breach duties are responsible for damage caused by the reasonably foreseeable consequences of their actions if they were a substantial cause of the harm and according to the percentage by which they are to blame for causing the injury at issue. Persons responsible for more than 50 percent of their own injuries recover nothing.

D. *Derivative Actions*

When a shareholder accuses the leadership of a corporation of mis-management, the law allows the shareholder to sue on the company's behalf "derivatively." Statutes and court rulings empower judges to con-trol the litigation to be sure the lawsuit is in earnest and in the com-pany's interest. Without litigation controls, a large corporation may become the victim of guerrilla warfare by minority shareholders using the lawsuit to leverage or extort the ruling powers. In derivative actions, the courts take an active role in governing who may sue and for what.

While the rules vary, generally judges decide if the lawsuit deserves derivative status. This means the judge must decide if the lawsuit may be brought, in effect, on behalf of the company itself to repair its af-fairs. Courts decide whether the people bringing the lawsuits are fit to bring them—Do they have the company's best interests at heart? If the suit is allowed, the court rides herd on it to ensure the lawsuit is about the company's best interests, not a private feud. At least the-oretically, that's how it's done.[6]

There are many problems with not following this notion, but the most problematic derivative suits today involve small, closely held companies—companies with two or three owners. These lawsuits are almost inherently personal. Yet they are often brought derivatively or attacked because they haven't been. Courts often don't but should permit these lawsuits to be direct actions as has been suggested by numerous commentators, including the American Law Institute.[7]

Courts of appeal could make this the rule. It would end an enor-mous tangle of lawsuits among the owners of mom-and-pop enter-prises who are forced to spend gigantic sums because of the vast complexity the courts have placed on their modest disputes.

E. *Civil Rights*

Perhaps only legislation can end this farce. The fictions in this area regarding who is suing whom for what in what capacity and for what relief is embarrassing to deal with as a lawyer or a judge.[8] It is not worth sorting through here. It is all about carving out limited exceptions to the immunity from suit of government officials. But because the rules are so unclear, the lawsuits get brought in large numbers, the complaints get battled over endlessly, and those who don't get the form-over-substance ritual right get tossed out of court, often with no notion of what they did wrong and no sense that their claim of government misconduct had anything to do with it. In short, like other things we have been looking at, the rulings are needlessly complex and undercut faith that our courts do justice.

If we were to try to put the matter plainly, when government agents negligently deprive citizens of their constitutional or statutory rights, the victims should be allowed to sue the government to stop the violations and possibly recover their attorneys' fees. When these agents act intentionally or recklessly, their victims should recover money damages and attorneys' fees from the government. Courts should award punitive damages against the government in cases involving egregious policies of wrongdoing when the extra damages will deter future wrongdoing.

We would do well to rid ourselves of talk about "individual" versus "official" capacities and the tortured business of defining with infinitesimal and subjective specificity what rights can be sued over. States that have their own parallel laws might lead the way by casting off this useless yoke.

F. *Discrimination*

Discrimination lawsuits are ensnared in the three-part test from *McDonnell Douglas Corp. v. Green*, which applies in cases of employment discrimination based on race, sex, and so on.[9] As noted, these tests almost always end up the same way, and appellate courts can readily reduce them to a single question.

Under the standard, first the plaintiff has to allege facts to support a claim. They almost always do. Then the employer has to assert a nondiscriminatory reason for their action. They almost always do. Then the plaintiff has to show that the reason was a mere pretext. They usually don't.

It's a nuisance. It has become more of a formalist ritual than a useful tool. It is, we can suppose, at least a barrier to entry for the uninitiated. If you don't know the test, you shouldn't be involved in one of these cases—we can suppose.

The question could be made simple: Was race, or what have you, the predominant reason for an adverse employment action?

Of course, sometimes an employer has more than one motive for taking some adverse action against an employee. The predominance standard would settle this. Courts that want a more plaintiff-friendly standard could adopt a rule saying that an action was discriminatory whenever it played a substantial, even though not decisive, role in the adverse action.

This approach gets rid of the hand-wringing appellate courts go through over direct evidence versus circumstantial evidence. In particular, too many federal courts over-lawyer and over-judge these cases.[10] These cases should be more about getting simply at the thing we don't like: discriminating against employees because of their race or what have you.

These six examples show how appellate courts might enhance their role in perfecting the law rather than merely repeating past descriptions of it. The examples we reviewed here stand in for dozens of the same ilk. In too many lawsuits, we find courts applying standards that are like many contemporary celebrities—famous for being famous. Like many of these celebrities, the standards are vacuous and easily replaced, and we are aware of them only because we keep seeing them.

We keep seeing them because appellate courts place too high a priority on the mere continuity of having these celebrities perform. They would be better off systematically improving, simplifying, and rationalizing the standards. Many times, this would mean no more than distilling a muddled idea to its essence.

Yes, there is always the danger of the ever-shifting standard. But most often, we need only recognize and make more understandable the unchanging principle at the root of a matter, not change it. Besides, the very reluctance of courts to do this suggests they are unlikely to abandon all cares and start scribbling madly over existing precedents. Indeed, they may not see the merit of doing it all or the way to gain the time to do it.

Deploying law clerks and technology to best advantage could surely help. Courts could aim these judicial resources at clarifying concepts and then creating simple web-based ways to keep up with the latest basic precedents on things like what a proximate cause is, what discrimination is prohibited, and other things the courts deal with every day.

45 : THE BEST
TRIAL COURT DECISIONS
GET STRAIGHT TO SAYING
WHO WINS AND WHY

Now let's consider how trial judges write their decisions and consider whether it's formalism that's making too many of their opinions take too long to write and read while educating us about nothing in particular.

When you read a trial court decision, do you skip to the end? Is the judge's written decision the primary source lawyers use to explain the case outcome, or must they interpret it or give alternative explanations—the judge doesn't like certain lawyers or doesn't like personal injury plaintiffs or always sides with workers?

To illustrate the state of the craft, we can use a trial court decision from California. Again, it's randomly chosen. It illustrates that needless complexity is routine in legal writing and why it reduces respect for the system.

The example is a decision in the California divorce case *McCourt v. McCourt*.[1] It suffers from the organizational mistakes of too many legal opinions.

The problems with the decision start with the law. Rather than discuss the legal standard when considering the facts, the court does the job three times. It includes a discussion and findings about the facts. There is a separate discussion of the applicable legal rules. Then there is a third discussion about the facts and the law together.

As with the Indiana appellate decision, we can read the desiccated recital of the facts, wondering the whole time which of them will be important.

Likewise, when it's introduced, the judge doesn't discuss how divorce law affects the case; he merely recites it at length and with breadth, leaving us ignorant of the role it will play in deciding the case. By the time the court discusses how the law applies to the facts, we have forgotten most of the facts and the law discussed so long before.

Unfortunately, this decision is more confusingly organized than most. It is called a "ruling on submitted matter." It opens with something called a "statement of decision." Is this section a summary of the ruling? Does it describe the whole document?

Anyway, this initial section helpfully points out that the decision is about the validity of three agreements the parties made after they got married (post-nuptial agreements). After that, the initial section is unavailing.

Like many trial decisions, this one starts by reciting docket entries that are exclusively electronic and readily accessible. There may have been a day when a judge's decision was a necessary resource to record the dates on which motions were filed, appearances given, decisions entered, and so on. Those days are long gone, so judges have no reason to distract their readers with this administrative trivia—except to give the appearance of substance through process.

The decision in the California divorce case is a good example of formalism in action. Early on it tells us that on December 9, 2009, the judge decided to try separately the issue of whether the agreements could be enforced. Do we need to know it was on December 9? Would it matter if it were the tenth? Does the date matter at all? The reader is left wondering if it does, so the date takes up a tiny place in the brain long enough to realize that it doesn't matter and neither do the four other specific dates in this short section.

Another digression follows as the decision lists the names of all twelve of the lawyers who participated in the proceedings for no apparent reason. Didn't they file appearances with the clerk? We never hear about them again, so they can't be terribly important to the decision.

From here we learn that oral evidence and documents were received, there was argument, the judge planned to explain his decision in the document, and he promised us that he considered "all the evidence, testimony, the demeanor and credibility of the witnesses the written and oral arguments of counsel, the material and authorities submitted by the parties, and the pleadings, papers and other documents filed with the Court."[2]

Is this useful? Are we reassured? We know the judge isn't the first to put this in a decision. We know it's boilerplate, and because of that, it doesn't likely build confidence. We might prefer to see the judge actually consider and explain the decision rather than read that the judge promises this was done. We see this and resume our search for the meat of the decision.

It doesn't show up quickly. Unfortunately, in its "summary of findings," the court starts by assuring us again that it has "considered the evidence and arguments submitted by the parties in this matter."[3] We wonder if the court protests too much.

Anyway, this summary section then goes on to give the game away without any supporting reasoning. The judge laid out all his conclusions. The upshot is that he invalidated the original agreement and its two supplements.

This section seems to have been written for an appellate court so that it can isolate the key fact conclusions for review. But for us, it's just another roadblock to drive around.

The court said the reason for the ruling amounted to this: the husband could not enforce the agreements because his wife didn't agree to convert—"transmute"—community property she would have a claim against in divorce into separate property she would have no claim against in divorce.

Rather than telling us this, the section has thirteen paragraphs. Several of them merely repeat that the judge found no agreement and that the agreements were set aside. But the decision also tries our patience by discussing arguments that, because of the main ruling, are moot—they don't matter anymore. The judge said the agreement's conditional terms aren't a problem. He found no undue influence. He rejected an argument for severing unenforceable provisions. He found no waiver.

This is the current fashion, but there's not much point to it. There was no agreement at all in the court's view, so why discuss and rule on issues that suppose there was an agreement? Usually, judges do this thinking so that an upper court might uphold their opinion on some alternative ruling they made.

It likely isn't worth the trouble. An alternative ruling might help when it's both distinct and of equal significance with the main ruling. But if a judge holds a case is barred by the statute of limitations, there is little reason for the judge to analyze the twenty-four lesser arguments a party might make. The judge can better use the same time thoroughly explaining the decision that ended the case.

After the judge in the California divorce case summarized his findings, he prepared a "summary of facts." This again is a staple of decisions both high and low. Like most decisions, this one doesn't focus on the facts salient to the decision—that the wife didn't intend the property covered by the agreement to be separate rather than community property.

Instead, it is crowded with meaningless dates and events—reflecting the mistaken notion that this is a kind of scientific data gathering. The case was filed on October 27, 2009. The motion to bifurcate was filed on October 27, 2009. The parties stipulated to the bifurcation on December 3, 2009. In this "summary" of the facts, there are over seventy entirely useless dates.

This fact section, like many others, suffers from another common flaw. It merely records what the witnesses said—data being gathered again. The court recited first the wife's testimony, then the husband's testimony, then each successive witness without suggesting any reason for doing so.

None of this is used in the court's *explanation* of its decision. The decision simply recites the testimony without explaining its significance to the judge. If we are concerned about appeals, courts have recordings and transcripts to tell us who said what at a hearing.

A judge's decision is best when it's written as the judge's opinion. What most people want from decisions are judges' explanations of why they ruled the way they did, not a truncated transcript of the proceedings. The facts could be blended together with the judge's view so we know the facts *and* why they matter. Here are two alternatives:

Formalist Way: The wife testified she was born in Cincinnati, went to school in Chicago, worked at the YWCA, and met her husband in 1979. There was a meeting in Vero Beach, Florida.

There were twelve drafts of the agreement. The wife saw three copies of the agreement and signed it four times.

Alternative: Jane Doe and John Doe may have signed something called an "agreement," but they never agreed. John Doe wanted to shield his business from his wife. Jane Doe wanted only to shield the house she believed they both owned from the debts of the businesses she believed they both owned.

For thirty years, the parties kept their business assets in one name and their family assets in another. Jane Doe was assured by the agreement's drafter that she was getting what she wanted — liability protection for the two of them — not a division of property between them. The document they signed didn't make it obvious she was wrong. Its drafter was inexperienced in California law and didn't use the language normally used to transmute property. And when Jane Doe finally found out what her husband believed the document did, she vigorously protested and demanded changes.

The next section of the court's actual opinion is also typical. Although it's called "discussion," it is dominated by a disembodied summary of the applicable law. As we read it, we never know the significance of the legal rules being recited to the decision about to be made. We try to keep as many of them in our heads as we can for later — in case we need them. In the end, we don't. The case was decided on an elementary ground.

This habit may reflect that judges — or their clerks — have cut and paste legal discussions about specific topics that they lift from other opinions and paste into opinions without integrating them with the facts of the case — one for personal injuries, one for contracts, one for unfair trade practices, and so on. We can suppose that it suggests to the inexperienced observer that the writer is a scholar well versed in the background of the applicable law no matter what the writer actually ends up relying on to decide the case.

But it's usually needless. As in so many cases, there is a basic principle on which the decision turns. A good trial decision can identify that principle precisely. It will be the hub from which the spokes of discussion emerge.

Here, that principle has already been stated simply: you can't force someone to honor an agreement they never made.

A single appellate court decision would have been enough to establish that proposition. But the decision's discussion of the statutes and cases instead takes us on a tour of California law, showing how thickly forested it is with the nuances of community property, transmutation agreements, five-factor tests, rules on the reformation of documents, and so on.

But this digression doesn't change that only one principle mattered—the disagreement about what was being done. This precept cuts straight through the five-factor test the court discussed and the basic rules of contract the court also dwelt on: courts don't enforce purported agreements when the parties don't agree on the same thing. Instead of the fifty to sixty paragraphs the court included on the law, two or three (or even one) sentences might have sufficed: "As the California Supreme Court held in 2005 in *Sherwood v. Redwood,* courts don't force parties to follow agreements they haven't made."

The court's reference to the wide range of law that *might* matter in a case like this reflects lawyers' and judges' tendency to imagine, defend, and dissect the largest numbers of theories they can construct. Again, perhaps it's because it makes them look thorough—scientific even.

But in most cases, courts need only focus on the one or two principles that snugly fit the facts. After that, they should explain in detail how the applicable principles apply to the case. The principles are usually easy to identify. The trial judge's larger task is to explain how the principles apply to the facts in evidence.

Here the legal question was whether the wife agreed to transmute. In personal injury lawsuits, the nature of the duty can usually take a back seat to the question of reasonable behavior. What makes someone's behavior reasonable under the circumstances is often the best focus. This is so in an auto accident—Was the driver paying proper attention? It's also true in the most sophisticated medical malpractice case—Would a reasonable surgeon have applied a clamp when the unanticipated bleeding started?

In contract cases, the parties' agreement is the polestar of the case. Most times, all a judge has to do is read the document to see what the parties agreed on.

Which leads to another thing about this divorce case. All the effort the court put into its decision presumes the document the parties signed was unclear. This may be the right judgment here, but in most contract cases, none of the evidence this decision dwells on need be admitted. The well-understood rule in contract cases is that with a completely integrated written contract, the plain language of the agreement controls the case, not what the parties say they thought it meant.[4]

Contract cases are too often complicated by the tendency of courts to accept evidence outside of the written agreement itself even when a reasonable reader has no trouble understanding what the parties meant. Some courts see it as a belt-and-suspenders way to get their decisions upheld—it comes out the same from the words as it does from the testimony.

But the testimony about what was "really meant" is often so distortedly self-interested that it merely absorbs time and money. Perhaps we can't plainly understand the meaning of a badly written document that doesn't reflect an understanding of the California rules about transmutation. But the transmutation case *may* be a rare exception. The trouble is that in too many ordinary cases the courts hear the testimony anyway and even needlessly pass the issue off to a jury.

Most cases can be decided by one or two legal principles applied to a limited range of facts. If lawyers and judges focused on them, the discussion of what matters might improve and the discussion of what doesn't matter might be eliminated.

Let's look at a few more trial court decisions. We can contrast how different courts handle the same issue.

The legal-writing consultant Ross Guberman showcased dozens of well-written opinions in *Point Taken: How to Write Like the World's Best Judges*.[5] One of them is by Southern District of New York Judge Jed Rakoff. Mr. Guberman says it is an example of what he calls the "teaser opener." Mr. Guberman's book considers a variety of styles in opening an opinion. Some feature the facts—some tease about the basic question, act as a trailer, or even offer a sound bite.

The syllogism is a favorite of some, including Bryan Garner. It can work well if it is coupled with a meaningful discussion. If it's not, it's mere formalism.

A ruling might use a syllogism this way: "Intentional infliction of emotional distress requires intentional or reckless conduct. The party suing here hasn't alleged any. Therefore, their complaint must be dismissed." Judge Richard Posner, Justice Antonin Scalia, and Chief Justice John Roberts regularly used them.

But there is no reason to adhere rigidly to any specific view. Instead, we should see it as a literary choice. It's art, not science. Some tales are best told from the beginning. Some tales aren't really tales at all. They explore an idea, and the tale is secondary. In other cases, to persuade, judges might first seek to disarm their audience by showing they understand their point of view. That's what Judge Rakoff seemed to be doing with Occupy Wall Street protestors in his 2012 civil rights decision in *Garcia v. Bloomberg*:

> What a huge debt this nation owes to its "troublemakers." From Thomas Paine to Martin Luther King, Jr., they have forced us to focus on problems we would prefer to downplay or ignore. Yet it is often only with hindsight that we can distinguish those troublemakers who brought us to our senses from those who were simply . . . troublemakers. Prudence, and respect for the constitutional rights to free speech and free association, therefore dictate that the legal system cut all non-violent protesters a fair amount of slack.
>
> These observations are prompted by the instant lawsuit, in which a putative class of some 700 or so "Occupy Wall Street" protesters contend they were unlawfully arrested while crossing the Brooklyn Bridge on October 1, 2011. More narrowly, the pending motion to dismiss the suit raises the issue of whether a reasonable observer would conclude that the police who arrested the protesters had led the protesters to believe that they could lawfully march on the Brooklyn Bridge's vehicular roadway.[6]

Judge Rakoff went on to deny some of the protestors' larger claims against the mayor of New York and his senior leaders—a ruling for the establishment against those who claim it's rotten to its core. But he softened the blow by placing the protesters in the pantheon with Thomas Paine and Martin Luther King. He softened it more by allowing parts of the claim to proceed against officers who failed to give them fair warning before arresting them.

Judge Rakoff did more than soften the blow with his ruling. He captured his audience with what Guberman calls a teaser. Readers are engaged because there is a greater issue at stake—one we could all consider. But probably the most important thing is what he didn't do. Unlike most courts, he didn't consign the central thing he had to say to oblivion by making the center of his decision needlessly complex.

Now let's look at how a typical civil rights ruling began from a different judge of the same New York federal court in 2021. The decision was about the same police department and concerned a similar complaint about abuse during an arrest:

> In August 2019, Plaintiff Aliyah Baker ("Plaintiff") brought this action under 42 U.S.C. § 1983 against five police officers and the City of New York (collectively, "Defendants"), alleging various constitutional and state law violations stemming from her arrest in June 2018. Defendants now move for partial summary judgment under Rule 56 of the Federal Rules of Civil Procedure. See ECF No. 41. Plaintiff opposes and seeks to amend her complaint for a second time under Rule 15 of the Federal Rules of Civil Procedure. See ECF Nos. 44, 45. For the reasons discussed below, Defendants' motion for summary judgment is granted in part and denied in part, and Plaintiff's motion for leave to amend is denied.[7]

Like the others, this opinion isn't outstandingly bad; it's just unfortunately typical. Who is this opening information for? The parties' lawyers already know all this. The parties themselves can't understand any of this. Those seeking to understand the law learn nothing from this.

It only gets less accessible as we soldier on through the opinion. As with the Los Angeles divorce opinion, it moved next to disembodied details about the facts and procedural posture. Do we need the precise address of the apartment? The date of the plaintiff's court dates? That she was released on her own recognizance? The precinct number of the officers? The names of officers uninvolved but present? Will we hear about them later? We do, but we have no way to know it when

FIGURE 45.1. *"Complexity made simple."*

they are introduced. Does the date the complaint was filed matter? Not this time—but how would we know?

Does it matter when the partial motion for summary judgment was filed? Again, we are left wondering why these things are important to the court's decision. We can pity judges who think they should drag themselves through lengthy procedural and factual irrelevancies, but we can place a reasonable bet they didn't do it—their law clerks did.

Now let's see how it might have begun. Here's an approach that introduces us to the facts, the legal standard, and the court's ruling in one long—but we can hope engaging—sentence. It then gives us the salient facts and a proper citation to the binding legal rule:

> During an arrest for a minor crime—where the officers were in no danger, where the accused says she cried out about a shoulder injury, where she claims she begged the officers to desist—the court should submit her brutality claim to a jury, especially when she swears the police manhandled her into cuffs, tossed her about needlessly, and twisted her arms.

This arrest was only for an illegal eviction. Aliyah Baker locked her frequently drunken husband out of their apartment, and the police arrested her for doing it. They never claimed she was a danger to them when they arrested her. They never claimed she was resisting. They claim only that she is exaggerating.

As the United States Supreme Court reminded us in 1989 in *Graham v. Connor*, the Fourth Amendment ban on unreasonable search and seizures bars the police from using excessive force when arresting people. The court in *Graham* said we can identify excess by considering the severity of the crime, the danger to police and others, and whether the accused is actively resisting arrest.

This opening is important to the lawyers. It should help them accept that the case is a good one for a jury. It can help the parties too. They can actually understand the words used, and they know which way the case is headed. For those who wish to learn about the law, the Fourth Amendment language is invoked—not just the rulings about it. We can learn in a single sentence, without seeing several courts cited as saying the same thing, what the nation's highest court says we should consider when deciding whether the amendment is violated. The actual decision cited six cases when one would have been enough.

Let's try one more area of the law—class actions. Let's consider how a trial court judge served up the red meat of the decision in his opening words. In most cases, it's a hungry hunt for it. Not so with Judge Richard Posner's 2015 opinion where he sat as a district court judge in *Johnansen v. GVN Michigan*:

> The defendant in this class action suit under the Telephone Consumer Protection Act has moved to dismiss the suit both as an individual suit and as a class action suit. The motion and supporting memorandum are intemperate and borderline frivolous, and I warn the defendant that if it persists in this vein of hyperbole and indignation it and its counsel will be courting sanctions, which I will not hesitate to impose.
>
> The defendant argues that the class is overbroad. This is both erroneous for the reasons explained by the plaintiff and premature. An overbroad class can be shrunk to eliminate

the overbreadth; overbreadth is thus not a per se ground for dismissal. The defendant's further argument that the TCPA can't be enforced by a class action is frivolous.

> The defendant also argues as a ground for dismissal that the plaintiff has not pleaded that he had not consented to the telemarketing calls that he claims violated the TCPA. He pleaded a violation of the statute; he didn't need to plead the affirmative defense of consent—the burden is on the defendant to plead affirmative defenses. Furthermore, far from consenting to the calls, the plaintiff had listed his number on the "National Do Not Call Registry."[8]

No need to explain what Judge Posner means.

Now let's take one last painful look at how most trial courts handle a similar job. We won't start where the opinion starts—no point in suffering through that again. Let's try instead to find the heart of what a trial court has to say about an attack on a class action lawsuit and see how it compares with Judge Posner's work. Picking at random as usual, we'll look at a 2020 decision of the US District Court for the District of Nevada. After all the preliminaries about the case's procedural posture and the already-familiar standard on a motion to dismiss, let's see how it addresses the question of dismissal of a class action under the same Telephone Consumer Protection Act:

> There are two salient issues in the instant motion. First, is whether Caplan has standing to bring this claim. Second is whether ringless voicemail messages ("RVMS") are "calls" under the TCPA.
>
> Budget argues that this court should dismiss Caplan's claims because Caplan consented to receiving the calls, therefore negating the injury-in-fact required for Article III standing. (See ECF No. 14). Caplan challenges that factual assertion by claiming he did not consent. (See ECF No. 24).
>
> Courts in the Ninth Circuit have not held that lack of consent is a requisite element of a TCPA claim. Consent is an affirmative defense to the merits of Caplan's claim, not a bar to his constitutional standing. See Van Patten v. Vertical Fitness Group, LLC, 847 F.3d 1037, 1042–43 (9th Cir. 2017); Grant v.

Capital Mgmt. Servs. L.P., 449 Fed. App'x 598, 600 n.1 (citing 23 F.C.C.R. 559, 565 (Dec. 28, 2007)). Therefore, Budget's argument that Caplan lacks standing as a result of his purported consent is misplaced. Caplan "need not allege any additional harm beyond the one Congress has identified" when bringing a TCPA claim. Van Patten, 847 F.3d at 1043.

The second issue is whether RVMS constitute calls under the TCPA. RVM technology allows a message to be placed in a recipient's voicemail without the recipient's phone ever ringing. (See ECF No. 14 at 2). The two incident "calls" Caplan claims violated the TCPA were RVMS. See id. at 3. Budget essentially argues that because there is no actual call or communication between the two parties, RVMS are not calls. See id. Caplan argues that leaving a voicemail is still an attempt to communicate, regardless of whether his phone actually rings. (See ECF No. 24).

This appears to be an issue of first impression before this court. The TCPA provides as follows:

It shall be unlawful for any person within the United States, or any person outside the United States if the recipient is within the United States—

(A) to make any call (other than a call made for emergency purposes or made with the prior express consent of the called party) using any automatic telephone dialing system or an artificial or prerecorded voice . . .

(iii) to any telephone number assigned to a paging service, cellular telephone service, specialized mobile radio service, or other radio common carrier service, or any service for which the called party is charged for the call 47 U.S.C. § 227. Courts in other jurisdictions have ruled that RVMS are calls under the TCPA. See, e.g., Saunders v. Dyck O'Neal, Inc., 319 F. Supp. 3d 907, 911 (W.D. Mich. 2018). While the Ninth Circuit has yet to address RVMS specifically, it has ruled that methods of communication other than traditional phones calls, like text messages, are calls within the scope of the TCPA. See Satterfield v. Simon & Schuster, Inc., 569 F.3d 946, 952 (9th Cir. 2009).

The Satterfield court reasoned that the TCPA was designed to stop invasions of privacy arising from any attempt to get in contact with the recipient related to their phone number; thus, an unsolicited text message would qualify as a call that the statute sought to prevent. Id. at 954. The Satterfield court construed the TCPA as primarily designed to prevent nuisance and invasion of privacy. Id. In addition, the TCPA is a remedial statute, and "should be construed broadly to effectuate its purposes." Saunders, 319 F. Supp. 3d at 911. Under that definition, RVMs are also calls under the TCPA.

Budget attempts to distinguish RVMs from phone calls, text messages, and traditional voicemails by asserting that RVMs are not delivered over the cell phone carrier's network, making them more akin to the broader "information services" category of communication not regulated by the TCPA. (See ECF No. 14 at 14). The FCC has previously extended the TCPA's coverage to include internet-to-phone text messaging, finding that a focus on the means used to initiate the communication "would elevate form over substance, thwart Congressional intent that evolving technologies not deprive mobile customers of the TCPA's protections, and potentially open a floodgate of unwanted text messages to wireless customer." In the Matter of Implementing the Tel. Consumer Prot. Act of 1991, 30 FCC Rcd. 7961, 8019 (2015).

This court finds that the TCPA is applicable to RVMs for the same reason. Focusing on the method of delivery, as Budget would have the court do, elevates form over substance. At bottom, RVMs are still a nuisance delivered to the recipient's phone by means of the phone number. RVMs are calls as defined by the TCPA. The court denies Budget's motion to dismiss.[9]

This is a typical trial court decision. It loses us in its attempt to appear thorough. It principally relies on other courts' decisions—even those that don't bind it—without saying why it followed them. It quotes more of the act than it needs—notice that Judge Posner explained what mattered in the act without quoting it at all. We can suppose if there was some likely contention over what the act said or something about the phrasing that mattered, then longer quotations might help. But most times readers don't doubt that legal writers—particularly judges—are stating the real terms of the law, and we don't have to set them forth at length to be credible.

The result here is that Judge Posner decided the question with 204 words and left us in no doubt as to what he was saying. The Nevada Court decided essentially the same thing with 767 words, and it was not only a chore to read, but it will be burdensome to convert what it says into plain language.

Here is what the Nevada judge could have said without losing anything a reader needs to know. The first issue is the claim that Caplan consented:

> Budget says Caplan has no standing to sue because he hasn't alleged lack of consent to the calls. But in 2017 the Ninth Circuit in *Van Patten v. Vertical Fitness Group, LLC* held that consent is a defense Budget itself must prove. Caplan doesn't have to allege that he didn't consent.
>
> Budget also claims a voicemail isn't a call—after all the phone didn't ring. But the act prohibits making "any call." It says nothing about ringing telephones or the call being answered. That's undoubtedly why in 2009, in *Satterfield v. Simon & Schuster*, the Ninth Circuit held that a text message is a call under the act.[10] There is no reason not to treat the two things the same way. The form of the message must not prevail over the reality of receiving it.

That's the heart of the dismissal decision in 130 words. Is there something important missing? On one question there is a binding authority. On that point, the lower court has no cause to debate the court that oversees it. On the second point, common sense prevailed in both versions. The act is designed to block annoying messages aimed at consumers—whether they hear the message live or on a voicemail recording.

The last call for a well-written opinion about telecommunication agitation was answered by Justice Neil Gorsuch in *Henson v. Santander Consumer USA Inc.* where he begins as follows:

Disruptive dinnertime calls, downright deceit, and more besides drew Congress's eye to the debt collection industry. From that scrutiny emerged the Fair Debt Collection Practices Act, a statute that authorizes private lawsuits and weighty fines designed to deter wayward collection practices. So perhaps it comes as little surprise that we now face a question about who exactly qualifies as a "debt collector" subject to the Act's rigors. Everyone agrees that the term embraces the repo man—someone hired by a creditor to collect an outstanding debt. But what if you purchase a debt and then try to collect it for yourself—does that make you a "debt collector" too? That's the nub of the dispute now before us.[11]

Whether it's about what goes in the complaint that initiates the lawsuit or the evidence that the parties present at trial, courts should push everything else out of the way and get to the salient facts. Trial judges who wish to rid their opinions of needless complexity should do at least seven things:

- Delete procedural-posture sections. Use only what's needed and only where it's needed in the opinion.
- Delete sections on legal standards. Weave the standard into your ruling.
- Delete summaries of the facts. Weave the facts that matter into the ruling.
- Begin with an engaging treatment of the main fact issue and how it relates to the key legal principle.
- Decide the case. Don't decide things not needed to decide the case.
- Use a single binding precedent where it's needed.
- Use nonbinding cases sparingly—only when the reasoning as opposed to the outcome is compelling.

The best technique may be for judges to start with how they might explain their ruling to someone sitting next to them on a park bench. This view is almost always a product of the judge's opinion of the facts against the content of a basic legal principle—lying, cheating, stealing, carelessness, and the like. The rest of the opinion gets built around the judge's plain statement of who won and why.

46 : NEEDLESS COMPLEXITY OBSCURES OUR BASICALLY HONEST COURTS

The legal profession shouldn't overlook the danger of growing deflection and complexity in the courts. Neither should the public.

But before we go further into this broader view of what's at stake, let's remember that American courts are an American strength. Indeed, to modify what some say Churchill said about democracy, American courts are the worst courts on earth until we consider the alternatives.

Legal systems in many of the world's largest countries aren't just flawed; they are corrupt. The United States is the only country among the world's ten most populous nations with basically honest courts. Consider China. Bribery continues to be pervasive in the Chinese courts at even the highest level.[1] Say what you want about our courts, you can't say bribery is their mainstay.

India is apparently worse. Transparency International says that India has the highest rate of bribery for public services, including in its courts, in all of Asia.[2]

Need we speak of Russia? Russia is the paradigm for how the absence of the rule of law—the lack of honest and reasonably efficient courts—can hold back an entire economy.[3] With no one's life or property safe from grasping oligarchs aligned with an autocratic and acquisitive state, hopes for a prosperous Russia have been dashed. When you invested in Russia, you gambled. Russia's invasion of Ukraine proved it was a bad bet. Businesses lost billions pulling out of that benighted land.

There is corruption in American courts. But it can't be called pervasive. Indeed, small sample sizes have made studying bribery in the

United States difficult and the that can't only be explained by the se-
crecy of the activity.[4] What corruption there is in American courts
is usually merely petty and is, at worst, only corrosive. Judges may
subconsciously favor lawyers they like. They may subconsciously give
in to the profit motives of those billing parts of the bar who prefer
inefficient courts, slow-moving cases, long trials, and repeated court
appearances. Elected judges may worry about alienating groups of
voters or contributors. Human biases are, of course, a problem too.

But no one can be perfectly neutral. Judges should acknowledge
their humanity and fallibility. They need only point out that our
constitution never set out to create a perfect union, only "a more
perfect union."

The trouble with our courts isn't real corruption. It's that after
flowing so many years, the mighty river of American law has dug itself deeper into the ground. It is less irrigating to commerce. It is
less accessible to the people. Its great arteries have become clogged.
Its edicts are muddy. Without a unifying, organizing vision of what
courts do, needless complexity clogs the system, and with needless
complexity comes needless obloquy.

None of this means that our courts' decisions are generally any
more wrong than they are corrupt. Another strength of American
courts is that they usually rule for the correct party—including, or
especially, juries. This is not to be understated. But, remember, the
trouble is that this only applies when a court makes a decision, and
the courts decide almost none of the cases that come before them.
The other problem is that when they do decide cases, court decisions
by judges too often hide their reasoning and focus almost entirely on
things besides the central issues of a case. Juries, of course, only pick a
winner. They might answer a few questions, but juries don't give reasons for their decisions and probably can't because individual jurors
might agree on the result without agreeing on the reason for it. The
problem with our courts is not that they are corrupt. It's not that they
make incompetent choices. It's that they too often make no choices at
all, and when they do choose, we can't understand why.

Reducing needless complexity in the courts can reverse this trend.
We could have human-centered justice—demystified, accountable,
and even faith affirming. We could have justice in which judges see

themselves as problem solvers—village elders who apply and pass on the lessons of experience through wisdom. If we did, we could potentially strengthen public confidence in the judiciary. Confidence in the judiciary may mean that this most modest branch could help buck up public faith in the other two branches of government. At least it could mean that the judiciary might escape their evident free fall in public esteem.

We can see the problem with what we're doing as we chart the growth of alternative ways to resolve disputes. This book has been about ways to do that. Now let's consider a few obstacles.

47 : LAWYERS MUST DISCARD OUTDATED BUSINESS MODELS

What can lawyers do to improve their prospects? Lawyers are court officers. They have ethical duties to promote justice. But we can't forget that most of them are also in business—they never do. And they are in a business with too much competition. There are too many lawyers chasing too few clients, and bigger law firms aren't necessarily better law firms.

Lawyers might consider a couple of ways to escape this dilemma. First, they might reduce the number of lawyers. They should be concerned about the certification of new law schools—especially those for profit. They should beware of many schools' lopsided concern with money rather than scholarship. They should help eliminate some schools' fraudulent claims to prospective students about job opportunities.

Law school troubles peaked following the Great Recession of 2007 to 2009, and applications since then have mostly declined, but the needless surplus of law schools and underqualified law school graduates remain a concern. In the wake of the worst of it, this glut led to stories like the *Atlantic*'s 2014 article "The Law School Scam" and the *New York Times* 2011 article "Is Law School a Losing Game?"[1] And one sure sign that the surfeit of needless graduates continued is that ten years after the Great Recession, unqualified law school graduates were still dragging down bar-exam passing rates.

Overall pass rates in California were 49 percent in 2009, and in 2018 they were 36 percent. Overall pass rates in Illinois were 84 percent in 2009, and by 2018 they had dropped to 66 percent. For the same period, New York overall rates fell from 65 percent to 56 percent, and North Carolina rates dropped from 67 percent to 47 percent.[2]

But this means the exam was doing its job. It's too bad that not everyone sees it that way. As of 2021, California and Rhode Island had lowered their cut rates, and other states were thinking of following suit.[3] They shouldn't. It won't increase public faith in the justice system to flood the bar with even more lawyers with even lower qualifications. Law schools should be more selective than they are now, and bar exams should remind those schools that merely graduating isn't enough to make their students lawyers.

About this, we should be offended by the idea pushed by some that that bar standards might be lowered to encourage greater diversity in the bar. It's insulting because it assumes that diverse potential lawyers are inherently less qualified than other potential lawyers and can't be taught.

A diverse bar is a better bar. But why encourage the talentless rather than find talent among desirable groups and get them to apply to law school and sit for the bar? Are you saying they aren't out there?

The bench and bar should see that young children in diverse communities understand the rule of law through school visits by judges and lawyers and court visits by school children. And financial considerations should never keep diverse students out of law school. The money spent by lawyers on diversity consultants, diversity policies at big firms, and advertising diversity in the legal profession would be better spent helping *qualified* prelaw and law students pay their tuition. Talent should be identified, encouraged, and welcomed from diverse groups.

The second thing lawyers might do is reconsider the billable hour before it destroys them. Most hourly wages are relics of the assembly line and the industrial age, when routine producers of goods had only a small, monotonous job to do all day—tighten a bolt, box a product, collect a toll, stamp a document. Since their output was predictably tied to the number of hours they spent at their routine, the hour was the best measure of their productivity. Jobs like this are mostly gone in the United States, and the rest are disappearing.

In many realms, a steady client rebellion has taken place against the billable hour. Lawyers who defend personal injury cases for insurance companies used to glory in the billable hour. They would charge a low rate. But they could grab a half dozen insurance-defense files, go off to court for some minor motion practice, and bill all six cases for the same block of time while waiting in line at the courthouse. One hundred dollars an hour became six hundred dollars an hour. Pure gravy.

If there are lawyers still doing this, they are the fortunate few. Most insurance companies won't accept that anymore and have imposed sharp restrictions on the number of hours defense lawyers may charge them. And it's not just insurance companies. In 2017, a report commissioned by Georgetown and Thomson Reuters reported the effective death of the commercial law billable hour, noting its nominal predominance but also the rise of budget caps that have left it a square peg seeking admission to a round hole.[4]

Many companies have taken matters entirely into their own hands, hiring in-house lawyers and paying them modest salaries to defend cases. Such lawyers are easy to find. With too many graduates chasing too few positions, it's a buyer's market for in-house legal talent. As a 2021 Harvard report about corporate law departments noted, "insourcing is among the most visible, discussed trends in the legal market in the past decade."[5] Doubtless, this trend will continue.

Commercial litigators are notable casualties in the demise of the billable hourly, not only because of caps that lower fees and lawyer increases at general counsel offices. Commercial litigation itself has been declining for years. Commercial litigators shouldn't scratch their heads over this. The economy has been up and down, yet even in the up years, the long-term volume of commercial litigation has been headed down.[6]

Commercial litigation is too expensive. It lasts too long. It punishes those who bring the litigation as much as those who receive it. Yet too many lawyers still think the answer is to bleed dry every billable commercial case they can get a hold of. They're only accelerating the extinction of their species.

Lawyers have bills to pay. We can understand why they give in to short-term pressures. But courts have no such interest. Indeed, courts are better off considering the long-term best interest of the justice system and acting accordingly.

This book shows how the courts can serve those long-term interests by clarifying the justice system, but it recognizes that things are getting worse instead of better. There's less litigation, but it's lasting

FIGURE 47.1. *"A third of the buck stops here."*

longer. Courts are moving slower, not faster, despite having greater resources, more judges than ever, and fewer trials.

So, what should lawyers do? Of course, there is a different dynamic in every field of the law. But let's deal with a few of the biggest. For them it's about aligning their interests more with their clients.

Lawyers who represent plaintiffs in exchange for a percentage of the recovery get closest to having things right. This approach is used in personal injury cases, in employment cases, civil rights cases, and even in some commercial cases. The faster the case is over and the bigger the recovery, the happier the lawyer is and the happier the client is.

But what about the other side? How can lawyers in these cases align their interests with their clients?

It depends on what their clients want. But many—maybe most— want to end litigation successfully, sooner rather than later, and for the lowest possible price. The real question is whether they can be persuaded to pay a premium to meet all these goals given that they aren't meeting any of them now.[7]

If they understand the dynamic at work, these clients should be willing. After all, they shouldn't punish their lawyers for winning big and winning early. But that's what happens with the billable hour, and most lawyers and some clients can't see beyond it.

If business clients know their own best interests, they will reward their lawyers for achieving a quick win. This can be done in several ways. First, they might negotiate a minimum fee—win or lose—with their lawyers. That number might be linked to the value of the dispute and the complexity of the case. How much money could it cost us if we lose? What percentage of that are we willing to pay to win instead? How many hurdles must be cleared to win? The more complex the hurdles, the higher the initial fee. The minimum fee shouldn't be so generous as to leave the lawyers indifferent to the outcome, and it shouldn't be so stingy that the lawyers would rather give the whole thing a miss than take a risk. The money must be enough for the lawyer to be willing to try the case to receive this sum—but with no incentive to intentionally drag it out.

That thinking might help in business litigation, but it could be a useful guide in divorce and other litigation. We know the fee in a divorce case is likely excessive when it exceeds the net worth of the parties, and yet this happens regularly. Unusually intricate custody matters might be an exception to this, but we should remember that too much of the money spent on custody fights is about the bitterness of the parties rather than the betterment of their babies. Lawyers should abet these abuses as little as possible.

Even the humble dog bite case can benefit from a realistic view of fees. What's the likely amount of damages? A lump sum fee could be set up front based upon a combination of a percentage of how much might have to be paid out in a loss and recognizing that the cases aren't likely to be complex. Damages likely around $40,000. Flat fee, win or lose likely around $15,000. The lawyer may prefer not to try the case, but the lawyer has lost the fee leverage they usually deploy to force a settlement.

And that's not quite enough. Lawyers might pick up further useful incentives from a series of win bonuses. One sum could cover any win and others could create bonuses for winning at ever-earlier stages. A client might pay a fixed sum for a dismissal with prejudice on the face of the complaint. About half that for winning on summary judgment after discovery. A sum based on settlement. And so on.

Of course, any approach like this assumes a savvy system in which those paying know how to weigh each potential payment against the backdrop of a unique case. But this might be good news. It might open opportunities for the legal profession. Experienced trial counsel—especially semiretired lawyers or retired judges—might charge a flat fee for evaluating cases and advising institutions on the structure to propose to law firms. Bidding might ensue.

Most firms have tried a variety of alternative fee arrangements, including this type. Those based upon success fit what are often called "value-based" fee arrangements. Many companies have caught on to this idea. But there is still a large disconnect between business clients and law firms. A 2021 Deloitte snapshot called "Value-Based Pricing: Aligning the Cost and the Value of Legal Services" noted that while corporate legal departments are anxious for alternatives to the traditional billable hour, most of them perceive law firms as clinging to the past. Eighty-six percent of corporate legal departments thought their law firms did a bad job at suggesting alternative fee arrangements that met their needs.[8] In other words, most firms have tried alternative fee arrangements because their clients demand it, not because the law firms themselves see it as a competitive advantage for themselves. Many firms fear they won't make quite as much on the individual case—in the short term—and institutionally that's as far as they can see.

What they may not see is that smaller fees and faster results might actually increase business. Rather than doing anything to avoid litigation—mediation, arbitration, or what have you—parties might be more willing to go to court. They could spend what they save on professional mediators or arbitrators on their lawyers.

Indeed, maybe courts could become a low-cost, speedy alternative to arbitration. This could happen just as the business of arbitration expands and strains itself—just as it's bound to take longer and cost more as arbitrators suffer from the same pressures and practices that have made the court system so sclerotic. International litigators have known this for a long time. As far back as 2008, a Pricewaterhouse-Coopers study revealed that 40 percent of in-house counsel complained that international arbitration was more expensive than litigation—arbitration was taking longer, filling up with experts, and costing more every year.[9]

And there is another thing. Law firm efficiency suffers from the billable hour. Nothing drives talent out of our largest law firms more than billable-hour quotas and the treadmill it puts a young lawyer on—early in the morning and late into the night. Lawyers measuring their lives in tenths of hours only see the years slipping away while they do things that take up time but aren't necessarily meaningful. This includes things like generating and responding to needlessly complicated discovery requests, filing and responding to needlessly complex and prolific motions, and writing and responding to needlessly complex briefing.[10]

No doubt lawyers will have trouble seeing this possible world. Some will see a thousand obstacles to realizing it. And, yes, there are obstacles to any kind of change. Still others may assure themselves they have already taken care of all this. Secretly they know that's not quite true.

In any case, a short time ago people also said that remote hearings and trials were an absurd notion—and yet now they're here to stay, and lawyers are taking them in stride. It took a pandemic to realize this. Maybe lawyers will realize there's a slow-moving disease killing off litigation right now, and they will start collectively and individually devoting more resources to reinventing themselves. Or maybe they won't.

48 : COURTS MUST REIMAGINE THEMSELVES

By virtue of their authority, judges are in the best position to change the way the courts do business. The trouble is that they have the least incentive to change. Judges have had full careers before they reach the bench. It's hard for them to change now. And, most of all, some of them might perceive that they have nothing to gain from routine-wrenching change.

But judges may see that some of the suggestions in this book can make their lives easier. Many factors create unnecessary work for judges: the long lags in briefing; the need to plod through transcripts; the seeming compulsion to decorate their decisions with tangential case law, endless procedural posturing, laborious recounting of the claims of both sides, all of which has to be scribed and proofread many times and sometimes—in courts of appeal—by many people.

If the judge's main job in writing a decision is to explain what they did and why they did it in plain language, the job might be easier. Judges might speak in their own voices and speak easier. Tedious written motion practice about discovery could disappear from their lives, and, drawing on experience, they might discern from the bench what is really being sought and decide whether it really ought to be had.

Judicial education is key. More resources in this area should be devoted to the nuts and bolts of judging. How to decide from the bench. How to schedule realistically. How to solicit agreement about what's uncontested, and how to manage the time at trial more proactively than in the past.

Most court systems have some form of judicial institute. Many have regular programs to introduce judges to nuances in the law or to intensify their understanding of contemporary problems. The Federal Judicial Center carries this out for federal judges, and there are many judges' organizations that do the same thing locally and nationally. New judges get lectures about everything from courthouse security to employee benefits. But not enough judicial education focuses on the nuts and bolts of being a judge. Every system should focus on having evolving, innovating annual programs on at least four things:

- innovative ways to manage pretrial discovery
- efficient decision-making
- efficient trial management
- efficient legal writing

49 : RETHINKING LAW CLERKING CAN REMAKE THE FUTURE

New lawyers, especially law clerks, might be the most important people. Law clerks are often the best and brightest of the next wave of lawyers. They are the accomplished litigators of tomorrow. They are the judges of the day after that. Most importantly, they aren't stuck in their ways.

Many of them served on law reviews. These too-little-read periodicals are a good place for the next generation of lawyers to start improving legal discourse by making them more relevant and readable.

Of course, law reviews must be scholarly, but they are too often obscure or obtuse. Too often, student work in particular comes out as a series of footnotes connected with a few lines of text. They are bastions of the past instead of a training ground for future innovation.

Yes, law review articles can still be complex; we can continue to welcome their frequent reliance on mathematical formulas, symbolic logic, and existentialist philosophy. But perhaps more effort should be given to more humanly relevant expression.

Fortunately, these venerable institutions have begun to recognize the problem themselves. As of 2022, the law reviews at Duke, Berkeley, Columbia, Cornell, Georgetown, Harvard, Michigan, Stanford, Texas, Penn, Virginia, and Yale joined in condemning the ever-expanding law review article and insisted that work submitted to their publications not exceed thirty-five thousand words.[1]

This is an achievement. But we shouldn't be gleeful. This means that an ordinary law review article is likely to remain almost half the length of this book. Still, the innovation was long overdue. Duke reported that it was inspired to change by a 2004 Harvard survey of law faculty indicating that 90 percent of them thought law review articles were too long. Perhaps they realized two things. One, too many law review articles were being read only by other law professors, and, two, if they were going to be forced to read them, they may as well go easier on their eyes.

Up to now, many law review articles have suggested to budding lawyers that scholarship exists for its own sake. Under the pretext of original insight, some of the densest things written by professors in law reviews seem to have as their only goal bending the brain in ways only a few can follow—like Judge Posner's Bayesian adventure. This process delights some writers and academics, but too often they inspire readers only to close the article and look elsewhere for insights—YouTube, for instance.

Law reviews should, more often than they are, be platforms for the development of law in court. We need only inject more life into them. If law students could publish and produce more relevant and more accessible law reviews including more matters linked to what's going on daily in court, it would be an excellent preparation for these future lawyers to write relevant, vital briefs and legal opinions. These

FIGURE 49.1. *"Thank you, Nathaniel. I think you, too, are a very scary young lawyer."*

soon-to-be lawyers can lead the way or join the herd. They are our best hope. They have no vested interest in the status quo.

They certainly don't need much incentive to resist prevailing practices. They need only consider what the current model for the best of them looks like: the caterpillar labors at the law review during school and enters the chrysalis of the judicial clerkship only to emerge not as a butterfly, but a moth, circling, circling the stupefying sacred flame of the billable hour only, after years of devotion, to burn out and up with a fizzling *phhht* noise from flying too close to that flame once too oft.

50 : RECOGNIZE NEEDFUL COMPLEXITY AND MEANINGFUL FORMALITY

Urging lawyers and judges in their own interest to eliminate needless complexity in court is not the same as promoting mindless simplicity and contemptuous informality. Far from it. The law is a faith-based business. *Needless* complexity, formulas that obscure the real reasons we do things, undercuts that faith.

But we shouldn't end our discussion without acknowledging that faith can be increased by recognizing needful complexity when it exists—by recognizing that not every question has an easy solution. We make trouble when we don't recognize easy solutions that exist, but we also make trouble when we don't explain the uneasy solutions we must sometimes accept. When judges and lawyers are honest about the difficulties of their positions—when they reflect those difficulties meaningfully in their analysis—they do us a service.

Recognizing complexity is a central theme in Wharton professor Adam Grant's 2021 book, *Think Again: The Power of Knowing What You Don't Know*. It urges that we can't solve complex problems—for our purposes, think abortion, the death penalty, the rights of the religious versus those of sexual minorities, and the like—by oversimplifying them. Certainly, we can't deal credibly with them by beclouding them with meaningless process and rigid assumptions. Instead, Professor Grant urges that we gain by admitting our own limitations by candidly recognizing and weighing the best arguments on both sides, by admitting we are fallible, even that we may be wrong. Sometimes we can help persuade people in new directions by asserting solutions and other times merely by raising questions. Above all, we make progress by being open to change, by remembering that our assumptions may be wrong.[1]

One goal of this persuasion process in law is to build confidence in our institutions. Professor Grant's is an enthusiastically scientific approach. But would he agree that science too has limits? It is called the "art of persuasion," not the "science of persuasion."

That kind of persuasion as practiced by lawyers and judges is most effective when it's aimed first at building faith in our courts—through deserving faith. That's why rethinking the mechanics of a lawsuit is the chief focus of this book. Once faith is earned, it can only help to show the inner article of faith outwardly by manifesting our respect for the court as an institution.

This means that opposing needless complexity isn't about removing the dignity from traditional court proceedings. On the contrary, we should ask ourselves just how much we might really lose if our society cast off any more of the outward shows of respect we give each other and our institutions. Is America stronger or weaker when the losing side in an election calls the winner "not my president," as members of both parties have done to the last two presidents?

Professor Grant would doubtless approve of the fact that it was not a church that a few years ago praised the value of rituals like those we observe when we refer to fellow lawyers as "counsel" and stand when judges and jurors enter a courtroom. Instead, it was two behavioral scientists from Harvard Business School, Francesca Gino and Michael Norton. To them, ritual can help with everything from empowering performance to assuaging grief.[2] Rather than tear ritual down altogether, we should reflect on how in court it can help reflect and reinforce public respect for legal institutions and the sense of duty to them held by judges and lawyers. In court, we address one another formally. We show respect for each other—even our adversaries, and even the guilty. We work in a formal place in a formal way. Yes, moments of levity can relieve tension. And we can show humanity while doing our best—though we sometimes fail—to keep our patience and our dignity.

The rise of remote court proceedings doesn't have to reduce our respect for court proceedings either. As it stands now, there are some challenges as remote court has become common even while lacking common protocol. Every judicial branch should consider rules for remote court.

We can all meet in virtual courtrooms by sharing a common background picture—wherever the judge is, the judge can appear on the bench and the parties can appear in the courtroom before the judge. No one should appear in court from a car—not to mention a moving one. Lawyers should continue to wear what they would wear in person in court, and if you wouldn't drink a big gulp soda or a mug of coffee in an in-person proceeding, you should question why it's any more appropriate to do so in a remote courtroom. Judges who used to gavel a room to order will now have the luxury of the "mute all" button to keep order. We must evolve, of course, but remember that evolving is best seen as the opposite of regressing.

And we should remember that in our contentious times, we will never win the faith of every person who interacts with the judicial system. Most people are simply trying to get on with their lives—to do their jobs and care for their loved ones. When we meet their needs in court, they won't need much persuading to support the institution of law. But there are a warped and wicked few who would trade our institutions for money and attention. The courts must firmly oppose them. First, by doing our job for the general public and making it less inclined to believe tales. This isolates these radicals from the rest—by a kind of algebra. Once isolated, these radicals can be dealt with as they deserve. For instance, we can be grateful to the lawyers and the judges who refused to allow our courts to become a vehicle for a coup d'état in the United States in 2020. Long may it be so.

51 : STEADY COURTS MAY
MEAN A STEADIER COUNTRY

And this leads us to the end and to the biggest stakes of all. The country has been unsteady in ways it hasn't been since the late 1960s and early 1970s. Americans are armed to the teeth and in a bad mood. Most still yearn for us to quiet their minds, but we have to restore their faith first.

We were last united after the attacks of September 11, 2001. But without a popular war to fight, it's as though we turned on ourselves and our institutions, including the courts. By 2021, only a bare majority of Americans were willing to say they had a "fair amount" of confidence in the Supreme Court—a thirteen-point drop from 2020. In *Dobbs*'s wake, this number doubtless dipped deeper—perhaps in part because of its pretense of objectivity.

Americans' faith was particularly challenged by the results of the 2016 and 2020 elections. The US House of Representatives twice impeached a president. A mob stormed the US Capitol in the name of a president with the goal of overturning the legitimate results of an election. As of 2022, Gallup polling concerning confidence in the executive and legislative branches showed that a majority of Americans had confidence in neither of these institutions.[1]

There was a bumper sticker that used to say, "The Irish only fight among themselves because they have no worthy opponent." Maybe America has been going through that too. Does it always have to be a war that unites a people? It's a pity if we can't do any better than that. We might fear this enough to work against its proving true.

America's troubles aren't about a lack of material goods. If material goods were enough, Americans should be positively giddy. No one in history has ever had more of them.[2]

But, with apologies to the law and economics movement, many

things that matter in court don't involve money. Money is corporeal, and like all corporeal things, all calculation, all measurement, and all process, it can only get you so far—a good distances, yes. But it won't get you home, and it might not get you peace.

Peace isn't always a matter of money. Hang around a family court sometime to see how little peace money will buy you. Consider irrational lawsuits over inheritances, minor boundary issues, major environmental lawsuits, and, of course, abortion. You can torture the choices made in them into an economic model, as Judge Posner did with witness credibility, but the analysis is a great struggle that sheds little light.

Honesty doesn't always involve only money. When we want others to show care in their physical dealings with us, it isn't solely to save money on doctors' bills. Respect for all these things can reflect a desire to live in harmony with each other and foster belief in the ways we deal with each other. Indeed, these values show that life is no mechanical exercise. Instead, there are many intangibles that contribute to our living in peace with one another:

Acceptance. Authenticity. Balance. Brilliance. Courtesy. Civility. Dignity. Decency. Empathy. Equanimity. Freedom. Forgiveness. Friendship. Honor. Honesty. Privacy. Tradition. Trust. Tolerance. Justice.

None of these things has a price per pound. But don't underestimate how important they are to courts and a country trying to make the public quiet and contented. It's the reason why a nation's gross national product isn't the best measure of its well-being. It's a useful measure, but as the only measure, it fails. Indeed, its limits have inspired the Human Development Index, the World Happiness Report, and other alternatives.

Consider Americans' nearly unanimous opposition to the 2022 Russian invasion of Ukraine. It cost Americans a fortune in aid to Ukraine. It increased inflation and led to oil and grain shortages, yet something hopeful seemed to come from it for a time. Briefly, at least, it rallied Americans and supporters of Western-style democracy just as the world had begun again a dubious dalliance with dictators. Did Americans really want a strongman like Russia's Vladimir Putin? Do loud-mouthed populists sweep aside corruption and incompetence, or do they merely sweep aside the rule of law and enthrone in its place hatred and struggle—the twin devils that keep tyrants in power?

The fate of dictators should teach Americans in times of crisis to cling to their legal institutions just as they would to their children. They should do it even when those institutions are in the hands of people with whom they don't agree—so long as they are ruled by law.

The English chancellor Thomas More said in the face of his own strongman, Henry VIII: "I would uphold the law for no other reason than to protect myself."

It cost him his head. The first rule of a dictator is that "thou shalt have no god before me." And Henry didn't want law. He wanted to say his legal marriage to his wife was illegal so he could get a new wife— only to behead her later.

But More's love for the rule of law won out. Nobody longs today to be ruled by Henry VIII, and Thomas More became a Catholic saint. Not only that, but the movie version of his sacrifice, *A Man for All Seasons*, won an Academy Award. In it More makes his case for the rule of law as he castigates his daughter's suitor:

> William Roper: So, now you give the Devil the benefit of law!
> Sir Thomas More: Yes! What would you do? Cut a great road through the law to get after the Devil?
> Roper: I'd cut down every law in England to do that!
> More: Oh? And when the last law was down, and the Devil turned 'round on you, where would you hide, Roper, the laws all being flat? This country is planted thick with laws, from coast to coast, Man's laws, not God's! And if you cut them down, and you're just the man to do it, do you really think you could stand upright in the winds that would blow then? Yes, I'd give the Devil benefit of law, for my own safety's sake![3]

Whatever our disagreements, most of us surely still want the rule of law. Indeed, most of us also know what we want from it. We want our courts corruption free. We want them to punish lying, cheating, stealing, and violence. We want people to live up to their promises. We expect neighbors, doctors, engineers, manufacturers, and contractors to be as careful with our lives as we would be with theirs. We

FIGURE 51.1. *"What do you do? I'm a lawyer. The law. I do law.*
I practice law. I'm an attorney. Something legal."

expect them to use reasonable care when we put our safety in their
hands. We prize our personal freedom and industry.

The system that ensures these things should win our respect. It's
a system we might call a system of "justice." The question is whether
we can with confidence call our courts a system of justice while we
make court proceedings longer, more confusing for the public, less
satisfying in outcome, less wedded to action on core issues, and more
engaged in diversion and dissimulation.

It's doubtful. Justice is not merely whatever a court does. Justice is incorporeal. Whether we have a system of justice is inextricably linked with the public's ability—and willingness—to perceive it as being just.

It's hard for them to do this when courts deflect and dismiss cases without reaching the central questions they raise. It's hard for them to do this given that, when courts do decide cases, they do so in a language we can't understand and with a rationale we either can't fathom, can't discern, or can't accept.

In 2022 before *Dobbs*, Justice Amy Coney Barrett told an audience at the Reagan Presidential Library that for reassurance the public should "read the opinions" before suggesting a decision was "purely results driven."[4]

That was a mistake. People can't get much of anything out of reading most judges' opinions. Most opinions aren't even related to the reason the lawsuit was brought. When they are, most lawyers struggle to get anything out of them. When they can, as in *Dobbs*, too often the decisions mask human judgment behind a pretext of objectivity. That's *Dobbs*. It turned on the unexplored, undefended assumption that the rights of the historically oppressed should be limited by their historical oppression.

Dobbs doesn't mean the American judiciary is corrupt. There is no reason to believe that Justice Alito is corrupt or malicious. Doubtless Justice Barrett was being sincere in what she said. But until the courts shed their formalist habits, their uninformative formulas and unspoken assumptions—until they speak to us in a human voice—the perception of justice won't be a regular enough consequence of what courts do.

And if it isn't, we will also miss a larger opportunity. Courts will miss the opportunity to teach.

Let's assume again that most people generally favor truth, personal freedom, nonviolence, respect for property, care to avoid harm to others, and fulfillment of promises. Courts can root these values deeper and grow them wider by illustrating how these values are brought to flower. In other words, most cases not only vindicate one of these values; they can also show how the value affects day-to-day conduct in ever-more specific contexts.

For example, a court might with a concrete case before it explain that respect for the truth sometimes means more than not telling a lie. If someone buying a basket of peaches asks you if the peaches are good, you haven't told the whole truth by answering "yes" when you should also mention that underneath the very good peaches is a very angry snake.

Likewise, a court might explain that you can't acquit yourself of responsibility for injuring a person solely by following the formal procedures prevailing in a profession, trade, or industry. The practices still must be reasonable, and matters not covered by formal procedures must still be addressed. So, where you follow forklift-safety procedures, you must still react sensibly and stop the vehicle for an unforeseen circumstance. Your hard hat, goggles, and flashing yellow light don't entitle you to drive at high speed into an oily patch.

Most judges are safe from everyday pressures. They have a degree of independence. Most of them also have long terms of office and long experience with the law and life. They can help reinforce our values and teach us how to apply them. They have a better chance of speaking authentically about how acknowledged values apply to everyday situations than the other government branches. Those branches face pressure day by day and minute by minute. If judges, with the cooperation of lawyers, can recognize this, they might increase public faith in justice. If it works, it might give the other branches of government ideas—or at least an anchor.

We don't have to feel joyful about the national prospect. But we needn't despair either. Perhaps, despite our deficiencies, the ill-wishes of some of our politicians, and the predictions of our adversaries in the world, the country will shake off its bad feelings—we have done it before—and once again trust our institutions. It will be up to us, and we aren't alone.

Many voices have called for clarity and change in the courts. There is no reason to assume courts will be dominated forever by an army of eager, busy-working law clerks facing off against an army of billing busy workers at law firms.

Bryan Garner's work on legal writing is a formidable tool for focusing briefs on what matters. Ross Guberman's compendium of decisions is full of fine judicial writing *and* thinking. Justice Breyer's reasoning and writing hit the mark most times. Justice Gorsuch writes lucid prose. Whenever he discussed human issues with human focus, Judge Richard Posner's writing and thinking is inspiring.

There are other, less known voices to consider as well. The Manhattan appellate judge Alfred Coxe took a firm stand against needless complexity. He wrote a compelling essay about the lost art of legal briefing. He complained about lawyers' "discursiveness" and "prolixity" along with their inability "to resist the temptation to argue every question which the record presents, no matter how inconsequential."[5] He understood the problem. Unfortunately, he said these things in 1908.

ILLUSTRATION CREDITS

Figure 43.1   "The ones just out of law school are especially frolicsome."

Figure 45.1   "Complexity made simple."

Figure 47.1   "A third of the buck stops here."

Figure 49.1   "Thank you, Nathaniel. I think you, too, are a very scary young lawyer."

Figure 51.1   "What do you do? I'm a lawyer. The law. I do law. I practice law. I'm an attorney. Something legal."

All figures, with the exception of Figure 26.1, are courtesy of CartoonStock.com.

NOTES

1. Prefer humanity to complexity

1. Jeffrey Q. Smith and Grant R. MacQueen, "Going, Going, But Not Quite Gone: Trials Continue to Decline," *Judicature* (Winter 2017), https://judicature.duke.edu/articles/going-going-but-not-quite-gone-trials-continue-to-decline-in-federal-and-state-courts-does-it-matter/.

2. Ibid.

3. For a discussion of conventional notions of formalism, see Richard A. Posner, "Legal Formalism, Legal Realism, and the Interpretation of the Statutes and the Constitution," *Case Western Reserve Law Review* 37 (1986): 179–217.

4. Dobbs v. Jackson Women's Health Organization, 142 S.Ct. 2228 (2022); Roe v. Wade, 410 U.S. 113 (1973).

5. *Dobbs*, 142 S.Ct. at 2244–45.

6. Ibid., at 2246.

7. *Roe*, 410 U.S. at 153.

8. *Dobbs*, 142 S.Ct. at 2257.

9. Griswold v. Connecticut, 381 U.S. 479 (1969).

10. Washington v. Glucksberg, 521 U.S. 702, 721 (1997).

11. See the concurring opinion of Justice Goldberg, with whom Chief Justice Warren and Justice Brennan join in Griswold v. Connecticut, 381 U.S. 479, 487 (1965), citing Snyder v. Com. of Massachusetts, 291 U.S. 97, 105 (1934).

12. Brown v. Board of Education, 347 U.S. 483, 492 (1954).

13. *Dobbs*, 142 S.Ct. at 2324–25 (Breyer, Sotomayor, and Kagan, JJ., dissenting).

14. Reed v. Reed, 404 U.S. 71, 76–77 (1971) (applying the equal protection clause to women); Obergefell v. Hodges, 576 U.S. 644, 673–74 (2015) (discussing coverture).

15. *Dobbs*, 142 S.Ct. at 2247.

16. Politico Staff, "Read Justice Alito's Initial Draft Abortion Opinion Which Would Overturn Roe v. Wade," *Politico*, May 2, 2022, https://www.politico.com/news/2022/05/02/read-justice-alito-initial-abortion-opinion-overturn-roe-v-wade-pdf-00029504.

17. *Dobbs*, 142 S.Ct. at 2257–58.

18. Ibid., at 2332 (Breyer, Sotomayor, and Kagan, JJ.).

19. Ibid., at 2301 (Thomas, J., concurring).

20. *Roe*, 410 U.S. at 113, 129 (1973).

21. Ibid., at 153.

22. Ibid.

23. Planned Parenthood v. Casey, 505 U.S. 833, 849 (1992).

24. *Dobbs*, 142 S.Ct. at 2258–59.

25. Kant's three critiques were his main works. See *Three Critiques, 3-Volume Set: Vol. 1: Critique of Pure Reason; Vol. 2: Critique of Practical Reason; Vol. 3: Critique of Judgment* (Indianapolis: Hackett Classics, 2002). Kant is notoriously inaccessible, so try instead Paul Guyer, *Kant* (London: Routledge, 2014).

26. Ronald Dworkin, *Taking Rights Seriously* (Cambridge, MA: Harvard University Press, 1978).

27. *Dobbs*, 142 S.Ct. at 2278.

28. H. L. A. Hart, *The Concept of Law* (New York: Oxford University Press, 2012).

29. Karl N. Llewelyn, *The Bramble Bush* (New York: Oxford University Press, 2008); Jerome Frank, *Law and the Modern Mind* (London: Routledge, 2009).

30. Francis Bacon, *Complete Essays* (Mineola, NY: Dover Publications, 2008); Cheryl Misak, *The American Pragmatists* (New York: Oxford University Press, 2013).

31. Stephen Breyer, *Making Our Democracy Work: A Judge's View* (New York: Alfred A. Knopf, 2010).

32. Southern Pacific Company v. Jensen, 244 U.S. 205, 222 (1917) (Holmes, J., dissenting).

33. See e.g., Alan Ryan, ed., *Utilitarianism and Other Essays* (London: Penguin Classics, 2004).

34. Buck v. Bell, 274 U.S. 200, 207 (1927).

35. Richard A. Posner, *How Judges Think* (Cambridge, MA: Harvard University Press, 2008).

36. Ibid., 66.

37. Tom Schulman, "*Dead Poets Society* ('Understanding Poetry' Scene)," Genius, www.https://genius.com/Tom-schulman-dead-poets-society -understanding-poetry-scene-annotated, accessed May 23, 2022.

38. Baskin v. Bogan, 766 F. 3d 648, 662 (7th Cir. 2014).

39. See, e.g., Paul J. du Plessis and John W. Cairns, eds., *Reassessing Legal Humanism and Its Claims* (Edinburgh: Edinburgh University Press, 2016). Roman law is a particularly important source of Scottish law.

40. Erich Maria Ramarque, *All Quiet on the Western Front* (New York: New York University, 1929; repr., New York: Ballantine Books, 1982), 56.

2. Rethink 90 percent of the typical complaint; make it about key facts, not law

1. Bell Atlantic v. Twombly, 550 U.S. 544, 564 (2007); Ashcroft v. Iqbal, 556 U.S. 662 (2009).

2. *Twombly*, 550 U.S. at 555.

3. *Iqbal*, 556 U.S. at 678.

4. "Federal Judicial Caseload Statistics," Statistics and Reports, United States Courts, accessed May 23, 2022, https://www.uscourts.gov/statistics -reports/analysis-reports/federal-judicial-caseload-statistics.

5. "Table CJRA 7—Detailed Reports Civil Justice Reform Act (CJRA) (March 31, 2019)," Statistics and Reports, United States Courts, https://www .uscourts.gov/statistics/table/cjra-7/civil-justice-reform-act-cjra/2019/03/31.

6. William H. J. Hubbard, "The Empirical Effects of Twombly and Iqbal" (working paper, Coase-Sandor Working Paper Series in Law and Economics, No. 773, 2016), https://chicagounbound.uchicago.edu/cgi/viewcontent.cgi ?article=2479&context=law_and_economics.

7. "Table CJRA 1—Civil Justice Reform Act (CJRA) (March 31, 2019)," Statistics and Reports, United States Courts, accessed May 23, 2022, https:// www.uscourts.gov/statistics-reports/march-2019-civil-justice-reform-act.

8. Christina L. Boyd, David A. Hoffman, Zoran Obradovic, and Kosta Ristovski, "Building a Taxonomy of Litigation: Clusters of Causes of Action in Federal Complaints," *Journal of Empirical Legal Studies* 10, no. 2 (2013): 253.

9. Traylor v. State, No. KNOCV135014624S, docket entry 199 (Connecticut Superior Court, July 9, 2014).

3. Address basic pleading and proof deficiencies with a single motion

1. The rise of outside legal auditors and its consequences are documented and discussed in Liberty L. Roberts, "Fee Audits Cut More than Fat out of Bills, Cutting the Heart of Insurance Defense," *Indiana Law Review* 34 (2000): 179–201.

2. See David Horton, "Infinite Arbitration Clauses," *University of Pennsylvania Law Review* 168 (2020): 633.

3. See Burton v. Commissioner of Environmental Protection, 291 Conn. 789 (2009) (overturning 2007 standing dismissal), 323 Conn. 668 (2016) (overturning 2014 mootness dismissal), 337 Conn. 781 (2021) (affirming 2018 trial decision).

4. For example, see the Eleventh Circuit decision in Gilreath Family & Cosmetic Dentistry, Inc. v. Cincinnati Insurance Company, 2021 WL 387097 (11th Cir. 2021). It disposed of this multibillion-dollar issue in a conclusory fashion consisting of two or three pertinent sentences.

4. Decide cases once; use agency remands sparingly

1. See, e.g., Seaman v. Virginia, 2022 WL 872023 *15 (W.D. Virginia 2022); Arc of Iowa v. Reynolds, 24 F. 4th 1162, 1172 (8th Cir. 2022).

2. Marbury v. Madison, 1 Cranch 137 (1803).

3. See e.g., Beshear v. Acree, 615 S.W.3d 780 (Ky. 2020); Casey v. Lamont, 338 Conn. 479 (2021); In re Certified Questions, 506 Mich. 332 (2020).

4. "State of Connecticut Supreme Court S.C. 19754 Brief," Supreme and Appellate Court Case Look-up, Connecticut Judicial Branch, accessed May 23, 2022, http://appellateinquiry.jud.ct.gov/DocViewer/DocumentInquiry.aspx?DocID=39633&AppID=1.

5. 328 Conn. 345 (2018).

6. Chevron U.S.A., Inc. v. Natural Resources Defense Council, Inc., 467 U.S. 837 (1984).

7. Stephen Breyer, *Making Our Democracy Work: A Judge's View* (New York: Alfred A. Knopf, 2010), 153.

8. See the discussion of the exhaustion problem in Judge Thapar's concurring opinion in Wallace v. Oakwood Healthcare, Inc., 954 F.3d 879 (6th Cir. 2020).

5. Reconsider standing challenges; they invite more lawsuits

1. See Mullins v. Pfizer, 23 F.3d 663 (2d Cir. 1994).

2. See In re Packaged Ice Antitrust Litigation, 779 F. Supp. 2d 642, 653 (E.D. Mich. 2011); Le v. Kohls Department Stores, Inc., 160 F.Supp. 3d 1096 (2016), in which another court rejected using standing to prejudge class action status.

6. Reduce fighting over subject matter jurisdiction; the unheard will not remain unseen

1. The Connecticut Supreme Court discussed this broadly accepted view in FDIC v. Peabody, 239 Conn. 93, 99 (1996).

2. See Safford Unified School Dist. #1 v. Redding, 557 U.S. 364 (2009).

3. You can see these arguments and claims about exhaustion unfold before the Texas Supreme Court in typical fashion in Rusk State Hosp. v. Black, 392 S.W.3d 88, 94–95 (Tex. 2012).

4. See Ashcroft v. al-Kidd, 563 U.S. 731 (2011); and the line of cases associated with it.

7. Order discovery when a case begins; police it without written motions

1. Ingram v. Quintana, 2014 WL 12966277 (C.D. Cal. 2014).

2. Too many courts pay lip service to this idea and then go about taking evidence outside of the document anyway, including about how the agreement was reached, the circumstances, and even the parties' self-serving views on what it says. When the text is clear, textualism should prevail. This needless complexity is discussed in Alan Schwartz and Robert E. Scott, "Contract Interpretation Redux," *Yale Law Journal* 119 (2010): 926.

8. Creatively manage complex cases;
no case should be too big to try

1. Katie Brenner, "Purdue Pleads Guilty to Role in Opioid Crisis as Part of Deal with Justice Dept.," *New York Times*, November 24, 2020, https://www.nytimes.com/2020/11/24/us/politics/purdue-pharma-opioids-guilty-settlement.html.

2. Brian Mann, "Corporate Opioid Payments Now Being Finalized Would Top $32 Billion," *NPR*, February 23, 2022, https://www.npr.org/2022/02/23/1082237366/corporate-opioid-payouts-would-top-32-billion.

3. Brian Mann, "3 of America's Biggest Pharmacy Chains Have Been Found Liable for the Opioid Crisis," *NPR*, February 23, 2022, https://www.npr.org/2021/11/23/1058539458/a-jury-in-ohio-says-americas-big-pharmacy-chains-are-liable-for-the-opioid-epide.

4. Amanda Holpuch, "Two Army Veterans Awarded $110 Million in 3M Earplug Lawsuit," *New York Times*, January 28, 2022. https://www.nytimes.com/2022/01/28/us/veterans-earplugs-3m-lawsuit.html.

5. NPR Staff, "15 Years Later Where Did All the Cigarette Money Go?" *NPR*, October 13, 2013, https://www.wbur.org/npr/233449505/15-years-later-where-did-all-the-cigarette-money-go.

6. Martha Bebinger, "The Purdue Pharma Deal Would Deliver Billions, but Individual Payouts Will Be Small," *NPR*, September 9, 2021, https://www.npr.org/2021/09/28/1040447650/payouts-purdue-pharma-settlement-sackler.

7. "Unfair Methods of Competition Unlawful; Prevention by Commission," 15 U.S.C. §45 (2018).

10. Streamline trials; they'll be more final, more credible

1. "Examining the Work of State Courts," Court Statistics Project, accessed May 23, 2022, https://www.courtstatistics.org/other-pages/examining-the-work-of-state-courts; *Caseload Highlights* 11, n. 3, https://www.courtstatistics.org/__data/assets/pdf_file/0014/30614/Trial-Trends-and-Implications-for-the-Civil-Justice-System.pdf, accessed May 23, 2022.

12. Increase juror numbers and diversity with remote jury trials

1. Huo Jingnan, "To Try or Not to Try—Remotely. As Jury Trials Move Online Courts See Pros and Cons," *NPR*, March 18, 2022, https://www.npr.org/2022/03/18/1086711379/as-jury-trials-move-online-courts-see-pros-and-cons.

13. Question the number of motions in limine

1. See Randy Wilson, "From My Side of the Bench," *The Advocate* 59 (2012): 74–75.

2. Bristol v. TSKP, Doc. No. HHDCV 176084696S (Judicial District of

Hartford, Connecticut). The case can be found on the Connecticut Judicial Branch website, www.jud.ct.gov.

14. Most exhibits prove undisputed facts; we don't need them
1. CCJEF v. Rell, 2016 WL 4922730 (Connecticut Sup. Ct. 2016), reversed in part, 327 Conn. 650 (2018).
2. Templeton v. Kannan, Doc. No. HHB FA196054337S (Connecticut Regional Family Trial Docket, Middletown, Connecticut, September 27, 2021).

15. Actively oppose cumulative and time-wasting testimony
1. "A Few Good Men," The Internet Movie Script Database, accessed May 23, 2022, https://imsdb.com/scripts/A-Few-Good-Men.html.

17. Consider common sense first in family court
1. Timothy Grall, "Custodial Mothers and Fathers and Their Child Support: 2017," Current Population Reports, United States Census, accessed May 23, 2022, https://www.census.gov/content/dam/Census/library/publications/2020/demo/p60-269.pdf.

18. Introduce time clocks to encourage efficient trials
1. Mathews v. Chevron, 2002 WL 826804 (April 23, 2002), result affirmed at 362 F.3d 1172 (9th Cir. 2004).
2. The decision recognizing the absolute privilege, along with some of the case background, can be found at Kelley v. Bonney, 221 Conn. 549 (1992).

21. Punish misconduct when it happens rather than in a separate proceeding
1. Corona v. Day Kimball Healthcare, Inc., Doc. No. X07HHDCV 156075511S (Connecticut Superior Court for the Judicial District of Hartford, September 20, 2018).

22. Cross-examine crisply, crushingly, or not at all
1. "A Few Good Men," The Internet Movie Script Database, accessed May 23, 2022, https://imsdb.com/scripts/A-Few-Good-Men.html.

25. Keep cases in the hands of a single judge from start to finish
1. To learn more about how the federal system evolved and the issues raised by different approaches, see Susan Willard, "The Assignment of Cases to Federal District Judges," *Stanford Law Review* 27 (1974–1975): 475.

*26. Speed cases to trial with judicial administration
instead of slowing them down*

1. Judicial Council of California, *2017 Court Statistics Report: Statewide Caseload Trends 2006–2007 through 2015–2016*, 2017, https://www.courts.ca .gov/documents/2017-Court-Statistics-Report.pdf.

2. "Administrative Structure of the New York State Unified Court System," Administration Overview, New York Courts, accessed May 23, 2022, https:// www.nycourts.gov/LegacyPDFS/admin/AdminStructure.pdf.

27. Accelerate and simplify justice with technology

1. Joseph Darius Jaafari and Nicole Lewis, "In Court, Where Are Siri and Alexa?" The Marshall Project, February 14, 2019, https://www .themarshallproject.org/2019/02/14/in-court-where-are-siri-and-alexa.

2. For instance, you can find the California system here: https://www .eldorado.courts.ca.gov/online-services/courtroom-live-streaming. And you can watch the Supreme Court of Ohio here: https://www.supremecourt.ohio .gov/JCS/courtSvcs/virtualCourt/default.asp.

28. Virtual proceedings should be the rule

1. The story of technology and the rise of remote proceedings during the pandemic is explored in Alicia Bannon and Douglas Keith, "Remote Court: Principles for Virtual Proceedings during the COVID-19 Pandemic and Beyond," *Northwestern Law Review* 115, no. 6 (2021): 1875–1920.

30. Cases are better resolved on their facts than on the law

1. You can find this concept discussed at, "Trade Secret," Legal Information Institute, Cornell Law School, https://www.law.cornell.edu/wex/trade_secret (last visited May 23, 2022).

2. Connecticut's is typical. You can see the alimony statute at Conn. Gen. Stat. §46b–82 (2021) and its statute listing similar criteria for property settlements at Conn. Gen. Stat. §46b–81 (2021).

3. For a look at the traditional view, see James Fleming Jr., "The Qualities of the Reasonable Man in Negligence Cases," *Missouri Law Review* 16, no. 1 (1951): 1–26.

*31. Deploy canons of construction sparingly—only when
they have a compelling reason to exist*

1. Antonin Scalia and Bryan A. Garner, *Reading Law: The Interpretation of Legal Texts* (St. Paul, MN: West Group, 2011).

2. Stephen Breyer, *Making Our Democracy Work: A Judge's View* (New York: Vintage, 2011).

3. See, e.g., Houghton v. Aramark, 90 S.W.3d 676 (Tenn. 2002).

4. See, e.g., Circuit City Stores, Inc. v. Adams, 532 U.S. 105, 115 (2001).

5. For an early recognition of this subjectivity, see Harlan F. Stone, "The Common Law in the United States," *Harvard Law Review* 50, no. 1 (1936): 12–14.

6. See, e.g., Crawford Fitting Co. v. J. T. Gibbons, Inc., 482 U.S. 437 (1987).

7. See, e.g., Barnhart v. Sigmon Coal Co., 534 U.S. 438, 459 (2002).

8. See, e.g., Woodruff v. Bretz, 218 P.3d 486 (Mont. 2009).

9. Charlie D. Stewart, "The Rhetorical Canons of Construction: New Textualism's Rhetoric Problem," *Michigan Law Review* 116, no. 8 (2018): 1485–1514.

32. Rarely resort to legislative history; it's often unreliable

1. United Steelworkers of America v. Weber, 443 U.S. 193, 201 (1979), citing the grandfather of all such cases, Church of the Holy Trinity v. U.S., 143 U.S. 457 (1892).

2. Stephen Breyer, "On the Uses of Legislative History in Interpreting Statutes," *Southern California Law Review* 65 (1992): 845.

3. Varity Corp. v. Howe, 516 U.S. 489 (1996).

4. Meinhard v. Salmon, 249 NY 458 (1928).

5. The court held that cheated plan participants could recover money against unfaithful fiduciaries in CIGNA Corp. v. Amara, 563 U.S. 421 (2011).

33. Reduce distractions by identifying fallacies

1. Oliver Wendell Holmes Jr., *The Common Law* (Boston: Little, Brown, and Co., 1881; repr., New York: Dover Publications, 1991), 1.

2. United States v. Deyoe, 2009 WL 4110440 *5 (N.D.N.Y November 20, 2009).

3. Kevin W. Saunders, "Informal Fallacies in Legal Argumentation," *South Carolina Law Review* 44 (1993): 343.

34. Don't blur laws to conquer facts

1. Beach v. Commonwealth Edison, 2003 WL 22287353 (N.D. Illinois, October 2, 2003).

2. Beach v. Commonwealth Edison, 382 F.3d 656 (7th Cir. 2004).

3. See Kenseth v. Dean Health Plan, Inc., 610 F.3d 452, 470–71 (7th Cir. 2010).

35. Endless consumer disclosures aren't doing us any good; they are just low-hanging fruit

1. Brad J. Bushman and Angela D. Stack, "Forbidden Fruit Versus Tainted Fruit: Effects of Warning Labels on Attraction to Television Violence," *Journal of Experimental Psychology: Applied* 2, no. 3 (1996): 207–226.

36. Reduce judicial testiness; use multipoint tests only when each point has meaning

1. Lemon v. Kurtzman, 403 U.S. 602 (1971).

2. The origin of this approach seems to be Johnson v. Georgia Highway Express, Inc., 488 F.2d 714 (5th Cir. 1974).

3. See for example, Weems v. Citigroup, Inc., 289 Conn. 769 (2008).

4. McDonnell Douglas Corp. v. Green, 411 U.S. 792 (1973).

5. Heard v. Sheahan, 253 F.3d. 316 (7th Cir. 2001).

6. Compare State v. CHRO, 211 Conn. 464 (1989) with Bouchard v. SERC, 328 Conn. 345 (2018).

7. Bodner v. Banque, 114 F. Supp. 2d 117, 134–35.

8. For the discussion of the issue, see "Memorandum of Decision Partially Granting Motion for Summary Judgement," Entry 171, 206125269, Superior Court Case Look-up, Judicial Branch, State of Connecticut, accessed May 23, 2022, https://civilinquiry.jud.ct.gov/DocumentInquiry/DocumentInquiry.aspx?DocumentNo=2076492.

37. Similar-sounding cases aren't precedent

1. Timothy J. Capurso, "How Judges Judge: Theories on Judicial Decision Making," *University of Baltimore Law Forum* 29, no. 1 (1998): 5–15.

2. William Blackstone, *Blackstone's Commentaries on the Laws of England* (New York: Oxford University Press, 2016); Herbert Broom, *A Selection of Legal Maxims, Classified and Illustrated*, 8th ed. (Clark, NJ: The Lawbook Exchange, Ltd., 2010).

38. The best legal writing is literature, not formula

1. Towne v. Eisner, 245 U.S. 418, 425 (1918).

2. United States v. Garsson, 291 F. 646, 649 (S.D.N.Y. 1923).

3. Robinson v. Pioche, Bayerque & Co., 5 Cal. 460, 461 (1855).

4. United States v. Ven-Fuel, Inc., 602 F.2d 747, 749 (5th Cir. 1979).

5. Jacob Gershman, "Why Lawyers Object to Making Legal Briefs Briefer," *Wall Street Journal*, March 12, 2015, http://www.wsj.com/articles/why-lawyers-object-to-making-legal-briefs-briefer-1426207344.

6. "Garner's Interviews," LawProse, https://lawprose.org/bryan-garner/videos/garners-interviews/.

7. Elizabeth Olson, "Judges Push Brevity in Briefs, and Get a Torrent of Arguments," *New York Times*, October 4, 2016, https://www.nytimes.com/2016/10/04/business/dealbook/judges-push-brevity-in-briefs-and-get-a-torrent-of-arguments.html.

41. Needless detail is . . .

1. Borrowed from a criticism of General Pickett in the movie *Gettysburg*. "*Gettysburg* Script," Drew's Script-O-Rama Database, accessed May 23, 2022,

http://www.script-o-rama.com/movie_scripts/g/gettysburg-script-transcript
-civil-war.html.

2. Bryan A. Garner, *The Winning Brief*, 3rd ed. (New York: Oxford
University Press, 2014); Bryan A. Garner, *The Elements of Legal Style*, 2nd ed.
(New York: Oxford University Press, 2002).

42. The best appellate decisions deeply
and plainly explain the law

1. City of Marion v. London Witte Group, LLC, 169 N.E.3d 382 (2021).

2. Ibid., at 390.

3. Ibid., at 394.

4. Ibid., at 397.

5. State ex rel. Nicely v. Wildey, 209 Ind. 1 (1935) (2,283 words); Eviston
v. Bradford, 100 Ind. App. 616 (1935) (1074 words); Martin v. Loula, 208 Ind.
346 (1935) (2714 words). All case-length calculations excluded headnotes but
included footnotes.

6. Schleicher v. Schleicher, 120 Conn. 528 (1935) (2313 words); Rogers v.
Doody, 119 Conn. 532 (1325 words); State v. Boucher, 119 Conn. 436 (1935)
(2029 words).

7. Ashmore v. Hartford Hospital, 331 Conn. 777 (2019) (12,577 words);
Sena v. American Medical Response of Connecticut, Inc., 333 Conn. 30 (2019)
(9,271 words); Boisvert v. Gavis, 332 Conn. 115 (2019) (13,653 words).

8. Schenck v. United States, 249 U.S. 47, 52 (1919) (citations omitted).

9. Republican Party of State of Conn. v. Tashjian, 770 F.2d 265 (1985).

10. Free Speech Coalition, Inc. v. Attorney General of U.S., 677 F.3d 519,
524–25 (2012).

11. Frigaliment Importing Co. v. B.N.S. Intern. Sales Corp., 190 F.Supp. 116,
117 (S.D.N.Y. 1960).

12. Starr Surplus Lines Ins. Co. v. Mountaire Farms Inc., 920 F.3d 111 (1st
Cir. 2019).

43. There is a better home for law clerks outside
of busy work and junior judging

1. Chad Oldfather and Todd Peppers, "Judicial Assistants or Junior Judges:
The Hiring, Utilization, and Influence of Law Clerks," *Marquette Law Review*
98, no. 1 (2014): 1–12, discussing Anthony Kronman, *The Lost Lawyer:
Failing Ideals of the Legal Profession* (Cambridge, MA: Harvard University
Press, 1993).

2. According to US Courts statistics, "fewer than 9 percent of total appeals
resulted in reversals of lower court decisions in 2015." See "Just the Facts: U.S.
Courts of Appeal," United States Courts, December 20, 2016, https://www
.uscourts.gov/news/2016/12/20/just-facts-us-courts-appeals.

44. Appellate courts should reform rusty rules

1. See, e.g., C.R. England v. Swift Transportation Company, 437 P.3d 343 (Utah 2019).

2. Restatement (Third) of Torts: Liab. For Econ. Harm §17 (2020).

3. See, e.g., Nobel v. Foxmoor Group, LLC, 868 S.E.2d 30 (N.C. 2022).

4. See, e.g., Callandro v. Allstate Ins. Co., 63 Conn. App. 602, 778 A.2d 212 (2001).

5. See, e.g., Doull v. Foster, 487 Mass. 1 (2021).

6. See, e.g., Sneed v. Weber, 58 Tex. Sup. Ct. J. 1009 (2015).

7. *Corporate Governance: Analysis and Recommendations* §7.01(d) (Am. Law Inst. 1994).

8. For a discussion of the problem of qualified immunity, for instance, see Joanna C. Schwartz, "After Qualified Immunity," *Columbia Law Review* 120, no. 2 (2020): 309–388.

9. McDonnell Douglas Corp. v. Green, 411 U.S. 792 (1973).

10. See, e.g., William R. Corbett, "McDonnell Douglas, 1973–2003: May You Rest in Peace?" *University Pennsylvania Journal of Labor and Employment Law* 6, no. 1 (2003–2004): 199–219.

45. The best trial court decisions get straight to saying who wins and why

1. McCourt v. McCourt, 2010 WL 5092780 (Superior Court of California, Los Angeles County, December 10, 2010).

2. Ibid., at *1.

3. Ibid.

4. For example, see Reyes v. Metromedia Software, Inc., 840 F.Supp. 2d 752 (S.D.N.Y. 2012).

5. Ross Guberman, *Point Taken: How to Write Like the World's Best Judges* (New York: Oxford University Press, 2015).

6. Garcia v. Bloomberg, 865 F. Supp. 2d 478, 482–83 (S.D.N.Y. 2012), aff'd sub nom. Garcia v. Does, 764 F.3d 170 (2d Cir. 2014), on reh'g, 779 F.3d 84 (2d Cir. 2015), and rev'd sub nom. Garcia v. Does, 779 F.3d 84 (2d Cir. 2015).

7. 551 F.Supp.3d 258 (S.D.N.Y. 2021).

8. Johansen v. GVN Michigan, 2015 WL 3823036 (N. D. Illinois June 18, 2015).

9. Caplan v. Budget Van Lines, 2020 WL 4430966 *3 (D. Nevada July 31, 2020).

10. The name of the case, the court name, and the date are important to the reader. The volume, reporter, and page are important to the researcher. The former is best in the text, the latter in a footnote.

11. Henson v. Santander Consumer USA Inc., 137 S. Ct. 1718 (2017).

46. Needless complexity obscures our basically honest courts

1. Yuhua Wang, "Court Funding and Judicial Corruption in China, *China Journal* 69 (2013): 43–63, https://scholar.harvard.edu/files/yuhuawang/files /wang_2013.pdf.

2. "Police, Then Judiciary Most Corrupt Public Institutions in South Asia," *Transparency International*, December 16, 2002, https://www.transparency .org/en/press/police-then-judiciary-most-corrupt-public-institutions-in -south-asia-reveal.

3. Maria Popova, "Putin-Style 'Rule of Law' and the Prospects for Change," *Daedalus* 146 (2017): 64–75, https://www.amacad.org/publication/putin-style -rule-law-prospects-change.

4. For an empirical study, see Stratos Pahis, "Corruption in Our Courts: What It Looks Like and Where It Is Hidden," *Yale Law Journal* 118 (2009): 1900–1943, https://openyls.law.yale.edu/bitstream/handle/20.500 .13051/9806/59_118YaleLJ1900_2008_2009_.pdf?sequence=2&isAllowed=y.

47. Lawyers must discard outdated business models

1. Paul Campos, "The Law School Scam," *Atlantic*, September 2014, https://www.theatlantic.com/magazine/archive/2014/09/the-law-school -scam/375069/; David Segal, "Is Law School a Losing Game," *New York Times*, January 8, 2019, https://www.nytimes.com/2011/01/09/business/09law.html.

2. "Ten-Year Summary of Bar Passage Rates, Overall and First-Time, 2009–2018," The Bar Examiner, accessed May 23, 2022, https:// thebarexaminer.ncbex.org/statistics/2018-statistics/ten-year-summary-of-bar -passage-rates-overall-and-first-time-2009-2018.

3. Sam Skolnik, "Bar Exams May Soon Be Easier to Pass," *Bloomberg Law*, March 29, 2021, https://news.bloomberglaw.com/business-and-practice/bar -exams-may-soon-be-easier-to-pass-as-states-eye-changes.

4. "2017 Report on the State of the Legal Market," *Thomson Reuters*, January 12, 2017, https://www.thomsonreuters.com/en/press-releases/2017 /january/2017-report-on-the-state-of-the-legal-market.html.

5. *General Counsel Imperative Series: How Do You Turn Barriers into Building Blocks?* Center on the Legal Profession, Harvard Law School, 2021, https://clp.law.harvard.edu/wp-content/uploads/2022/10/ey-general-counsel -imperative-series-how-do-you-turn-barriers-into-building-blocks.pdf.

6. Mark Herrmann, "Is litigation in 'Secular Decline?'" *Above the Law*, August 14, 2017, https://abovethelaw.com/2017/08/is-litigation-in-secular -decline.

7. Aric Press, "Can 'Value' Pricing Replace the Billable Hour?" *Bloomberg Law*, May 30, 2017, https://news.bloomberglaw.com/business-and-practice/ can-value-pricing-replace-the-billable-hour-perspective.

8. "Value-Based Pricing," Deloitte Development, 2021, https://www2

.deloitte.com/content/dam/Deloitte/us/Documents/Tax/us-tax-value-based
-pricing-aligning-the-cost-and-value-of-legal-services.pdf.

9. Joseph R. Profaizer, "International Arbitration Now Getting Longer and
More Costly," *The National Law Journal* 30 (2008): 51.

10. Susan Saab Fortney, "The Billable Hours Derby: Empirical Data on
the Problems and Pressure Points," *Fordham Urban Law Journal* 33, no. 1
(2005): 101–122; Erika Holmes, "Evils of the Billable Hour," September 18,
2020, in *Modern Law Revolution*, produced by Colorado Bar Association,
podcast, YouTube, https://www.youtube.com/watch?v=A1J7t-UlOw4.

49. Rethinking law clerking can remake the future

1. "Article Length," Duke Law Journal Policies, *Duke Law Journal*,
accessed May 23, 2022, https://dlj.law.duke.edu/about/submissions/.
The author has fond memories of his days on the editorial board of the
Connecticut Law Review.

50. Recognize needful complexity and meaningful formality

1. Adam Grant, *Think Again: The Power of Knowing What You Don't Know*
(New York: Viking, 2021).

2. Francesca Gino and Michael I. Norton, "Why Rituals Work," *Scientific
American* (May 14, 2013).

51. Steady courts may mean a steadier country

1. Megan Brenan, "Americans' Confidence in U.S. Institutions Dips,"
Gallup, July 14, 2021, https://news.gallup.com/poll/352316/americans
-confidence-major-institutions-dips.aspx.

2. The *New York Times* usefully explored discontent amid good
material news in 2022: Max Fisher, "Is the World Really Falling Apart, or
Does It Just Feel That Way?" *New York Times*, July 7, 2022, https://www
.nytimes.com/2022/07/12/world/interpreter-world-falling-apart.html
?searchResultPosition=1.

3. James Wall, "Thomas More: 'I'd Give the Devil Benefit of Law, for My
Own Safety's Sake,'" *Wall Writings*, April 30, 2009, https://wallwritings
.me/2009/04/30/thomas-more-id-give-the-devil-benefit-of-law-for-my-own
-safetys-sake.

4. Michael R. Blood, "In Simi Valley, Justice Barrett Says Supreme Court
Decisions Aren't Politically Driven," *Los Angeles Times*, May 4, 2022, https://
www.latimes.com/world-nation/story/2022-04-05/justice-barrett-supreme
-court-decisions-not-politically-driven.

5. Alfred C. Coxe, "Is Brief-Making a Lost Art?" *Yale Law Journal* 17, no. 6
(1908): 413–421.

INDEX

BRANDEIS SERIES IN LAW AND SOCIETY

Rosalind Kabrhel, J. D., and Daniel Breen, J. D., Editors

Justice Louis D. Brandeis once said that "if we desire respect for the law, we must first make the law respectable." For Justice Brandeis, making the law "respectable" meant making it work in the interests of humankind as a help rather than a hindrance in the manifold struggles of persons of all backgrounds to achieve justice. In that spirit, the Law and Society Series publishes works that take interdisciplinary approaches to law, drawing richly from the social sciences and humanities, with a view towards shedding critical light upon the variety of ways in which legal rules, and the institutions that enforce them, affect our lives. Intended for practitioners, academics, students, and the interested general public, this series will feature titles that contribute robustly to contemporary debates about law and legal reform, all with a view towards adding to efforts of all sorts to make the law "respectable."

*For a complete list of books that are available in the series,
visit https://brandeisuniversitypress.com/series/law*

*The Common Flaw: Needless Complexity in the Courts and
50 Ways to Reduce It*
   Thomas Moukawsher

We're Here to Help: When Guardianship Goes Wrong
   Diane Dimond

Education Behind the Wall: Why and How We Teach College in Prison
   Mneesha Gellman

*When Freedom Speaks: The Boundaries and the Boundlessness
of Our First Amendment Right*
   Lynn Levine Greenky

*Pain and Shock in America: Politics, Advocacy, and the
Controversial Treatment of People with Disabilities*
   Jan A. Nisbet